The Lake Michigan beach in Grand Mere State Park

Fifty Hikes
in Lower Michigan

The Best Walks, Hikes and Backpacks
from Sleeping Bear Dunes to the Hills of Oakland County

Jim DuFresne

Photographs by the author

A Fifty Hikes™ Guide

Backcountry Publications
The Countryman Press, Inc.
Woodstock, Vermont

An Invitation to the Reader

Over time trails can be rerouted and signs and landmarks altered. If you find that changes have occurred on the routes described in this book, please let us know so that corrections may be made in future editions. The author and publisher also welcome other comments and suggestions. Address all correspondence to:

Editor, *Fifty Hikes*™ Series
Backcountry Publications
P.O. Box 175
Woodstock, VT 05091

Published by Backcountry Publications, a division of The Countryman Press, Inc., Woodstock, Vermont 05091

Cover and series design by Wladislaw Finne
Trail maps drawn by Richard Widhu

Cover photo: Backpacker on North Manitou Island by Jim DuFresne

Library of Congress Cataloging-in-Publication Data

DuFresne, Jim.
  Fifty hikes in lower Michigan: the best walks, hikes and
backpacks from Sleeping Bear Dunes to the hills of Oakland County/
Jim DuFresne; photographs by the author.
    p. cm.
    Includes bibliographical references
    ISBN 0-88150-189-1
    1. Hiking—Michigan—Guide-books. 2. Backpacking—Michigan—Guide
-books. 3. Michigan—Description and travel—1981- —Guide-books.
I. Title. II. Title: 50 hikes in lower Michigan.
GV199.42.M5D84 1991
917.74′0443—dc20   90-29145
                                                          CIP

To Donna

*And her enthusiasm for new challenges, her
quest for adventure, her passion for the wilderness.
Routines are for the everyday people.*

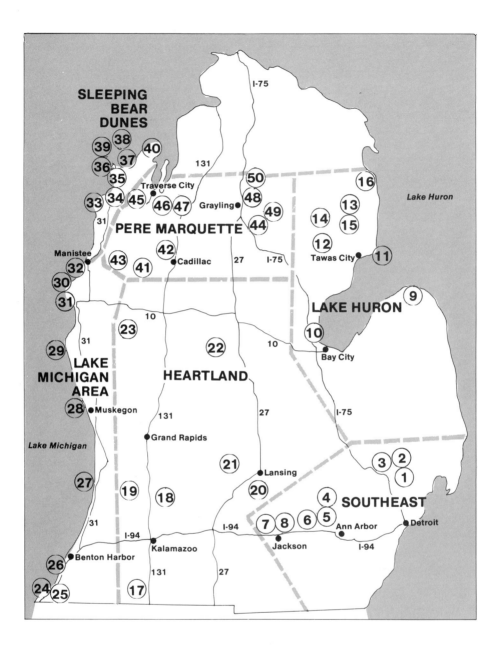

SLEEPING BEAR DUNES

SLEEPING
BEAR
DUNES

I-75

131

(38)
(39) (37) (40)
(36)
(35)
Traverse City
(33) (34) (45) (46) (47) Grayling
(50)
(48)
(49)
(44)

PERE MARQUETTE

(42)
Manistee
(32) (43) (41) Cadillac
(30)
(31)

10

31
(29)
(23)

LAKE
MICHIGAN
AREA

(22)

HEARTLAND

(28) ●Muskegon

Lake Michigan

131
●Grand Rapids

(27)

(21)
(19) (18)
●Lansing
(20)

31
(26) ●Benton Harbor
I-94
Kalamazoo

(24) (25)

131

(17)

27

Lake Huron

(16)
(13)
(14) (15)
(12)
Tawas City (11)

LAKE HURON
(9)
(10)
Bay City

10

I-75

(3) (2)
(1)
(4)
SOUTHEAST
(7) (8) (6) (5)
Ann Arbor ●Detroit
Jackson I-94

I-94

27

Contents

Lake Michigan 127

Sleeping Bear Dunes 167

Pere Marquette 205

Foreword

When Jim DuFresne first told me that he was writing a guide to 50 hikes in the southern portion of Michigan, I said, "You've got to be kidding. There aren't that many."

Being a hiker and having lived in southern Michigan most of my life, I thought Jim was starting to suffer from a little too much fresh air. And, in fact, some will probably question the finer points of where lower Michigan begins and ends, but what is clear after reading through the following pages is that this guide is an eminently useful resource.

Outdoor pursuits have never been as diverse and widely popular as they are today. With the increasing urbanization of lower Michigan and growing complexity of living in a society steadily moving away from the land, there are corresponding stresses which prompt in many of us a need to return to a natural environment.

Social scientists and bio-engineers have long understood that the presence of plants can have a soothing effect on the human psyche. In recent years the findings from their research have led corporate leaders and city planners to incorporate more of nature into the day to day scheme of things, whether by encouraging workers to bring plants to the office, building lush atriums for coffee breaks in corporate headquarters, or giving increased attention to landscape planning on corporate grounds and in city and neighborhood parks. Today, even at the somewhat sterile NASA laboratories of Johnson Space Center in Houston, research is underway on how greenery might be incorporated into future space stations to take advantage of the many benefits it provides.

That is where this book comes in — as an easily read and carried window of opportunity for those who periodically feel the need to get away. For people who like to hike occasionally, the first question is usually where to go. *Fifty Hikes in Lower Michigan* provides the answers, whether you only have time for a two-hour jaunt nearby or can take a day or weekend to visit some of Michigan's most scenic walks.

For the hiker who enjoys getting away from city life regularly, this book will provide still other benefits. With its topographic trail maps and detailed descriptions of the topography, trails, and how to get to them, it offers a quick reference to the qualities of various hikes and what hikers might observe on them. A compilation of information important to hikers, it is easy to carry along in a daypack and will serve well as a guide on the trail.

Anyone who has spent time and money on stamps, envelopes or long-distance calls to obtain trail maps and information from various land managing agencies knows what a hassle that can be. Easy to use, thorough, and very readable, this book eliminates the misery of rummaging through file boxes or drawers of stray maps and trail information. When Saturday or Sunday morning arrives and the urge hits to be on a trail, you can just flip through the pages and pack a lunch, toss your boots in the car, and go.

—Howard L. Meyerson, Outdoors Editor
Grand Rapids Press

Acknowledgments

I like to hike. More than any other outdoor activity, more than tossing a dry fly in the AuSable, skiing on a groomed trail, or kayaking around Isle Royale's rugged coast, what I enjoy most in the out-of-doors is a quiet walk in the woods. It's simple enjoyment that sets free the soul and allows the mind to escape the daily routines of life in the city. This project was not just another book in the on-going effort to pay the bills but was an opportunity for me to share with others what I love most about Michigan.

I'm deeply indebted to many people who have assisted me in this book and others over the years. I thank Dana Gleason of Dana Packs, Sandy Graham of Kelty, Inc., and Herb Lindsay of Gore-Tex, Inc., for the equipment that allowed me to be comfortable outdoors regardless of the weather conditions.

I appreciate the support of my editors at *Booth News Service* in Lansing and at the *Saginaw News,* where tales of these walks first appeared in the pages of "Venture Outdoors." I also thank Chuck Spriggs of the Benchmark in Farmington, where others read about hiking in *Tracks & Trails.* Likewise, without the encouragement of Carl Taylor at Backcountry Publications, this project would never have been completed.

But most of all, I will always remember fondly my hiking partners and the others I met along these trails, if only for a brief instant to share information or swap exaggerated tales. Now, Mark, tell me again . . . How heavy was that pack of yours on North Manitou Island?

Introduction

Walking in the woods with my four-year-old son, I suddenly stopped, stared at the two paths that confronted me, looked around for a trail sign, and finally pulled out the map.

Michael stared at me before asking the inevitable question, "Are we lost?"

"Absolutely not, I know where we are."

"Where?"

"In Michigan," I said, and then told my four-year-old son to pipe down while I studied the map we had picked up at the Department of Natural Resources field office in Baldwin.

Lost in the woods? No, as my old scoutmaster used to say, just "geographically displaced." And it shouldn't really have surprised me. We were hiking along Pine Valleys Pathway in Pere Marquette State Forest, planning to spend a night at the walk-in campsites on the shores of . . . Lost Lake. Like many foot travel areas in Michigan's state forests, hikers share the area with horseback riders, mountain bikers, and skiers, while snowmobilers have their own trail passing through. Throw in a couple of old logging tracks and the dirt road to Stewart Lake, and it's quite understandable why we were geographically displaced.

No problem. One nice feature of this eight-mile trail network is how well it's been posted with trail signs. We merely retreated one hundred yards to the last blue bootprint we passed and corrected our error.

Another nice aspect of this pathway was that we didn't see another person on the trail that afternoon. Three wild turkeys, a ruffed grouse, and deer prints by the dozens, but no other backpackers. But the best part of the trip was emerging on the edge of a wooded bluff and "finding" Lost Lake for the first time. There wasn't a soul on the small lake. It was all ours. We descended to the shoreline, pitched our tent so we could view the whole lake from our sleeping bags, and spent most of the evening sitting on the bank watching our bobbers on the still surface.

While enjoying our own little lake, for the first time that day we truly felt lost . . . from everybody and everything. And isn't that what hiking is all about?

Hiking in Southern Michigan

It should be no surprise that Michigan, with the world's greatest collection of freshwater sand dunes, with the best trout streams east of the Mississippi, with 3,200 miles of Great Lake shoreline, has the trail network and scenery every hiker dreams about. A hike in the Great Lakes State is not just a walk down a dirt path but the means to see some of the country's most spectacular natural treasures. From sand dunes without even a blade of grass to the towering monarchs of Hartwick Pines' virgin forests, from miles of beach that turn to gold with every Lake Michigan sunset to one of the eleven thousand inland lakes where on a still evening bass rise to the surface like trout, all these wonders of the Midwest can be reached by hiking foot trails.

The scenery is as varied as anywhere in the country, and so are the trails. Michigan's paths include a major part of what, when completed, will be the longest trail in the country, the 3,200-mile-

Beaver dam seen along Reid Lake Foot Travel Area in Huron National Forest

long North Country Trail, and range down to short hikes such as the mile-long Ledges Trail, which skirts the famous rock cliffs along the Grand River and provides hikers with a front row seat of daredevil rock climbers. The hikes can be classified as "walks," short and easy trails that are usually under three miles in length, "trails," which include a variety of terrain and are often five to eight miles in length, and "foot travel areas," a network of trails that usually offers backcountry camping.

All three types of trails are in this book, which seeks to reveal the best fifty hikes in southern Michigan. The region covered is basically Michigan south of the 45th parallel, the halfway point between the equator and the North

Pole, along with the Leelanau Peninsula. The region might also be described as south of the straight county line that forms the northern border of Alcona, Oscoda, Crawford, and Kalkaska counties, plus Leelanau County, an important addition. Although it might be slightly out of place, the peninsula had to be included in the southern region to keep Sleeping Bear Dunes National Lakeshore in one volume. This federal preserve, which stretches from Crystal Lake to North Manitou Island offshore of Leland, is one of Michigan's four greatest hiking areas, offering a variety of trails, backpacking opportunities, and superb scenery. The other three consist of Pictured Rocks National Lakeshore, Porcupine Mountains Wilderness State

Park, and Isle Royale National Park, but Sleeping Bear Dunes is the only one of the four in the Lower Peninsula.

The other reason for dividing the state at this point deals with driving time. From Michigan's major urban areas — Detroit, Grand Rapids, Lansing, Flint, Jackson, and Kalamazoo — most of the hikes in this book are within a two- to three-hour drive and are almost always under four hours away. The majority of them are thus possible day hikes, and almost all of them can be weekend destinations. A Detroit hiker cannot reach north of the 45th parallel, and especially the trails in the Upper Peninsula, in a day and, even on a weekend outing, would spend most of his or her time driving there, not walking.

Topography and terrain: There are no mountains in southern Michigan, but there are hills (some steep ones), many ridges, and, of course, sand dunes. All of them are the results of the several continental glaciers that covered Michigan during the Pleistocene era, which ended only twelve thousand years ago. The forward movement of the glaciers rounded off the tops of hills, gouged out the Great Lakes, and deepened valleys to give them their U-shapes.

As the great ice age melted northward, water was everywhere. New river channels cut through sands and gravel, carving sculptures like the ledges of the Grand River, before draining into broad lowlands and filling the Great Lakes. Massive chunks of ice became kettle lakes, while winds and waves gathered up glacial drift and created the beaches along the Great Lakes and the dunes bordering Lake Michigan.

Today in southern Michigan, hikers find a region with a variety of topography — from the broad river valleys in the heart of the state to the vast stretches of wetlands that border Saginaw Bay and the state's most famous stretches of dunes. Within this region is the dividing line between the hardwood forests of broad-leafed trees, whose leaves turn brilliant colors in the fall, and the transitional forest. Commonly referred to as the North Woods, here beech and sugar maples of the southern forest grow side-by-side with red pine, white pine, and hemlock, trees typical of the boreal forests of Canada.

Because of this variety, the fifty hikes in this book have been divided into six areas:

Southeast: Although dominated by Detroit, an urban wasteland to most hikers, the edges of this seven-county region contain some excellent hiking opportunities. It's not wilderness, by any means, and sometimes it's hard to escape the sights and sounds of a mushrooming metropolitan area, but many people are surprised at the rugged terrain, scenic lakes, and rewarding trails they can find within an hour's drive of the city. There are even backpacking opportunities, including a three-day trek along the Waterloo-Pinckney Trail that climbs over several scenic vistas and passes almost a dozen lakes. The best short hike of the region is Silver Lake Trail, a 2.3-mile loop in Pinckney Recreation Area.

Lake Huron: This region extends from the Thumb and Saginaw Bay north along the Great Lake and includes most of Huron National Forest. It's characterized by the wetlands along the Saginaw Bay, the AuSable River and other fine trout streams, and the most undeveloped Great Lake shoreline found anywhere in the southern half of the state. Included in this book are eight trails in this area, several with backcountry camping opportunities. The best backpacking trip is the West Loop of the Hoist Lakes Foot Travel Area. The most unusual day hike is the walk out to South Point in Negwegon State Park.

Heartland: The only region not abutted by a Great Lake, this section of Michigan extends from the borders with Ohio and Indiana to Isabella County, the heart of the Lower Peninsula. The area is characterized by numerous rivers and the broad valleys they flow through on their way to the Lakes, including the Grand River, the longest waterway in Michigan at 260 miles. Four of the seven hikes border rivers, including two on the Grand. Best day hike—Wildwood Pathway in Deerfield County Park near Mt. Pleasant with its distinctive covered bridge. Best backpacking trek—the Baldwin Segment of the North Country Trail.

Lake Michigan: This is dune country. Michigan's shoreline is a showcase of 275,000 acres of freshwater sand dunes, and the vast majority of them are found here and in the Sleeping Bear Dunes region. These towering hills of sand, which often rise to almost two hundred feet above Lake Michigan, make for an intriguing topography and for outstanding hiking. There are nine hikes featured in this region, and eight of them wind through the coastal dunes along the Great Lake, where it's often possible to combine a trek in the morning with stretching out on a remote beach in the afternoon. Best backpacking adventure—the Michigan Trail in Nordhouse Dunes Wilderness. Best day hike—the route to Lake Michigan in Silver Lake State Park.

Sleeping Bear Dunes: This is the smallest region in the book, covering only Benzie and Leelanau counties, but the best hiking and, without a doubt, the most spectacular scenery is found here. Seven of the eight hikes described lie in Sleeping Bear Dunes National Park, whose towering perches of sand may be the most famous dunes in the country. Trails often climb one hundred feet or more to scenic vistas, where you can gaze over the rugged coastline to the islands out on Lake Michigan or, if you time it right, toward a sunset melting into a watery horizon. Best backpacking adventure—North Manitou Island. Best day hike—South Manitou Island.

Pere Marquette: Hiking abounds in this nine-county region, for much of it has been preserved in two great forests: the Pere Marquette State Forest and the Manistee National Forest. To most people in Michigan, here is where you enter the North Woods, that fabled spot where pines lean over banks of crystal clear streams and trout are rising just around the bend. Vast forests, spring-fed rivers, and trout characterize this area, home of such scenic and wild rivers as the Pere Marquette, Little Manistee, Pine, and Boardman. The best backpacking adventure—North Country Trail, Manistee segment. Best day hike—Wakeley Lake Foot Travel Area.

When to Hike

You can undertake these trails any time of the year, and during a mild winter, you need not even worry about encountering much snow south of Lansing. Most people, though, regard the hiking season in lower Michigan as extending from late April to early November. Depending on the year, there is often good hiking in April and May. Streams may be swollen and trails a little muddy in places, but the wildflowers are blooming in profusion, fiddleheads are emerging from a damp layer of leaves, and ducks and geese are migrating through the region. Everything in the forest seems to be awakening, hikers included. Best of all, there're no bugs, not yet. Temperatures can be cool—in the fifties and sixties—and rain showers are a frequent occurrence. Pack a rain suit and don't worry about getting your boots muddy.

June through August is summer hiking, the most popular time if only because children are out of school and treks into the woods are often part of the family vacation or camping trips. Temperatures can range anywhere from a pleasant seventy degrees Fahrenheit in June to a blistering ninety in August. Sunny weather and blue skies are the norm, but keep an eye out for sudden thunderstorms that roll off Lake Michigan or across the state. Many state park campgrounds are filled for the weekend by Thursday night, and, of course, summer is insect season. Mosquitoes begin appearing by late May in southern Michigan and usually peak sometime in late June. Deerflies filter through later (how convenient) and seem to be most annoying in late July and early August.

If bugs and crowds annoy you, there are trails that provide an escape from both. The dune country is an excellent choice. Step out of the woods and into the open dunes and watch the bugs diminish. Hike a mile or two from the road, and there's a beach to stretch out on or a walk-in campsite without a single recreational vehicle.

Few argue, however, that the best time to hike lower Michigan is September through October. Temperatures return to those pleasant levels below seventy degrees. Showers are common (especially on the weekends it seems), but so are those glorious Indian summer days when the sky is a deep blue, the forest dry, and the temperature peaks in the mid-sixties. And then there are the fall colors. The hardwoods in this part of the state begin changing in mid-September and peak anywhere from the first week of October around Traverse City to the end of the month at the Warren Woods Natural Area near the Indiana border.

There're no bugs, there's great color, it's common to spot deer and other wildlife, and on a Saturday afternoon, half the state is glued to the television watching the University of Michigan football game. Without a doubt, Michigan autumns were made for hikers. The unofficial end of the hiking season for many is November 15, the first day of the firearm deer season. Not caring to add "hunter orange" to their wardrobes, people tend to put the boots away and, by the time the sixteen-day season is over, are too busy with other activities to return to the woods.

Clothing and Equipment

Too often people undertake a day hike with little or no equipment and then, two hours from the trailhead, get caught in a rain shower wearing only a flimsy cotton jacket. Or, in the worst possible scenario, they get lost and are forced to spend a night in the woods without food, matches, or warm clothing. To hike without a soft daypack or rucksack containing the essential equipment is like driving your car without putting on the safety belt. The risk just isn't worth it.

Always carry what many refer to as the "ten essentials." They are (1) food, either lunch or high-energy snacks such as trail mix, raisins, fruit, or chocolate; (2) rain protection in a windbreaker or Gore-Tex garment and, depending on the season, extra warm clothing, especially a wool hat and mittens; (3) water; (4) a pocket-sized flashlight; (5) a compass; (6) an appropriate map; (7) matches in a waterproof container; (8) insect repellent; (9) a small folding knife (the Swiss Army knife being the classic choice); and (10) a small first-aid kit that contains items (moleskin, bandages) to take care of blisters that suddenly develop three miles from the trailhead.

Perhaps the most important piece of equipment is your footwear. For years the traditional choice was the heavy, all-leather hiking boot that was smeared on the outside with half a can of bees wax. Today you rarely see such boots on Michigan's trails. Most hikers opt for the new, ultra-light nylon boots made by sporting-shoe companies such as High-Tec, Nike, and Vassar. These are easier on the feet, do not need half as much time to break in, and provide enough foot protection for the trails in lower Michigan. Normal tennis or running shoes, on the other hand, do not provide sufficient ankle support for most trails.

Depending on the season, other gear might be necessary. In the summer, you will want to carry along sun screen, sun glasses, and a wide-brimmed hat, especially when hiking trails in dune country. In November or December, mittens, stocking cap, and a warm sweater or sweatshirt are needed to avoid chilling when you stop for a break or lunch. If it's deer season, whether the firearm or the archery hunt, which extends from October 1 to December 31, add a piece of "hunter orange" clothing, if only a stocking cap.

Backpacking and Camping

Backpacking opportunities, off-trail camping, and walk-in campsites are described for fifteen of the fifty trails included here. The "highlights" listing at the beginnings of chapters indicates which trails offer such camping opportunities. Backcountry camping offers hikers a rustic setting that can only be reached by trail, with sites containing at most a fire ring, hand pump for water, and maybe a vault toilet. Many spots are simply a scenic spot to pitch a tent. When considering such an adventure, follow the new wilderness ethic of minimum-impact camping being promoted by the U.S. Forest Service and many other groups.

Either pitch the tent in designated campsites or select a level area with adequate water runoff. Use a plastic ground cloth to stay dry rather than ditch around the tent. Position the tent so that it blends in with the environment, and never set up camp within two hundred feet of natural water or the trail. Wash, brush teeth, and clean dishes one hundred feet from all water sources. Never use soap or clean up directly in streams or lakes. Cook on pack stoves and, if you must have a fire, keep it small, using only downed wood. Totally dismantle the rocks used for the pit and cover up the ashes with natural material. Leave the axe at home.

It's best to hike and camp in small groups that have less impact on wildlife and terrain. Forego the boomboxes and radios. And, most important, not only pack out all your own garbage but pick up and carry out any litter you encounter on the trail. If hikers don't pick it up, who will?

Water and Ticks

Unless the water comes out of a hand pump or has been posted as safe to drink, consider it not. Water from all lakes, streams, and rivers must be treated before you drink it. The increasing occurrence of backcountry dysentery caused by *Giardia lamblia* clearly demonstrates the frequency of water pollution in parks and state land. To ensure your safety, boil water a full minute

Tracks in the dunes

or run it through a filter whose screen is small enough to remove microscopic organisms along with other impurities.

For many hikers, an even greater fear than bad water is Lyme disease. The bacterium that causes Lyme disease is transmitted to humans through the bite of a deer tick, which is found on all types of vegetation but especially in the woods. The very small deer tick is orange and brown with a black spot near its head. Even more common is the wood tick, which is considerably larger and has white marks near its head but is unlikely to transmit the disease.

The best way to deal with Lyme disease is to avoid the tick. The tick is most active in the spring and early summer but is also present in the fall. Many bug repellents work well against the insect, especially those containing a high percentage of diethyltoluamide (DEET).* Treat shoes, socks, and pant legs as well as skin to repel ticks. Wear long sleeves and long pants, make periodic checks for ticks, and when the outing is over, bathe as soon as possible to wash off any tick you might have come in contact with. A hot shower and a good scrub with a wash cloth is probably the best precaution against ticks, which need up to twenty-four hours to attach.

A diagnosis of Lyme disease is best left to a doctor, but common early symptoms include a ring-shaped rash that can occur four to twenty days after the bite. You might also experience fatigue, mild headaches, muscle and joint pain, fever, and swollen glands. Some victims believe they have nothing more than a mild case of flu, while others suffer joint inflammation and other arthritis-like symptoms. Fortunately, the disease is rarely fatal and if detected early can be treated with antibiotics.

Most important, don't give up hiking or other outdoor activities because of Lyme disease. Some common sense and a few precautions will prevent most encounters with deer ticks.

How to Use This Book

It is not the intention of this guide to give hikers a step-by-step narration of a trail. Some might wonder why it's even necessary to provide walkers with anything more than the location of a trailhead and the length of the path. The answer is simple—time constraints. In this hectic world of raising families and maintaining houses and marriages where both spouses work, we never seem to have enough time to venture outdoors. What little time we do carve out for a hike or a weekend backpacking trip is rare and valuable.

So valuable that it can't be wasted on an ill-planned adventure. That's the reason for this guidebook. I once drove three hours for a hike that turned into an afternoon of walking through clearcuts and past discarded cars and washing machines—not my idea of a quality trek. If you only undertake a handful of hikes each year, or even a dozen, you want each one to be a good outdoor experience. You want to be spellbound with the scenery, to climb through hills, or to find a backcountry lake to spend the

---

*There has been recent concern about repellents containing DEET, principally because of reports of neurological problems in children associated with excessive use of these repellents. Given the effectiveness of DEET products in reducing the spread of Lyme disease, state health departments have not recommended against using them. They do, however, recommend that you avoid using repellents containing more than 30% DEET on children, avoid prolonged and excessive use (no more than 1 to 2 applications a day), and apply repellents to clothes rather than skin whenever possible. People with skin problems should also use DEET products sparingly.

night at . . . you don't want to be buzzed by a pack of off-road vehicles.

This book leads you to those treks. It doesn't tell you what's around every bend, but it does cover the highlights of each trail and, in some cases, the low points. It provides facts on the natural or human history of the area for a better appreciation of the land you're walking through. It mentions if there are fish the lake so you can pack your rod, and notes the campsites along the way so you can plan to spend an evening. Each description lists the length and difficulty of each stretch—most important details. Ill-fated outings usually begin when hikers select a trail too long or too hard for their capabilities.

What makes one trail better than another? Many times your assessment of a trail results from unpredictable circumstances surrounding the hike—good weather, a lucky sighting of a deer or a flock of wild turkeys, or, alternatively, a swarm of mosquitoes that drives you back to the car after only a half mile. But good trails do share many tangible characteristics.

They provide excellent scenery. On many, you climb to a highpoint and are rewarded with a panorama that's well worth the drive and the struggle to the top. Others skirt lakes that are not encircled by cottages and docks, follow streams, or wind through a wooded hollow. They offer a variety of terrain—hills and ridges to climb, beaches to follow, wetlands to skirt. Often a change in topography makes the hike almost as interesting as reaching a scenic vista. The trails in this book were also chosen because they are generally well posted and maintained. You will thus spend most of your time studying the scenery or looking for wildlife rather than staring at a compass or a topographical quad.

Finally, some trails were selected simply for their location. The Penoska Trail in Brighton Recreation Area is an amazing route if for no other reason than that, within thirty minutes of downtown Detroit, there is a place to hike five miles in the woods. And that's a most important characteristic of a good trail— an escape from the concrete jungle at home. The escape doesn't have to be into a true wilderness, in fact you'd be hard pressed to find such in lower Michigan; it just has to be a route away from the sights, sounds, and golden arches of our society—if only for an hour or two.

The most important use of this book is for choosing the right hike. At the beginning of each description, you'll find a listing of total distance, hiking time, a difficulty rating, and maps that can be helpful.

Total distance includes a round-trip hike unless otherwise noted. Mileage is based on actual distance hiked as opposed to a measurement taken from a United States Geological Survey (USGS) quad. This figure is the most useful for hikers, since it takes into account climbing hills or following a series of switchbacks into a ravine. None of us follow a route "as a crow flies."

Hiking time is an estimate; your actual hiking time will depend upon your walking speed. The estimate is based on the fact that reasonably fit hikers cover two to three miles an hour on level ground and less than two miles when moderate uphill walking is involved. The figure does not include an hour for lunch or an afternoon spent trying to land a bass out of a remote lake.

Rating is even more subjective than hiking time. In general, though, you can consider those treks rated "easy" to be walks under three miles in length on somewhat level ground and along well-maintained trails, where bridges and boardwalks cover wet areas. "Moderate" hikes usually include some climbing, and their length—from 4 to 7 miles—demand that you carefully plan sufficient time to complete the outing. "Challenging" treks include not only some rugged terrain but might also involve poorly marked trails where a USGS quad is a necessity. Many challenging trails are also long and require an overnight in the backcountry.

Maps listed are either the proper USGS topographic quad of the 7½' series or a map available at the park or nearest ranger station. Judge for yourself which you feel more comfortable with.

Finally the question of rating trails. I say why not? We rate movies and cars and books, even washing machines and motels. Why not trails? As a lifelong resident of Michigan, as an avid hiker since my Boy Scout days in Troop 1261, and as an outdoor writer most of my working days, I've hiked hundreds of trails in lower Michigan. What I am presenting here is one man's opinion of the best fifty walks, hikes, and backpacking treks of varying lengths and locations around the state. It's the opinion of a person, you might say, who's been down the trail.

If I was only spending a summer here or were soon moving out-of-state, here are the best five hikes in southern Michigan, not to be missed:

1. South Manitou Island—the views from the top of the perched dunes here are breathtaking, while the artifacts from the island's past, from a shipwreck to a historic lighthouse, make this trek one of the most interesting day hikes in the state.

2. Manistee Segment of the North Country Trail—a long trail at more than twenty miles, but the scenery and the remoteness of the backcountry intrigue you from the first step to the last.

3. Michigan Trail in Nordhouse Dunes—the entire federal wilderness is a hiker's delight, but this stretch, where you follow a bluff while looking down on the Lake Michigan shoreline, is a scenic trek every step of the way.

4. West Loop of Hoist Foot Travel Area—Byron Lake has some the most scenic backcountry campsites in the state, while the vista the trail climbs to south of the lake provides an excellent panorama.

5. South Point in Negwegon State Park—the park is hard to reach, but the trail winds past the most remote beaches on Lake Huron. The scene at the tip of South Point is worth the 2.5-mile walk.

Southeast

1

Paint Creek Trail

Place: Rochester to Lake Orion
Total Distance: 9 miles one-way
Hiking Time: 4 hours one-way
Rating: Easy to moderate
Highpoints: Trout stream, cider mills
Maps: USGS Utica, Rochester, and Lake Orion; Paint Creek
*   Trail map from Rochester-Utica Recreation Area*
*   headquarters*

You will frequently see houses along the Paint Creek Trail; you have to wander through downtown Rochester as well as cross seven other roads while hiking the entire route; and the trail parallels Orion Road so closely in places you can hear the traffic as commuters rush home at day's end. Still, Paint Creek Trail is an amazing avenue. Within the rapid development of Oakland County, one of the fastest growing areas of Michigan, is this nine-mile trail that, for the most part, is a wooded path winding along a trout stream. It touches ponds, grassy meadows, wetlands, even prairie habitat, where wildlife such as muskrats, herons, snapping turtles, and an occasional deer can be sighted. But most of all for those walking or jogging along the gravel path, Paint Creek is a quiet escape from the bulldoze mentality of developers who are scraping clean this hilly region north of Detroit and turning it into a land of strip malls and subdivisions.

Paint Creek Trail extends from the Clinton River at the Rochester-Utica

Recreation Area to Lake Orion, interrupted only briefly in downtown Rochester. It was the first rails-to-trails project to be opened in Michigan, where there are now a half dozen either in the planning stages or nearing completion. The concept behind this national movement is to purchase abandoned railways, strip off the rails and ties and resurface the gravel beds, construct bridges where needed, and post signs prohibiting motorized vehicles.

Paint Creek was the corridor for the Penn Central Line, and leftover railroading artifacts, including rails, wood ties, even communication boxes, still litter the area. The trains also had another interesting impact on the landscape. Paint Creek drops three hundred feet in elevation between Lake Orion and Clinton River, and naturalists say that the old trains spewed forth a lot of hot cinders while working their way back up this incline. The result was numerous grass fires, which have resulted in the small patches of rare prairie habitat found here today.

The entire trail takes a good four to five hours to hike, so, being a point-to-point path, there is a need for two vehicles or some other plan for returning to the trailhead. The trail is accessible from almost a dozen spots where it crosses a road, and most people tackle only a section of it. One of the most scenic segments is the 2.4-mile stretch from Tienken Road to Gallagher Road and Paint Creek Cider Mill, an appropriate place to end a walk.

The trail can easily be handled in tennis shoes and is, in fact, a popular route for joggers. Anglers might want to carry a rod and reel and a container of leaf worms, for the creek is stocked annually with rainbow trout by the state's Department of Natural Resources. The best time to tackle the trail, without a doubt, is the fall when the hardwood forests of predominately oak, maple, and hickory are blazing with autumn colors.

Access: The southern trailhead is directly across from the Yates Cider Mill in the Rochester-Utica State Recreation Area. The recreation area is located on the corner of Dequindre and 23 Mile Road (Avon Road) just east of Rochester, and can be reached from MI 59 by heading north of the Dequindre exit. The northern trailhead is an unmarked path that departs from the backside of a supermarket parking lot on the corner of MI 24 and Atwater Street. The trail is also posted in Lake Orion at the end of Newton Street south of Atwater.

Other good spots to pick up the trail are Rochester Municipal Park at Pine Street just north of University Avenue, Tienken Road west of Rochester Road, Silver Bell Road west of Orion Road, and at the corner of Clarkston and Kern roads in Bald Mountain Recreation Area. At all these points, the trail is posted, and there's space to park a vehicle.

For more information on the Paint Creek Trail or to pick up a trail map, stop at the Rochester-Utica Recreation Area headquarters at 47511 Wooddall Road, off Auburn Road in the southern portion of the park. The office (313-731-2110) is open from 8 A.M. to 4:30 P.M. Monday through Friday.

Trail: Paint Creek Trail technically begins within sight of the big red barn of Yates Cider Mill, the first of two cider mills along the trail and one of the most colorful and popular mills in southeastern Michigan. Built in 1863, it began its long history as a grist mill and has been a water-powered operation ever since. In 1876 it began making cider, and today the water wheel still powers the apple elevator, grinders, and press, as well as generating electricity for the lights inside. The mill (313-651-8300) is open daily from 9 A.M. to 7 P.M. from September through November, and noon to 5 P.M. Saturday and Sunday from December through May.

Across Avon Road is the posted trailhead for Paint Creek Trail, but you quickly dead-end at a washed-out railroad bridge at Clinton River. For this reason, most hikers park at the Rochester-Utica Recreation Area and pick up the trail by traveling over a wooden footbridge to the west bank of the Clinton River. At this point, the trail is a wide path covered with large gravel and parallels the Clinton River, not Paint Creek. Throughout most of the walk, however, you are in the woods and out of sight of the water. The river does pop into view twice, the second time being a scenic spot where the Clinton makes a sweeping curve to the east, reached .8 mile from the trailhead. The trail skirts the river briefly, then departs and follows a straight course along the powerlines, where on one side of you is a hardwood forest and the other, a grassy strip.

At 1.2 miles you reach the Clinton a

third time and cross it on a bridge, only to discover that the trail ends at a railroad track that has hardly been abandoned. To continue, you must follow the line .3 mile to Second Street, the first road to cross the tracks. Turn right onto the road. After passing over Paint Creek, Second merges into Third Street, which is followed west. Two blocks past Main Street (Rochester Road), turn north (right) on Pine Street and follow it three blocks to the banks of Paint Creek, rippling gently through the heart of Rochester Municipal Park.

The park is a maze of sidewalks, and the trail follows its northeast side. It is easiest to relocate it where Ludlow Road crosses the creek at the northernmost point of the municipal park. Here the trail is well posted on both sides. Heading north, the trail quickly crosses the creek again and arrives at a stairway leading into Dinosaur Hill Nature Preserve. Named after a hill that children said looked like a sleeping brontosaurus, this sixteen-acre preserve is located on the northern edge of Rochester and is bordered on one side by Paint Creek. Dinosaur Hill (313-656-0999), which includes an interpretive center and three self-guided nature trails, is open from 9 A.M. until 2 P.M. Monday through Thursday, and 10 A.M. to 1 P.M. on the weekends in the summer. During the school year hours are 9 A.M. to 5 P.M. Tuesday through Friday, and noon to 3 P.M. Saturday and Sunday. There is no admission charge.

From the preserve, you follow the trail for only .3 mile before crossing Tienken Road. After switching to the creek's north bank, you pass within view of the backside of a subdivision, then gradually leave the sights and sounds of Rochester behind. The sights that remain are of a gurgling trout stream, as you wander through the woods. Within 1.5 miles of Rochester Municipal Park, the trail crosses the creek a second time. Just beyond the bridge are a series of steps leading down to the water; a quiet place to soothe the mind.

From the steps you quickly reach Dutton Road, where there are bridges crossing the creek on each side of the road. The trail maintains a level and straight course here, and, on the way to Silver Bell Road, crosses the creek twice more. In many places here, the streambanks have been reinforced by logs. The work of a local Trout Unlimited Chapter, these logs and rocks were placed to stabilize eroding portions of the stream, which were making the water too silty for trout eggs to hatch. Natural reproduction now occurs, and along with annual plantings makes Paint Creek a destination for anglers. Though it's rare to see a fly fisherman here, occasionally you run into an angler who is simply baiting a small hook with a worm and floating it in the current through pools and eddies. Most angling activity takes place between Dutton Road and Gunn Road, but only because this is where Paint Creek flows closest to Orion Road. Generally the trout are not big, though I once watched a young angler land a fifteen-inch rainbow.

Silver Bell Road is reached 2.5 miles from Rochester Municipal Park. On the north side of the road the trail becomes a wide, gravel path that parallels the creek. The stream swings close to the path several times, and in .5 mile you come to another set of steps that overlooks an S-bend in the creek. It's a scenic spot to toss a line in or just sit and while away the afternoon.

Just before reaching Gallagher Road, 3 miles from the municipal park, you will see the backside of Paint Creek Cider Mill along the stream. Needham Hem-

Hikers in Paint Creek

ingway built the first mill here in 1835, then dug a raceway a half mile up Paint Creek to power his fifteen-foot water wheel. The original mill was torn down in the 1940s but quickly was replaced and remained a water-powered operation until 1960. Located on the corner of Gallagher and Lake Orion roads in the hamlet of Goodison, the mill (313-651-8361) is best known today as a fine restaurant where many tables overlook the water wheel and raceway. But from September through Christmas, the mill makes apple cider and is open from 9 A.M. to 6 P.M. daily. During the summer, it switches to selling ice cream and is open 11 A.M. to 8 P.M. Tuesday through Saturday, and until 6 P.M. on Sunday. Either one is a refreshing treat that can be enjoyed near the banks of the creek.

The scenery changes in the next stretch as you pass a handful of impressive homes to the east, some with their own ponds, and wetlands to the west. Paint Creek never actually appears, since it flows through private property and is fenced off. The trail crosses Gunn Road 3.5 miles from Rochester Municipal Park and in another quarter mile, the trail crosses a bridge to the creek's east side. The terrain is open but undeveloped here, with the exception of a scenic faded barn. Shortly, the creek swings by, while on the east side of the trail is a large pond. Another half-dozen ponds are spotted before you reach Adams Road, and all should be surveyed for the variety of wildlife they attract, including nesting herons.

Adams Road is reached 4.5 miles from Rochester Municipal Park, with the trail resuming on the other side as a narrow, dirt path. Within .25 mile you pass a sign warning of the approaching Royal Oak Archery Club. The sight of some target bales, no more than fifteen yards away from the trail, has undoubtedly quickened the heartbeat of a few hikers. But any nervousness quickly disappears as the trail approaches its most scenic and isolated section. Less than .25 mile from the club, you begin to hear the creek and then see its gently flowing waters. For the next half mile, the trail stays within sight of the creek, which gurgles and sweeps through bends, looking all the world like a blue-ribbon trout stream up north. You have to remind yourself that you're in the fringes of one the largest metropolitan areas in the country.

You cross a bridge to the west side of Paint Creek 5.5 miles from Rochester Municipal Park, and soon break out of the hardwood forest at the intersection of Kern and Clarkston roads. The trail crosses Clarkston Road high above the creek, evidence of the constant grade you've unknowingly been climbing all day. The trail is now passing through a small parcel of the Bald Mountain Recreation Area, and just beyond Clarkston Road is the last set of stairs down to the water.

The last segment of Paint Creek Trail heads northwest into the town of Lake Orion along a very straight route. Along the way, you pass the largest pond of the day. On the fringe of town, the trail uses an old railroad trestle to cross both a road and Paint Creek. Houses quickly pop into view, and the trail ends in a rather undramatic fashion, along the backside of a supermarket.

Graham Lakes Trail

Place: Bald Mountain Recreation Area
Total Distance: 3.6 miles
Hiking Time: 1 hour
Rating: Moderate
Highpoints: Lakes, scenic vistas
Maps: USGS Lake Orion; Bald Mountain Recreation Area
*   North Unit Trail Guide*

In 1983, the Department of Natural Resources staff at Bald Mountain Recreation Area built a loop around Graham Lakes and marked and promoted the new trail for cross-country skiing. Located in hilly northern Oakland County, the lake-studded area seemed a natural for skiers, providing numerous long, downhill runs. To the surprise of the DNR staff, skiers returned the following summer as hikers to discover what the new trail would be like on foot.

What they discovered was one of the most scenic and enjoyable foot trails in southeastern Michigan, and today the route is as popular with hikers spring through fall as with skiers in the winter. There is no actual "Bald Mountain" here, or anywhere else in the state recreation area, but the trail does ascend a number of ridges and hills, climbing sixty feet at one point, to several scenic overlooks of lakes. Hikers are left feeling physically invigorated at the end. Depending on the time of year, the wildlife encountered ranges from grouse, cottontail rabbits, and a variety of waterfowl, including Canada geese, to deer,

which are most often spotted in early spring or September. In spring, the patches of wildflowers abound near the wetlands; in the autumn, the ponds are highlighted by the fall colors of hardwood trees. Summer is nice, too, but keep in mind that these stagnant bodies of water are natural hatcheries for mosquitoes, especially late May through June.

The other attraction of the 4,637-acre state recreation area's northern unit is the fishing to be found in the walk-in lakes, and the trail provides access to a dock on the best one, West Graham Lake. Anglers can also wet a line in East Graham and Prince Lake with hopes of landing species ranging from bluegill and other panfish to smallmouth bass.

Access: The northern unit of the recreation area is a forty-five-minute drive north of Detroit. Located east of Lake Orion, the tract can be reached from MI 24 by following Clarkston Road, an especially scenic route where it forms an S-turn to cross Paint Creek. After 2 miles, turn north (left) on Adams Road,

which ends at Stoney Creek Road. Head east (right) 100 yards, then turn north (left) on Harmon Road which leads into the park. There are four trailheads and parking areas to the loop, including one at the end of Harmon Road, another near the corner of Predmore and Lake George Road, and a third further north on Lake George Road. This hike, however, is described from the trailhead at the East Graham Lake boat ramp, reached by turning right onto Predmore Road from Harmon and heading east for .25 mile. By starting here and walking counterclockwise, you put the heavily forested stretch in the middle of the hike and save the best view for the end. The park headquarters (313-

693-6767) is located in the southern unit and can be reached by departing east from MI 24 at Greenshield Road.

Trail: A large wooden display sign marks the trail. Heading east (right), you quickly break out into the back yard of the park manager's residence, where there is a dock onto East Graham Lake. The path re-enters the woods, then arrives at a wooden bridge over a stream, .5 mile from the parking lot. To the north is one end of East Graham Lake, to the south, the marshy shoreline of Dorn Lake, a gathering spot for waterfowl in spring and fall. The trail winds away from the lakes, returns to the woods, and within the next mile climbs over several hills. The footing is dry, but to the west is a low-lying area of ponds and swamps, undoubtedly the source of whatever is buzzing around you in July.

Eventually you climb to the highest point of the day, 1,020 feet, though it doesn't seem like it, pass a map-posted spur to the Lake George Road trailhead and swing due west. Remaining in hardwoods, the trail descends a long hill and finally breaks out of the trees at the edge of an arm of Duck Pond, a rather shallow and marshy pond. The best

The dock on East Graham Lake

view of the large pond is in another .5 mile, or 1.9 miles from the boat launch, where a skiers' bypass has been built. Here you ascend to an overlook, and a bench on top of a hill, with Duck Pond to the north and the surrounding hills to the west.

The trail continues west until it breaks out of the trees at Prince Lake, roughly the halfway point and a logical spot for an extended break or lunch on the shoreline. The lake has a boat launch on its west end, and a few anglers are attracted to it for panfish and bass. Avoid the trails that wander around the lake. Soon you'll enter a pine plantation whose towering trees are in perfect rows and that is marked in the middle by another bench. Within .6 mile from Prince Lake, the trail passes the only private home seen along the way, a rather amazing fact for this rapidly developing region of Oakland County, and then reaches the end of Harmon Road 2.7 miles from the beginning.

The trail loop heads south from here, crosses a wooden bridge over a stream that flows between Shoe and West Graham lakes, and begins to ascend the best hill of the day. On the way up, you pass a view of Shoe Lake and then actually "top out" at a clearing where there is a bench and panorama of West Graham Lake and many of the surrounding ridges you've already walked over. You quickly descend the other side and pass an old road heading east. This path is the trail to a fishing dock located on the southwest corner of the large lake. Shore fishermen can do well in West Graham from mid-May to mid-June when bluegill gather in their spawning beds in this shallow corner of the lake. During the rest of the summer, the bluegill are usually found in the middle of the lake where the depth reaches twenty-five feet. The most successful anglers at that time have squeezed a boat or canoe through the narrow stream that connects East Graham Lake with West Graham.

The descent off the hill ends in an open field where you pass post 11, the junction to the loop trail on the west side of Harmon Road. From here, the trail swings east into the woods and in .4 mile emerges at the boat launch parking area, having come full circle from where it started.

Springlake Trail

Place: Independence Oaks County Park
Total Distance: 3.1 miles
Hiking Time: 2 hours
Rating: Moderate
Highpoints: Nature center, inland lake
Maps: USGS Ortonville; Independence Oaks County Park
  map

Glaciers were good to Oakland County. In the northern portions of one of the state's most populated counties, these ancient rivers of ice scoured the land and left behind ridges, hills, and, most of all, potholes that became a patchwork of inland lakes and ponds. These qualities make for interesting terrain, diverse habitat, and excellent hiking wherever the land has been preserved from urban sprawl.

Independence Oaks County Park is such a place. Established in 1976, it's the largest unit in the Oakland County Parks system at 1,062 acres. The eastern half of the park, where visitors enter, has been developed, with shelters, a boathouse concession, tables, grills, fishing docks, and a swimming area. The western half is a series of rugged ridges and low-lying wetlands that can only be seen from the park's ten-mile network of foot trails. The natural barrier separating the two halves is Crooked Lake, a sixty-eight-acre lake with crystal clear water that is free from the summer buzz of motorboats.

The route described here is a 3.1-mile hike along most of the Springlake Trail to the south end of the park, with a return along the Ted Gray Trail, a portion of the Lakeshore Trail, and the Rockridge Trail. You begin and end at the Independence Oaks nature center, which is an ideal starting point for many hikers. Because of its terrain, the park supports a wide range of habitat, and hikers pass through upland forests of oak and hickory, pockets of cedar in the bog areas, and maple/beech climax forests surrounding the lake in the floodplains. This diversity of habitat and the wildlife it supports is explained through an excellent series of displays within the nature center.

Although the loop is not long, you do end up climbing more than one hundred feet along two main ridges, actually old glacial moraines. During the winter, these hills and trails attract cross-country skiers from throughout southeastern Michigan. In the summer, hikers climb the same ridgeline, where they often find a bench and a pleasant view of the park's interior. In this somewhat isolated section of the park, you can sit on

Geese on Crooked Lake

a quiet hilltop and not even know that on the other side of the lake there are picnickers, volleyball games, and family reunions taking place.

Access: Independence Oaks is located north of the village of Clarkston and can be reached from I-75 by exiting at Sashabaw Road (exit 89). Head north for 2 miles to the posted entrance. After entering the park, the road heads both north and south. To the south the park road ends at Hidden Lakes swimming area and a boathouse that rents out canoes, rowboats, and pedalboats, and sells bait during the summer. Turn north (right) to reach the nature center, open daily 10 A.M. to 6 P.M. Memorial Day to Labor Day, and Tuesday through Sunday 10 A.M. to 5 P.M. the rest of the year.

The park is open from 8 A.M. to dusk, and there is a vehicle entry fee for both residents and nonresidents of Oakland County. For more information call the park headquarters at (313) 625-0877.

Trail: A large sign with a park map marks the trail in the nature center parking area, and a few steps away is the posted junction of the Springlake Trail and the Rockridge Trail. Springlake departs to the north (straight) and is a wide path designed to accommodate both hikers and skiers. It begins with a descent into the first marsh of the day, which is crossed on a long boardwalk. Cattails are on both sides of you as the trail crosses the low-lying wet area and then climbs out of it to a ridgeline. You descend briefly, then climb again to the first bench, .5 mile from the parking lot.

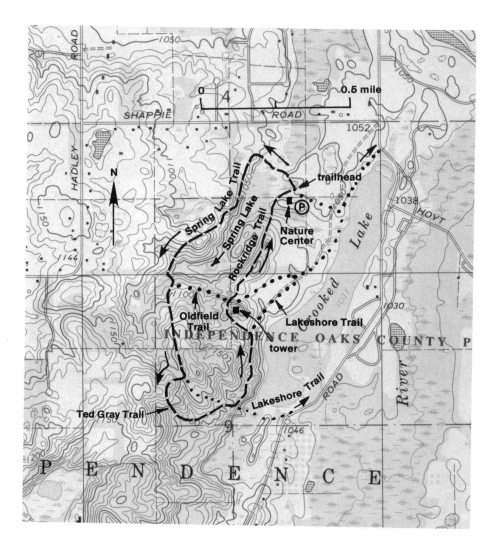

If the leaves aren't too thick, you can view the marsh area, which stretches from Spring Lake to Crooked Lake.

The trail quickly resumes climbing and passes another bench, a few steps off the path and easily missed. This one features a railing since it's perched on the steep side of the ridge, making the view an especially scenic one in mid-October when the fall colors are peaking. Beyond the bench, the trail continues to follow the ridgeline, rising and dropping with its crest, until you reach the posted junction with Oldfield Trail, a mile from the nature center. Head down Oldfield a few steps for your only view of Spring Lake, from a stand of tamarack. The small pond is a dying lake, slowly being filled in and covered up by the carpet of moss and bog plants that encircle it.

Back to Springlake Trail, which curves sharply away from the lake and begins a steady climb to the crest of another ridge, the one that is so clearly seen when driving Clarkston Road to the south. You follow the ridgeline for a short spell before topping out at almost 1,200 feet or more than 150 feet above the lake surface, where the junction with the Ted Gray Trail is posted. This spur is a bit longer than the last leg of the Springlake Trail but far more interesting. It descends sharply off the ridge, climbs back to almost 1,200 feet, and then drops sharply again in a stretch where more than one skier has lost control and ended up in the trees. It ends in a scenic marsh area crossed by a long boardwalk, where during the fall the surrounding hardwoods will be burning with reds and oranges while the cattails next to you are exploding in a mass of light brown fluff.

After .75 mile, Ted Gray returns to Springlake, which quickly merges into the posted Lakeshore Trail. Turning east (right) leads to the east side of Crooked Lake and the boathouse. Head north (left) to return to the nature center, first following the shoreline along the lake's south end. Here Crooked Lake forms a small, shallow bay that attracts both waterfowl and anglers in the spring. The lake supports bass and northern pike but is best known for its panfish. This section can be productive waters, especially in May when the fish are spawning in the shallows, and anglers often tease the fish into striking with rubber spiders or small poppers.

At one point the trail passes a picnic table on a small knoll overlooking the lake, a great place to eat your lunch. In .4 mile from the junction with the Springlake Trail, you reach the south end of the Rockridge Trail. Turn left onto Rockridge. This segment begins with a steady climb to the overlook tower, where another picnic table is located. The tower provides a view of the surrounding ridges outside of the park to the east, but ironically it's tough to see Crooked Lake right below you through the trees bordering the shoreline.

From the tower, the trail drops to the posted junction with Oldfield Trail and then begins a steady climb up "Devil's Elbow," a well-named stretch as far as skiers are concerned since the pitch is quite steep at one point. Rockridge tops off at 1,100 feet, where you can see both sides of the ridge from the trail before descending to the creek that runs from Spring Lake to Crooked Lake. You cross a bridge here and then quickly break out of the woods to arrive at the nature center, .6 mile from Lakeshore Trail.

4

Pen-O-Sha Trail

Place: Brighton Recreation Area
Total Distance: 5 miles
Hiking Time: 2.5 to 3 hours
Rating: Moderate
Highpoints: Hardwood forest, fall colors
Maps: USGS Brighton and Hamburg; "Hiking Trails at
  Brighton Recreation Area" map

Thanks to an ice age twenty-five thousand years ago and some unsuccessful farmers in the 1930s, today there is still a place in southeastern Michigan where people can escape the concrete and go for a walk in the woods. Brighton Recreation Area is a five thousand-acre unit of the state park system located in the rolling hills of southeast Livingston County. The park is blessed with an interesting terrain, ten lakes, and the Pen-O-Sha Trail, a five-mile trek in a hardwood forest of maple, hickory, and oak.

The glaciers of the Pleistocene epoch, which ended twenty-five thousand years ago, were responsible for the topography here, which features moraines and ridges, steep-sided kettles, and numerous lakes and ponds. Indians from the Potawatomi and Saginaw Chippewa tribes were its original occupants, before European settlers arrived in Livingston County in 1828. As towns such as Brighton and Howell grew, woodlands were cleared, and farms developed but were never very productive. It was a challenge to make a living by plowing land characterized by glacial drift and wetlands. During the depression of the 1930s, it became impossible, and farmers began selling out or, in many cases, simply abandoning their property. The state purchased much of Brighton Recreation Area between 1944 and 1949 and continues to add parcels from year to year. The unit still has a patchwork appearance, though, for private lots break up its continuity.

The largest contiguous section lies on the east side of Chilson Road and is the site of the park's four campgrounds, frontier cabins, and trail system. Pen-O-Sha is the Chippewa word for long, as opposed to Kaw-Chin, which means short and is the name for the two-mile loop that shares the same trailhead.

Although there is one scenic overlook, Pen-O-Sha is not a spectacular walk, and the backpacker's campground that was once located along it is gone. But the land is interesting and the trees impressive, and together they provide for a pleasant forest walk with only a few man-made intrusions in view. Wildlife in this area includes whitetail deer, foxes, pheasants, quail, and partridge, but to spot any you have to take to the trail in the early morning or at dusk and maintain a quiet pace. Most Saturday afternoon outings will flush out little more than a few squirrels or a raccoon.

The trail is well marked in blue bootprints, blue dots, and an occasional Department of Natural Resources (DNR) pathway triangle. It's easy to follow, and the brush along many stretches is even mowed at times (for reasons I don't understand). There is no question about the best time of year to hike it—in the fall. Leaves begin turning between late September and early October, peaking at the end of that month and lingering on well into November. The trail receives its heaviest use during that pe-

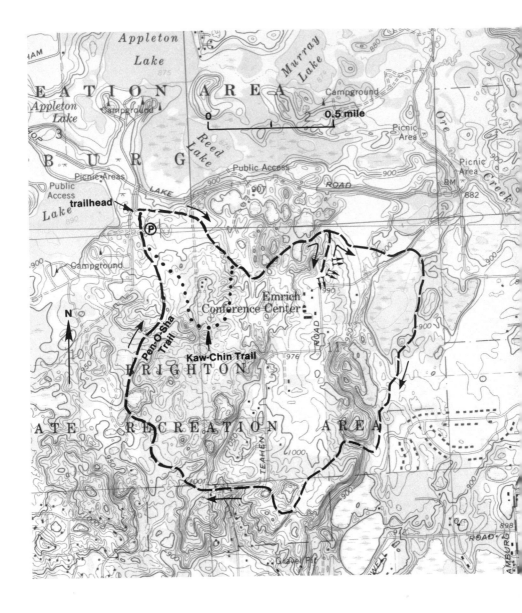

riod, but even on a bright and crisp weekend, you'll see only a handful of other hikers.

The main trail continues east beyond the spur and passes through more regenerating fields, semi-open forests with large maples and hickory trees, and kettles on both sides of the path. Eventually, you parallel Teahen Road from above, finally descending to the dirt road via a staircase. On the other side of the road, 1.4 miles from the trailhead, the path is marked by a "Wheeled Vehicles, Horses Prohibited" sign. You briefly pass through a thick growth of saplings, witness the trail split and rejoin quickly, and then re-enter the older forest, wondering when you'll spot Deidrich Lake.

You never do. You come close to its east side, but the forest is thick here and the leaves prevent you from spotting the small body of water most of the year. For the next mile, the hike remains in the forest and becomes a stroll along the hilly terrain. At one point, you skirt the base of a steep slope. Then, 2.2 miles from the beginning, the trail makes a 180-degree turn and ascends to the

Hikers on the Pen-O-Sha Trail

top of the heavily forested ridge for the most interesting stretch of the day.

You pass a log home at 2.5 miles and then more open fields, which become a vista of color in the fall. The knee-high grass of the meadow turns to gold in October, highlighting a few green pines in the middle of the old farm field that is framed by the reds and oranges of the surrounding hardwood forest. The trail curves north from the field and at 3 miles arrives at Teahen Road for the second time. Head south (left) for .2 mile to a trail sign next to a dirt driveway. The trail skirts two parcels of private land, hugging a fence and passing one home as it climbs a hill. It then drops back into the state recreation area.

In less than a mile from Teahen Road, the trail climbs steadily again. It skirts a large meadow from above and then a smaller one. In the morning or evening, search these areas carefully for any signs or sounds of wildlife. Especially in the evening you can occasionally be rewarded for sitting quietly on the edge of the meadow. The natural openings are followed by a stand of pines, a rare sight on this walk, and then another steady climb to a semi-open hilltop (but no view). From here, the trail gradually descends through open areas with scattered trees for the remaining .7 mile. Just before breaking out at the parking area, Kaw-Chin Trail, marked by blue DNR pathway triangles, merges into the main trail.

Silver Lake Trail

Place: Pinckney Recreation Area
Total Distance: 2.3 miles
Hiking Time: 1 to 2 hours
Rating: Easy
Highpoints: Inland lakes
Maps: USGS Pinckney; Pinckney Recreation Area map

Although it might be hard to believe when you're fighting crowds in the middle of the city, within an hour's drive of Detroit there are dozens of places to hike, and one of the best is Pinckney Recreation Area. The 10,842-acre state park unit was scoured by glaciers that left numerous lakes, ponds, and marshes lying between ridges and hills. Forested primarily in hardwoods, the park features a rainbow of wildflowers in the spring, spectacular fall colors in October, and a diversity of wildlife year-round, including deer, fox, pheasants, and usually a large number of waterfowl. From the hilltops and ridgelines you can also get an occasional extended view of this rugged slice of Michigan.

Although Pinckney is spread out and includes many parcels of private land (the typical, patchwork appearance of most recreation areas in this part of the state), there is enough public land for a forty-mile network of trails, including opportunities for backpackers. The Potawatomi Trail is a 17.3-mile route that includes a backpacker's camping area on Blind Lake. Also located in the park

is the eastern half of the Waterloo-Pinckney Trail, which at forty-six miles is the longest footpath in southern Michigan (see Hike 7).

Despite their lengths, though, either of these paths would be hard pressed to match the scenery experienced along the much shorter Silver Lake Trail. Only 2.3 miles in length, this route includes views of three lakes, passes by a handful of ponds, and climbs several hills to make the walk invigorating as well as visually enjoyable. The trail can easily be hiked in tennis shoes. The loop starts at the Silver Lake day-use area, where there is a swimming area, picnic tables, bathhouse, and grills.

The path is wide and well marked, and there's not a house within sight the entire route, something that most trails in the southern half of the state can't claim. The only possible drawback is the heavy numbers of mountain bikers that Pinckney Recreation Area draws. Although the cyclists seem to prefer the longer trails of Crooked Lake and Potawatomi, you should be prepared to encounter a few on Silver Lake during most weekends from May through Octo-

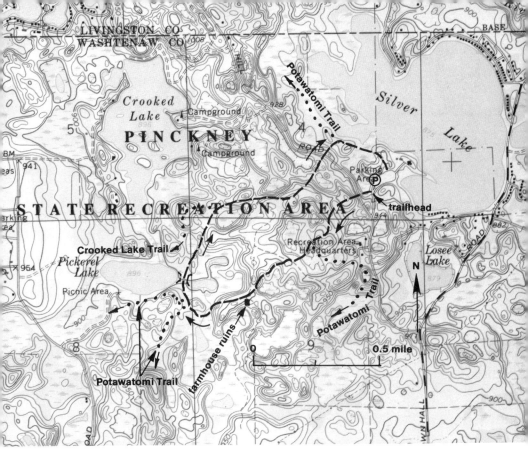

ber. Wildflower enthusiasts will enjoy this hike most if they arrive from late April through early May.

Access: The park is northwest of Ann Arbor and straddles the border between Livingston and Washtenaw counties. From I-94, depart at exit 159 and head north on MI 52 for 6 miles to North Territorial Road, where you turn right (east). The Silver Lake day-use area is reached by turning left (north) on Dexter-Townhall Road, which is reached in 5 miles, and then left at Silver Hill Road where the park entrance is posted. Dexter-Townhall Road can also be reached north of Ann Arbor from US 23 by departing west on North Territorial Road (exit 49) and heading west for 12 miles, or by exiting I-94 at Baker Road (167)

and continuing north on Dexter Pinckney Road to North Territorial.

Just before entering the day-use area, you pass the park headquarters (313-426-4913), where information about the park's trails, campgrounds, or other facilities can be obtained.

Trail: To avoid conflicts between mountain bikers and walkers, park officials established directional regulations in 1990. Cyclists need to follow the loop in a counterclockwise direction, and hikers, in a clockwise direction by beginning at the trailhead in the lower parking lot of the day-use area. The other trailhead is in the upper lot, and both have large display maps outlining all the trails in the park. From the lower lot, the trail enters the woods only to cross Silver Hill

Trillium wildflowers

Road and continue on the other side, where it ascends a hill. This first climb of the day will certainly not be the last, something that surprises those unfamiliar with this area.

In .5 mile you climb over another ridge and ascend a hill where, under a lone pine at the top, you can view the short stretch just hiked. The well-posted junction with the Potawatomi Trail is only a few steps further. Silver Lake Trail departs to the right (west), levels out somewhat, then skirts a bluff above a pond that is full of chirping frogs in the spring. Just around the bend, the trail comes to an old stone chimney and what appears to be a fruit cellar. Park rangers believe the old farmhouse might have been built in the nineteenth century by the Irish families who first settled here.

Quickly you come to a view of two small lakes before the trail descends to a creek and finally crosses it a mile from the trailhead. The creek heads south to a third small lake that is seen only briefly by those alert enough to be looking for it. The trail, however, heads

north to skirt the lake that drains directly into Pickerel Lake. You pass a second junction with the Potawatomi Trail and then descend to cross a wooden bridge over a stream. This is a scenic spot. From the middle of the bridge you can view the length of Pickerel all the way to the fishing pier at its west end, or you can turn around to see what waterfowl is gathering on the small lake to the east.

Beyond the bridge, you climb through the midst of a small stand of trees and then drop down to cross another swamp area, where there is a profusion of wildflowers every spring and, unfortunately, an equal number of mosquitoes in June. The trail departs the marsh to re-enter the woods and at 1.5 miles arrives at the posted junction with the Crooked Lake Trail (see Hike 6). By heading .3 mile west (left) along Crooked Lake Trail, you can come to another large footbridge from which you will be able to view both Pickerel and Crooked lakes.

Continue east along Silver Lake Trail to follow a ridge that looks down on a marsh pond to the south and then passes another pond on the north side of the trail. You finally climb a hill to the highest point of the day at 970 feet, but the trees preclude any view. The trail then descends steadily until you again cross Silver Hill Road. On the other side of the road, you pass yet another small pond and then break out at an arm of Silver Lake. If it's spring or fall, study the inlet carefully as it often attracts a variety of waterfowl, especially Canada geese.

The trail has now merged with the start of the Potawatomi and Crooked Lake trails, which continue north. To return to the day-use area, head south (right) to cut through an interesting cattail marsh before climbing to the upper parking lot.

Crooked Lake Trail

Place: Pinckney Recreation Area
Total Distance: 4 miles
Hiking Time: 2 hours
Rating: Moderate
Highpoints: Inland lakes, scenic vista
Maps: USGS Pinckney; Pinckney Recreation Area map

As pointed out in the description of Silver Lake Trail (Hike 5), the best hiking in southeastern Michigan is in Pinckney Recreation Area, and the Crooked Lake Trail is another reason why. This four-mile loop is a pleasant walk that traverses hardwood forests, marshes, and grassy hillsides. Along the way, you pass three inland lakes, climb to 1,008 feet for a view of Crooked Lake, and plunge down a ridge forested in hardwoods that makes this path an especially scenic one in October.

But the nicest feature of this trail is its proximity to several urban areas, including Jackson, Ann Arbor, and western Detroit. Because of Pinckney Recreation Area, hikers from here don't have to drive all day just to find a scenic trail on state land. Unfortunately, this location also draws large number of mountain bikers that are looking for suitable terrain to pursue their activity. These off-road cyclists began appearing in the mid-1980s, and when the sport mushroomed a few years later, so did the number of incidents between walkers and riders in Pinckney Recreation Area. In an effort to find a solution to the problem, the state park staff instituted regulations in 1990 that required bikers to follow Crooked Lake in a clockwise direction and recommended that hikers walk in the opposite direction.

By following these regulations, at least you have time to react to bikers speeding towards you. If encounters with even conscientious cyclists who pull over to allow hikers to pass disturb your walk, find another trail. Crooked Lake and the park's Potawatomi Trail draw more mountain bike activity than any other routes in southeastern Michigan and maybe any other trail in the state.

Along with October, when fall colors peak, mid-May is a pleasant time to walk this trail, when the ponds and marshes are ringed by wildflowers and waterfowl can often be sighted on the lakes. These same low-lying areas make the area a little buggy in late June through July, although not excessively bad.

Access: The park, which lies in both Livingston and Washtenaw counties, is 15 miles northwest of Ann Arbor. Head north on US 23, then west on North Territorial Road (exit 49) for 12 miles. The

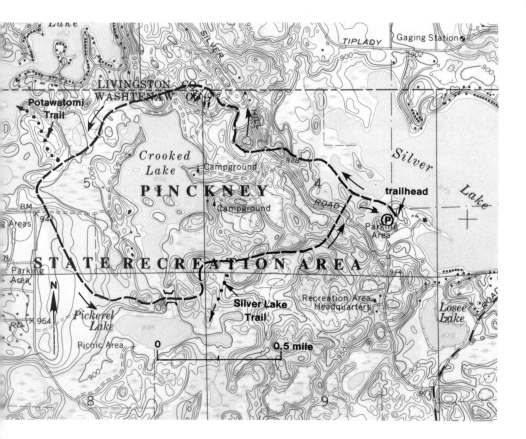

trailhead is located in the Silver Lake day-use area, reached from North Territorial Road by turning north (right) on Dexter-Townhall Road, then left at Silverhill Road where the park entrance is posted. From I-94, depart at exit 159 and head north on MI 52 for 6 miles to North Territorial Road, then head east (right).

Just before entering the day-use area, you pass the park headquarters (313-426-4913) where information about the park's trails, campgrounds, or other facilities can be obtained.

Trail: There are two posted trailheads in the day-use area, with the Crooked Lake one at the display map off the upper parking lot. Actually, this trailhead

marks the beginnings of both Potawatomi and Crooked Lake trails and the end of Silver Lake Trail (see Hike 5). The trail heads north to skirt Silver Lake, weaving between low-lying wet areas and young stands of trees and then passing the return trail. You continue straight. Although you can hear boaters and water skiers on the main body of the lake, the trail is following a narrow inlet of its western shore where in spring and fall a variety of waterfowl can be sighted.

Within a half mile of the start, the trail swings west and begins a long ascent away from the lake to cross Silverhill Road. On the other side of the road, the trail cuts through an older stand of oak and breaks out on a grassy ridge, where you have a good view of Pinckney Recreation Area's rugged interior. The trail crosses a second dirt road, and the first mile of the journey ends at a highpoint of 1,008 feet, where there is an excellent view of Crooked Lake and the surrounding ridges. The only obtrusion here is a powerline that passes through.

From the viewpoint, the trail makes a .5-mile descent, passes a mile 9 post and a few more glimpses of the lake along the way, and bottoms out at a bridged creek that flows between a small pond to the north and Crooked Lake. Just beyond this creek, you arrive at a well-posted junction 2 miles from the beginning. Hikers continuing on the 17-mile Potawatomi Trail should head north (right), while the Crooked Lake Loop swings south. The latter trail crosses another bridge, then makes a gentle climb to Glen Brook Road, a private drive.

On the other side of the road, the trail remains in the woods as it winds towards the south end of Crooked Lake. Eventually you swing east and skirt a ridge while overlooking Pickerel, the third lake passed along the way. The structure at the west end is a fishing pier, and that at the east end is a footbridge along the Silver Lake Trail. You descend the ridge to an even more impressive footbridge across the small river between Pickerel and Crooked lakes. The bridge makes a nice spot to sit and enjoy the view of the two lakes and surrounding ridges.

From the stream, you climb a pair of hills and in .3 mile come to the posted junction of Silver Lake and Crooked Lake trails. Continue east (straight), and soon you'll be following a ridge and looking down at marsh ponds on both sides before ascending to a highpoint of

Deer in the woods

970 feet. The trail makes a steady descent from here and soon crosses Silverhill Road for the second time. On the other side of the road, you pass yet another small pond and return to a junction with the first leg of the trail along Silver Lake, where the upper parking lot trailhead is reached by heading south (right).

7

Waterloo-Pinckney Trail

Place: Waterloo and Pinckney recreation areas
Total Distance: 35 miles
Hiking Time: 3 to 4 days
Highpoints: Scenic vistas, backpacking opportunities
Maps: USGS Chelsea, Grass Lake, Gregory, and Pinckney;
Waterloo-Pinckney Trail map from the Department of Natural
Resources

The longest trail in Michigan is called the North Country Trail and, when completed, that trail will extend 872 miles, bisecting Michigan. The most popular long-distance route is the Greenstone Ridge Trail, the forty-mile path that runs the length of Isle Royale National Park and attracts thousands to the Lake Superior island every summer. Isle Royal is about as far north as you can go in Michigan. But not all backpacking trips in Michigan are synonymous with the north. One of the finest routes, a three-day trek through rugged hills, past ten inland lakes, and up to three scenic vistas, is neither in the Upper Peninsula nor even north of Lansing. In fact, the east end of the Waterloo-Pinckney Trail is only an hour drive from Detroit; the west end is less than ten miles from Jackson. But along this thirty-five-mile trail, you'd never know you were anywhere near a metropolitan area. From the trailhead on Big Portage Lake, you don't pass a house or any other structure for six miles, and you encounter less than a dozen during the entire three-day hike.

Much of this walk is spent climbing hills and ridges or plunging into forests of oak, maple, and beech. The interesting terrain includes numerous marshes and ponds, along with grassy fields that were farmed in the early 1900s but were abandoned by hard-luck families during the Great Depression of the 1930s. The land eventually reverted to the federal government, which handed it over to the state in 1943. Waterloo and Pinckney recreation areas were created the following year, and trail development followed, with much of it laid out since 1965.

What made the trail a backpacking reality was the final two-mile link connecting the twenty-two miles of trail in Waterloo with the equal-sized network in Pinckney. This link was completed by 1984, after two private property purchases were funded by the National Resources Trust Fund and the Washtenaw County allowed the trail to traverse its Park Lyndon. The trail dedication was held in October of 1986, and there has been hikers on it ever since.

Although the entire network of trails covers forty-six miles, the main route from Big Portage Lake in Waterloo to Silver Lake in Pinckney is a thirty-five-mile trek that most people cover in three days. The most common itinerary is to begin at Portage Lake and hike either to a rustic horsemen's campground or to the modern Sugarloaf Lake campground the first night, a walk of 14 to 15 miles. The following day you can either hike 8 miles to Green Lake Rustic Campground or go 15 miles to the less desirable walk-in campground on Blind Lake in Pinckney. From the Green Lake campground, the final leg is a 13-mile trek to the day-use area on Silver Lake. Another option for lodging is to rent a frontier cabin in Waterloo Recreation Area, which must be reserved in advance.

If 15 miles is too much for one day, consider beginning at Clear Lake Road in Waterloo. A vehicle can be left in a small pulloff just north of where the trail crosses the road, and the first day to Green Lake would be a 10-mile trek past Pond Lily Lookout and the scenic overlooks at Crooked and Mill lakes. The second day would be a 7-mile walk to Blind Lake, and the third, a 6-mile trek to Silver Lake. The most scenic stretches are from Clear Lake Road to Mill Lake in Waterloo and from Blind Lake to the east trailhead in Pinckney, but there is a tremendous sense of accomplishment that motivates people to complete the entire 35 miles.

The trail is well marked with a variety of symbols, but you watch mostly for mileage posts and blue DNR pathway triangles. The route, though well posted, should not be taken lightly. Numerous bridle paths and old roads in the recreation areas can get you turned around. It's not so much that you're lost in the woods, it's just that you haven't seen a trail marker for awhile. The other problem is that hikers share the route in Wa-

terloo with horseback riders, which can often result in muddy and badly eroded stretches. In Pinckney, you will encounter mountain bikers.

It's virtually required to walk the route from west to east due to mountain bike/hiking regulations implemented in 1990 in Pinckney. These regulations require walkers to cover the Potawatomi Trail, which makes up the last stretch of the long route, in a counterclockwise direction. By ending at Silver Lake, you are also in sync with the mileage postings. Summer is probably the most popular time for hikers on the trail, but keep in mind that the numerous ponds and wetlands make many sections a bug heaven. Some prefer to ski the route during the winter when they can rent a cabin in Waterloo's Mill Lake Outdoor Center. If you can arrange three days in mid-October, you can enjoy spectacular fall colors and encounter few if any other trail users. For my money, hiking doesn't get any better than this in southern Michigan.

Access: For all practical purposes, the Waterloo-Pinckney Trail parallels I-94 between Jackson and Ann Arbor. The Portage Lake Day-Use Area—the western trailhead—is reached by departing the interstate at Race Road (exit 147) and heading north to Seymour Road. The lake entrance is just a mile east (right) on Seymour, and you'll find the trail posted by the boat launch. Depart I-94 at MI 52 (exit 159) and head north to reach the Silver Lake Day-Use Area. Within 6 miles, turn east (right) on North Territorial Road and then north (left) again on Dexter-Townhall Road, where the park entrance is posted.

There are pulloffs, however, on almost every road that the trail crosses. Good places to leave a car include the parking area to Sackrider Hill on Mt. Hope Road, at Waterloo's horsemen camp-

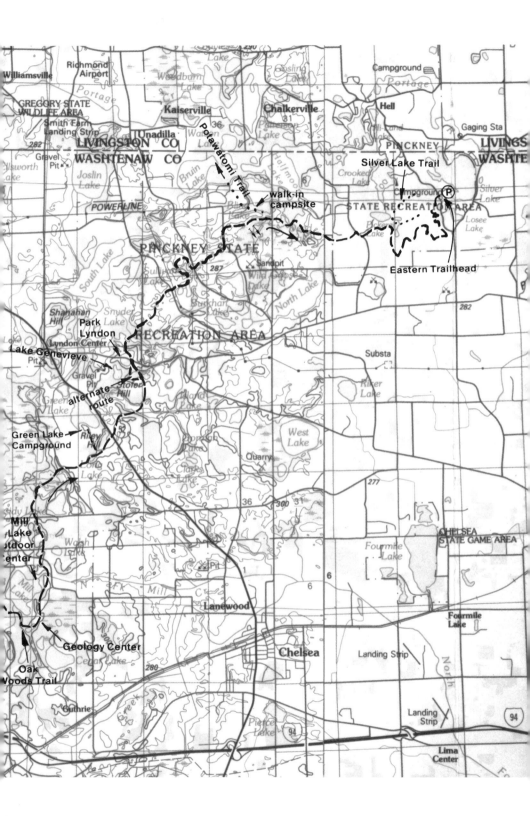

ground just off Loveland Road, near Clear Lake, across McClure Road from Waterloo headquarters, at Green Lake Rustic Campground, at a small pulloff south of the trail on Goodband Road, and at the Pickerel Lake boat ramp off Hankerd Road in Pinckney Recreational Area.

The headquarters for Pinckney Recreation Area (313-426-4913) is located on Silver Hill Road, just before you enter Silver Lake Day-Use Area. The headquarters for Waterloo Recreation Area (313-475-8307) is on McClure Road. The trail winds past the Waterloo headquarters, or you can reach it by departing I-94 at Kalmbach Road (exit 156) and following the signs. Both offices are open Monday through Friday, 8 A.M. to 5 P.M., and are where you pay park entry fees and campground fees or arrange for a cabin reservation. You can also pay entry and site fees at Sugarloaf Campground.

Trail: The Waterloo-Pinckney Trail described here is a 35-mile trek from Portage Lake to Silver Lake. A hiker in excellent shape and with a light load can actually cover it in two days by walking 23 miles the first day and spending the night at Green Lake. The vast majority of people plan to be on the trail for at least three days.

First Day

The trail begins near the Big Portage Lake boat launch and is marked by a display sign announcing that Green Lake is only 23 miles away. You begin by skirting a ridge for some nice views of the lake below. You then swing south, staying in the woods except to cross a dirt road at .6 mile. The first climb of the trip, but certainly not the last, comes right before the trail crosses paved Seymour Road at 1.2 miles. South of Seymour, the trail quickly crosses a small grassy area and powerline right-of-way, then re-enters the woods. For the next mile you climb low hills and ridges and descend to pass a marsh, pond, or other low-lying wet area. This area is interesting, even though it can get a little buggy in late June or early July.

List Road is crossed at 2 miles, and at 2.5 miles, the trail arrives at an old and very overgrown road. Signs direct you to swing north (left), where you move out of the forest and into a grassy clearing. Within .7 mile of reaching the old road, you arrive at Willis Road. A parking area lies next to the trail here, while on the other side of the road is Portage Pond, the largest body of open water seen since Portage Lake. A footbridge crosses the north end of the pond over the dam, and from there you climb back into the forest.

The post for Mile 4 is past before you descend to a large marshy area and cross it where the trail is planked. You return to the forest, then descend again to emerge at Glenn Road. On the other side of the road is more climbing, which now gets serious with the trail reaching close to 1,100 feet. The path levels off on the crest of a ridge, and, at one point, you stand on the edge and stare fifty feet or more straight down into a forested ravine. At 5.3 miles, the trail makes a sharp descent off the ridge, breaks out of the trees, and begins its climb of Sackrider Hill. The view gets better with every step, and by the time hikers finally reach the cross that marks the 1,128-foot top, many are a little stunned. There are finer panoramas in Michigan, in the Upper Peninsula no doubt, but for those who just hiked the last 6 miles and climbed 130 feet, this one is remarkable. You can see 360 degrees, but the view to the southwest is the best. Below you are miles of Michigan, including rolling farm fields, other ridges, barns, and I-94 (after all, this is southern Michigan).

The trail quickly drops off the hill and skirts Mt. Hope Road, though many hikers end up in the parking lot for Sackrider Hill. If you do find yourself in the parking lot, just head south on the paved road and watch for the next trail marker on the left side. Trail posts lead you up Katz Road and past the first house of the trip. Soon the woods closes, and within .8 mile, the trail departs east from Katz Road at a spot posted for both equestrians and hikers. You climb away from the road, shortly to come to an old vehicle track. For the first time that day, the trail is poorly marked. Head south (right), and the track will swing north and emerge at Glenn Road. The other side of the road is well posted for both horseback riders and hikers, so for the next 5 miles, you will be looking for a boot and horseshoe symbol.

The trail continues north from Glenn Road as a wide, eroded path in the woods. After passing the post for Mile 9 and then a well-marked junction for horseback riders, the trail swings east and cuts through the first of many extensive, grassy fields. Most of the open areas are old farm fields from when settlers arrived in the early 1800s with plows and axes in hand. The glaciers that created the ridges and lakes also left a topsoil of predominately sand and gravel that hindered the effort of most farmers in the region. During the Great Depression, the families turned to the federal government and were moved to more productive land as part of a relocation relief measure.

The trail skirts the edge of a horse farm before arriving at Baldwin Road. Here you jog north (left) on the road briefly before picking up the next trail marker on the east (right) side of the road. Within .5 mile of the road, you cross a stream on a footbridge where, to the south, is a dam and a huge flooded area. Keep an eye out for waterfowl and wildlife on the water. The terrain remains mostly grassy fields. Several times bridle paths enter and leave the trail, but all junctions are clearly posted and there is little doubt as to which way hikers should head.

Clear Lake Road is crossed 12 miles from Portage Lake. On its east side, you finally return to the forest. Within .5 mile of the road, you cross a Y-junction with some dirt roads and then begin climbing. It's a steep climb of almost 140 feet; at one point, there are even switchbacks in the trail, making it probably the sharpest ascent of any trail south of Lansing. Eventually you reach the top, known as Prospect, where there is a USGS marker. There is no view here, but after you descend slightly and climb a ridge, the trees clear to allow a scenic vista of the farm fields to the southwest as well as Pond Lily Lake to the south. This spot is called the Pond Lily Lookout. From here, you begin a rapid descent to reach Loveland Road, 14 miles from Portage Lake.

On the east side of Loveland Road is the Mile 14 marker, a huge sign announcing that Green Lake is another 8 miles east and Sugarloaf Lake Campground is 1 mile north. The modern campground has 180 sites in an open, grassy area near the large lake. There are modern bathrooms with showers and a small swimming area. The campground is reached by heading north (left) on Loveland, then east (right) on an entrance drive. Along the way, you pass the horsemen's campground, a rustic facility with vault toilets, a hand pump for water, and twenty-five sites in a wooded setting. The horsemen's

Backpacker on the top of Sackrider Hill

campground is a considerably closer walk then Sugarloaf Lake and less expensive. Near the rustic campground are Burns Cabins, two, twenty-bunk structures hemmed in by woods and featuring wood-burning stoves, tables, chairs, and mattresses.

Second Day

For most hikers, the second day is either an 8-mile walk to Green Lake Rustic Campground or a 15-mile trek to the walk-in campground at Blind Lake. The trail begins with a number of bridle paths veering off. Soon you leave the bridle paths behind and cross McClure Road for the first of three times, just before the Mile 15 post. At this point, the trail heads south along an old road, then curves away from it to the east. It's easy to miss this last junction; if you emerge onto the dirt road to the Crooked Lake Day-Use Area, backtrack and watch for trail markers.

The trail climbs a number of hills, drops past a few marshes, and crosses McClure Road two more times before merging onto Hickory Hills Nature Trail. This mile-long loop begins near the Waterloo park headquarters and includes twenty interpretive posts and an accompanying brochure. You join it near interpretive post 13, where the trail breaks out to a view above Crooked Lake, a body of water scraped out by glaciers ten thousand years ago. As is typical with nature trails, there are benches every one hundred yards. The one right on the shore of the lake makes a scenic spot for lunch or an extended break. At interpretive post 17 are the remains of an old pumphouse, used by Sylvan Estates Country Club forty years ago.

The trail passes through a clearing, part of the golf course before the club went bankrupt during the Great Depression, then arrives at the park headquarters. Outside the building is water, trash barrels, vault toilets, and a large display sign. If the office is open (Monday through Friday 8 A.M. to 5 P.M.), you will find more maps, brochures, and information inside.

The trail resumes across McClure Road from the park headquarters, in an area also marked for cross-country skiers who share portions of it. You quickly cross Lowry Road and resume hiking on an old road. The next stretch is level and straight, an unexpected sight for hikers on this route. Within 1.2 miles from the headquarters, you come to the posted junction with the Oak Woods Trail from the Gerald E. Eddy Geology Center. The Waterloo-Pinckney Trail follows the west side of this loop (see Hike 8), breaking out of the loop south of the interpretive center. The trail resumes on the Old Field Trail. If the center is open, take the time to view its displays. The exhibits present an interesting look at Michigan's geology, as well as explain why it seems that you have been walking uphill for the last two days.

DNR pathway triangles clearly indicate where to depart from the Old Field Trail. You quickly cross the entrance drive to the geology center and pass by the entrance to Mill Lake Outdoor Center. Within this center and Cedar Lake Outdoor Center a mile south on Pierce Road, the park maintains semi-rustic cabins that can be rented by backpackers. The cabins feature electric lights and stoves (bathrooms are still outside). By planning ahead, then, you can spend one night at Burns Cabins and another one here and not have to carry a tent, though that arrangement would involve 15-mile hikes both the first and third days.

At Mile 19 you cross Bush Road and

begin climbing. This hill is steep, but on top it levels out. You follow the crest of a ridge to view a scenic marsh below to the west. The trail eventually descends and crosses Waterloo Road, following a level course for a short spell. You pass a "Prison Zone" sign, indicating that you are passing near Cassidy Lake Correctional Facility.

After climbing a few hills, you cross Cassidy Lake Road and cut through rolling, grassy fields to the dirt entrance drive to Green Lake Rustic Campground, reached just beyond Mile 22 of the trip. The campground is .3 mile north along the road and has twenty-five sites in a lightly shaded, grassy area. Some sites are on a low bluff overlooking the lake, a splendid place to camp. The facility also has vault toilets, water, and a boat ramp to the lake, and overall is a better choice to spend the night than the walk-in campground at Blind Lake.

Third Day

The trail continues on the other side of the entrance drive to the campground by climbing almost eighty feet to the top of Riley Hill. It then descends to MI 52, where it finally leaves Waterloo Recreation Area. The route heads northeast, skirts a pond and marshy area, and at Mile 24 enters Park Lyndon, a preserve administered by the Washtenaw County Parks and Recreation Department. From the wooden gate and "Park Rules" sign at the boundary, it's an uphill climb to the first junction in a network of trails within the park.

DNR pathway triangles mark the Waterloo-Pinckney Trail, which follows an old road to head directly to a crossing on North Territorial Road. Alternatively, follow the green tree symbols to the

west (left), thereby skirting Lake Genevieve and passing an observation platform along its shore before emerging at the Park Lyndon South Unit. Here is a hand pump for water, vault toilets, and tables. Park Lyndon North has more tables and a shelter. Camping is not allowed anywhere in the county park.

The trail crosses North Territorial Road, cuts through the fields and forests in the north unit, and leaves the county park at Mile 25. Here it swings almost due east to cross a creek from Snyder Lake. At this point, you enter Pinckney Recreation Area. In the next mile, you cross Embury and Joslin Lake roads, both rural, dirt roads. The trail continues northeast, then curves due north as it skirts the base of a 1,020-foot hill. To the east is a huge cattail area, but the trail stays dry even when it swings east to cross the marsh on a footbridge over a sluggish stream.

The trail heads south at this point, and within .4 mile of the bridge, you cross Hadley Road. DNR pathway triangles lead you up a grassy hill on the other side of the road and eventually back into the woods. You skirt the south end of an unnamed lake, which you do not get a very good view of. At one point, though, you pass the post for Mile 28 and descend sharply. At the bottom of the ravine, you get a glimpse of the lake, which appears to be almost totally covered by lily pads.

The trail skirts a parking area off Goodband Road, then crosses the road itself to begin a gentle climb on the other side. You top off at only 970 feet, but it's high enough to provide the third spectacular vista of the trip. To the southwest, you look over the rugged terrain of Waterloo Recreation Area and can see no less than ten forested ridges in different shades of green. The trail descends sharply off the ridge and arrives at the junction with the Potawatomi Trail, a seventeen-mile loop that lies totally in Pinckney Recreation Area. To the west (left) is the walk-in campsite on Blind Lake, a grassy area with a trash container and vault toilets. Although a walk-in campsite on a lake is usually an inviting place to spend an evening, this one is not. Blind Lake is ringed by cottages, and at the height of the summer, the lake is buzzing with motorboats, water skiers, and, worst of all, jet skiers. Green Lake is a much better choice for pitching the tent.

To the east, the trail plunges into a thick hardwood forest, then climbs slightly to follow the crest of a narrow ridge. On both sides of you is a steep drop to a ravine, where a variety of wildlife—deer, raccoons, even flocks of wild turkeys—might be spotted. You skirt Dead Lake just beyond Mile 30, or 1.5 miles from the walk-in campground, and

then emerge at Hankerd Road in another mile.

The trail resumes just to the south (right) at the Pickerel Lake Access. It parallels the access road, then skirts the scenic lake from a high bank. You can see a popular fishing pier at the lake's west end. Near Mile 32, you come to the well-posted junction with the Silver Lake Trail. If you're eager to get back to your car, follow this short loop to the left. Within a mile, you'll be in the parking lot of the Silver Lake Day-Use Area. The Silver Lake Trail is actually a more scenic walk (see Hike 5) than the final stretch of the Waterloo-Pinckney Trail, and you'll clip off 2 miles.

Purists, however, will want to finish the remaining 3.5 miles. This last leg heads southwest and weaves its way along the edges of numerous marshy areas and ponds before rejoining the Silver Lake Trail. From there, it's .5 mile to the eastern trailhead.

Oak Woods Trail

Place: Waterloo Recreation Area
Total Distance: 2 miles
Hiking Time: 40 minutes to an hour
Highpoints: Geology center, scenic overlooks
Maps: USGS Chelsea; Gerald E. Eddy Geology Center
  brochure

Short trails through a diverse terrain, the interesting plant life, and an interpretive center attract hikers from throughout southern Michigan to the Gerald E. Eddy Geology Center. The center is located in the southeast corner of the Waterloo Recreation Area, a state park lying between Jackson and Ann Arbor. It includes almost twenty thousand acres of lakes, wetlands, and some of the most rugged country in this corner of the state.

Originally a nature center that was closed due to state budget constraints, the facility was reopened in 1989 as a tribute to Gerald Eddy, a former chief of the Geological Survey Division. At one time, Eddy was also the director of the Department of Conservation, the forerunner to the DNR. The center reflects his career in geology and his dedication to preserving Michigan's natural areas.

The state interpretive center features two main exhibit rooms, with the first devoted to Michigan's geological history. Displays describe the difference between igneous, metamorphic, and sedimentary rocks and explain each of the state's different geological eras. Magnifying glasses provide a close view of crystals, hunks of pure copper, and Petoskey stones and other fossils. Nearby, murals depict a scene of Michigan buried under a glacier or when American mastodons ruled the forests, complete with a display case containing fossilized molars and the ribs of the giant, elephant-like mammals.

The second exhibit room is devoted to the natural history of the state recreation area. There are three-dimensional displays on the beaver, on Waterloo's Native Americans, and on the variety of wildlife that might be seen along any trail in the park. You will also see a collection of live turtles, displays on birds, insects, and wildflowers in the area, and a hands-on exhibit to help you identify the various species of trees in southeastern Michigan.

All this new knowledge can be put to good use with a hike along one of the center's six trails. The longest is the Oak Woods Trail, an hour-long walk through an upland woods of oaks and hickories. The trail plus the walk in from the parking area to the center is a 2-mile journey, making this an excellent destination for families with young children.

Access: Located among the rolling hills of Waterloo Recreation Area, the center is between Jackson and Ann Arbor. It is reached from I-94 by departing north onto Pierce Road (exit 157). Brown park signs lead you north along Pierce Road, then west (left) on Bush Road to the entrance of the parking area. The center (313-475-3170) is open daily during the summer from 9 A.M. to 5 P.M.

Trail: Halfway along the paved path between the parking lot and the geology center are the posted trailheads for five of the six trails, including Oak Woods, which is the only one departing to the west (right). The trail makes an immediate descent and quickly passes the first bench at an overlook of the south end of Mill Lake. It's a scenic view, framed in by the branches of several hardwood trees. From here, the trail levels out and passes several interpretive signs pointing out such species as sassafras, red-osier dogwood, and white oak.

At .5 mile, you pass a spur to a scenic view that you will reach on the return trail and then skirt the base of the ridge, actually a glacial moraine. The glaciers of the last ice age swept through here ten thousand years ago,

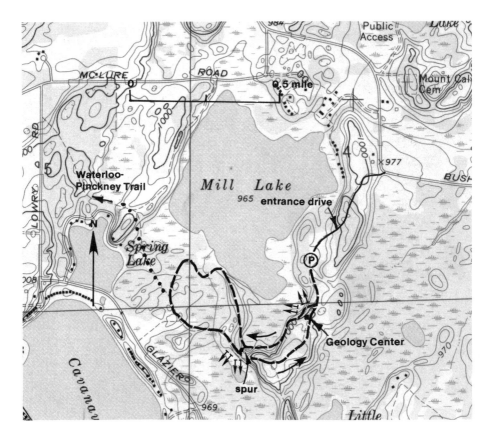

then retreated to leave the rugged hills and ridges found throughout Waterloo Recreation Area as well as lakes such as Mill Lake. Within .2 mile past the spur to the overlook, the trail climbs the

Trail Post

moraine and traverses it for a short distance to provide good views of the main body of the lake, arriving at another bench along the way.

At one point, you pass a post with a blue pathway triangle on one side and a number on the other, indicating to hikers coming from the other direction that they have reached mile 18 of the Waterloo-Pinckney Trail. That long-distance route stretches thirty-five miles from Portage Lake in Waterloo Recreation Area to Silver Lake in Pinckney Recreation Area (see Hike 7). The junction where the long-distance trail splits off west is reached a mile from the trailhead.

Oak Woods heads east (left). You soon arrive at the third bench and overlook, where you gaze down on a small pond. The open water is slowly being covered up by a bog—a floating layer of plants, mosses, and shrubs, including the carnivorous pitcher plant. From the bench, you see just part of one of the largest concentrations of bogs in southern Michigan, lying south of Mill Lake and the moraine you are following. The best trail for viewing this environment is the center's Bog Trail, often referred to as a "floating trail" because it ends as a boardwalk on the delicate layer of plants. The trail is only .6-mile long, and from the boardwalk you can actually reach down and push on the bog as if it was a waterbed.

The Oak Woods Trail continues by swinging north, as it follows the crest of the moraine through oaks and hickories and past sections of a split rail fence built in the 1960s. It ends at the geology center, where there are more benches with a view of Mill Lake. It's a .2 mile walk along the paved path to the parking lot.

Lake Huron

Port Crescent Trails

Place: Port Crescent State Park
Total Distance: 2.3 miles
Hiking Time: 1.5 to 2 hours
Rating: Easy
Highpoints: Sand dunes, overlooks
Maps: USGS Port Austin West and Kinde West; Port Crescent
* State Park map*

To historians, Port Crescent was a thriving lumbering and fishing town in the mid-1800s. To summer travelers, Port Crescent is a state park with one of the most beautiful beaches on the east side of the state. But to hikers, this preserved tract of wind-blown dunes, wooded hills, and Saginaw Bay shoreline is the destination for the most scenic and interesting hike in the Thumb region of Michigan.

The sand dunes here and elsewhere along Lake Huron are nowhere near the stature of those along the west side of Michigan. But in Port Crescent they are high enough to provide sweeping panoramas of the bay, of the miles of shoreline, or of the valley carved by the Pinnebog River. Most people never expect to find such overlooks in the flatland of the Thumb. Hikers take to the trails March through December, relinquishing them only to skiers in the winter. October is unquestionably the best time, since the park is empty of campers and sun worshippers and the fall colors of the oaks and maples that forest the dunes reach their brilliant

peak. If you come in the early morning or at dusk during the fall, you might even spot a deer or two feeding on the acorns along the path.

The trail, a 2.3-mile loop with a .3-mile cutoff spur, lies in an area of the park completely surrounded by water, with the Pinnebog River to the west, the Saginaw Bay to the north, and the Old Pinnebog River Channel everywhere else. The access point used here is from the campground where a chimney monument and display board recounts the story behind Port Crescent, the town. The town's heyday was in the mid-1800s when there were almost seven hundred residents working at Pack Woods Sawmill and two salt mines. The town vanished by the 1930s, with only a portion of the sawmill's 120-foot chimney remaining as testimony to its industrial past.

What replaced "progress" was nature in the form of the 565-acre state park that was dedicated in 1963. Port Crescent features three miles of beach of almost pure white sand, the tallest dunes on Lake Huron, a shoreline campground, a day-use area, and the network of trails—often the only place to escape the summer crowds that fill the park. By using the cutoff spur, you can shorten the hike to either a 1.3- or 1.1-mile walk, but you would then miss some of the overlooks. The entire loop is an easy trek with only gentle climbing that can be handled by children as young as five or six years old.

Access: The park (517-738-7656) is located 5 miles west of Port Austin on MI 25 and is split in half by the Pinnebog River. The trail area is in the eastern half of the park. One trailhead is the old iron bridge at the corner of MI 25 and Port Crescent Road, providing direct access to both the blue loop (1.3 miles) and the red loop (1.1 miles). The other trailhead, where this description starts, is located in the campground whose entrance is posted on MI 25. Begin the hike across from the modern restroom, between two beachfront sites. If the campground is not overflowing with too many vehicles and campers for your pleasure, this is the best place to begin the loop.

Trail: From the beautiful beach on Saginaw Bay, you kick off your shoes or boots and scramble through the mouth of the Old Pinnebog River Channel towards the yellow post at the start of some small sand dunes. The yellow

Young hiker exploring the dunes

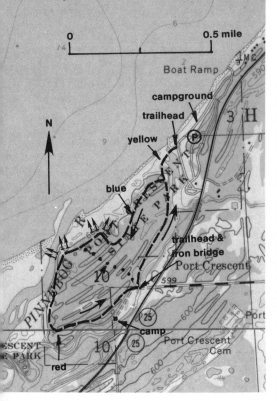

Boat Ramp

campground

trailhead

N

yellow

blue

trailhead & iron bridge

Port Crescent

camp

Port Crescent Cem

ESCENT PARK

red

Port

Follow the red poles and diamonds, and shortly the trail will emerge at another bench with a panorama of the mouth of the Pinnebog River, the sandy shoreline of the Saginaw Bay, and a long line of open and grassy dunes that stretch to the west. This vista is the best in the park, maybe in all of Michigan's Thumb, and even more remarkable considering the flat fields of corn and navy beans you drove through to get here. At your feet is a steep slope of sand leading down to the river, while on the opposite riverbank are usually a handful of anglers trying their luck for perch or panfish. If it's September or October, they are probably fishing for Chinook salmon that spawn up the river.

For the next .4 mile, the trail continues along this sandy bluff above the river until it reaches one final bench, where you can see much of the Pinnebog River Valley and the wetlands that border it. At this point, the trail swings to a southerly direction, and then to the east, becoming a walk through woods. Follow the red diamonds carefully, for there are numerous "unofficial" paths cutting through the open forest of oaks and maples. If it's early or late in the day, hike quietly and be alert; deer are occasionally seen feeding along this stretch.

In another .4 mile from the last bench, you reach the organization campground (vault toilets and a picnic shelter) and then the junction at the old iron bridge, now used only by hikers and skiers to reach the second trailhead and parking area. Entering from the north (left) is the cutoff spur. Continue along the blue loop by dropping down towards the bridge to pick up the trail that skirts the old channel closely. Eventually the trail begins to climb gently again, and within .5 mile, tops off at the first overlook and bench, where the yellow spur leads back to the campground.

spur quickly rises to the first scenic vista and bench where you get a view of the old river channel, the chimney monument, and the campground below. From here, the blue loop begins, with posts descending south along the old channel or west through a wooded ravine. Turn right (west) to begin the most impressive section of the trail.

The trail passes through a ravine of sorts, forested in hardwoods, and away from the water and sand for .3 mile. Keep an eye out for blue diamonds on the trees, for the trail takes a sharp turn to the north to reach an overlook of the bay, shoreline, and the open dunes that border it. In another .25 mile, you'll reach the junction of the red and blue loops, marked by a large pole and another bench. Head south (left) to return to the yellow spur and reduce the walk to 1.7 miles; but continue west (right) for more views.

10

Tobico Marsh Trail

Place: Bay City State Park/Tobico Marsh State Game Area
Total Distance: 4 miles
Hiking Time: 2 hours
Rating: Easy
Highpoints: Wildlife observation towers, birding
Maps: USGS Kawkawlin; Tobico Marsh State Game Area map

When it comes to counting, my three-year-old son Michael isn't very steady beyond twenty, so he ran out of numbers three times while climbing the sixty-step observation tower at Tobico Marsh. When we reached the top of the thirty-foot tower and looked out at the hundreds of birds bobbing gently on the water in the marsh, well, he didn't even try to count. He just stood on the railing, watched this migration of waterfowl, and exclaimed, "There sure is a lot of ducks out there."

That about sums up Tobico Marsh Interpretive Area, a wildlife refuge just north of Bay City State Park and almost within sight of the city itself. Access into the interpretive area is through a pair of loop trails one and four miles in length that make for a pleasant forest hike any time of the year. But during the fall and spring migrations of waterfowl, they are excellent outings that combine a walk in the woods with birding—the fine art of observing and identifying wildlife.

The refuge covers more than half of the two thousand-acre Tobico Marsh State Game Area and contains a variety of habitat, from small pockets of cattail marshes and oak/maple climax forest to Tobico Lagoon, a nine hundred-acre body of water and the largest remaining wetland along Saginaw Bay. The entire area is home to deer, beaver, muskrat, and mink, but it's the wide variety of birds, especially waterfowl, that makes this refuge so spectacular. During the fall more than four thousand ducks and geese gather in the marsh, with the number increasing to almost ten thousand during the peak of migration from the third week of October to early November. In all, more than two hundred species of birds have been sighted in the game area.

It is this seemingly endless supply of geese, fish, and other wildlife that has led archaeologists to believe that the area was inhabited by prehistoric tribes, known as "Paleoindians," several thousand years ago. The marsh was also the frequent site of hunting camps for the Sauk and Chippewa tribes, and the name Tobico itself is derived from the Chippewa word "Pe-to-be-goong," which means "little lake by the big lake."

Native Americans remained until 1837, and a few served as local guides for duck hunters even as late as 1925. By 1844 a timber cruiser had already passed through the area, which eventually endured intense logging before six lumber barons purchased the lagoon in 1907. Recognizing the true value of the marsh as a waterfowl refuge, the six men set up the exclusive Tobico Hunt Club for their own private hunts.

By 1956 there were only two surviving members of the club, and they offered the marsh to the state as a wildlife refuge. The forty thousand dollar sale was approved, and the Tobico Marsh State Game Area was created that year. In 1976, the U.S. Department of Interior designated the area a Registered Natural Landmark, and since then 1,109 acres have been declared a refuge to provide full protection for its unique features.

The Jennison Nature Center, within Bay City State Park, is a required stop for this hike, if for no other reason than to pick up the key to unlock the refuge's entrance gate. But a few minutes in the

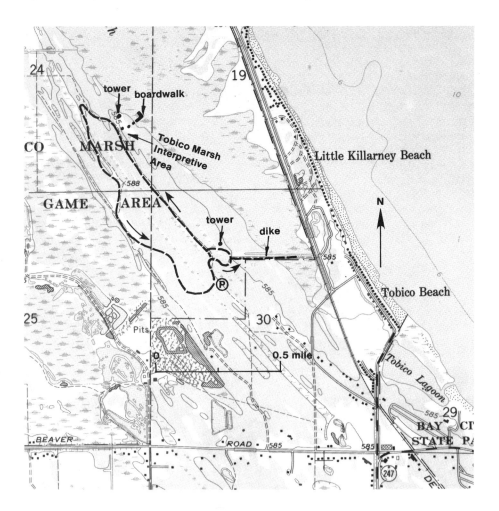

interpretive center makes for a much more interesting walk in the woods. The center has twenty permanent displays and several seasonal ones, including a fine selection of mounted birds and ducks for close inspection and tanks of live fish and reptiles taken from the marsh. Every exhibit furthers your understanding of the unique wetland habitat that will be viewed from the trails. The center can also supply a bird checklist of 127 species, for those who take their birding seriously, and a trail map.

Access: The state park is 5 miles north of Bay City and reached from I-75 by departing at exit 168 and heading east on Beaver Road. It's almost 5 miles to the park entrance, just past the intersection with MI 247. The nature center (517-667-0717) is open Tuesday through Friday from 10 A.M. to 4 P.M., and Saturday and Sunday from noon to 5 P.M. A vehicle entry fee is required to enter the state park.

To reach the Tobico Marsh from the nature center, backtrack to MI 247 and head north (right) for .5 mile and then west on Killarney Road to the posted entrance. Within the parking area, beyond the gate, are vault toilets, a small shelter, and a plaque commemorating Tobico as a natural landmark, appropriately placed on a boulder brought south by a glacier thirteen thousand years ago.

Trail: The trail departs from the shelter and quickly comes to the first junction between the two loops. Head east (right) for the short loop, where the trail crosses three bridges, each spanning an old beachline left behind by a retreating Lake Huron centuries ago. In less than .5 mile, you come to the dike at the south end of the lagoon that was built in 1946 as a water retention measure. By hiking along it, you'll reach a

spot where the cattails are cut periodically for easy wildlife observation and that is marked by an interpretive sign about the creation of the marsh. You're guaranteed to see signs of wildlife here, for there's a beaver lodge twenty yards out.

The most abundant bird inhabiting the marsh is probably the redwing blackbird, and during spring and early summer you can witness the male proclaiming his territory and nesting spot. Other species to be sighted are herons—including great blue, black-crowned night, and little green—long-billed marsh wrens, and warblers. During the migrations, the most commonly recognized waterfowl are pintails, green-wing teals, widgeons, and the green heads of drake mallards.

Retrace your steps off the dike and continue on the short loop. The trail soon passes the first of two thirty-foot observation towers, though the view from this one is blocked by the surrounding trees. You then return to the long loop at another junction, this one marked by a display sign explaining maturing forests. From here the trail heads north (right) as a straight and wide path through a tunnel of towering trees. The tree species range from red and white oak to red maple and poplar, making this stretch especially brilliant during fall colors in mid-October.

At .8 mile from the junction, the trail passes a bench and soon enters a clearing posted "Tobico Marsh Interpretive Area," featuring vault toilets, a boardwalk, and the second tower. This area is the site of the Tobico Hunt Club, which, according to the extant records, never had more than eight members during its existence from 1907 to 1956. The exclusive club was never lacking, however, for it featured cottages with porches and fireplaces, boathouses,

View of Tobico Marsh from the top of an observation tower

blinds scattered throughout the marsh, and a caretaker who lived here year-round with his wife and children.

A three hundred-foot boardwalk extends beyond the thick growth of cattails along the shoreline to the edge of the open lagoon, where you can view acres of marsh. Just as impressive is the sight from the top of the tower. It's a climb of sixty steps, but you can see a good portion of the lagoon, including a grassy islet in the middle that attracts waterfowl in spring and fall.

From the tower, the trail continues north. It then curves south 1.3 miles from the junction with the short loop and quickly passes between two cattail marshes decorated with several wood duck boxes hanging in the trees. In another .5 mile after re-entering the woods, you pass a grove of paper birch on the west side of the trail whose white trunks are impressive, almost dazzling, during autumn colors. If it is autumn, chances are it's also duck season, and while hiking this back stretch, you'll occasionally hear pop of a hunter's shotgun off in the distance and maybe even his bird dog scrambling out of the boat to retrieve the fallen bird.

The terrain becomes more open after the stand of birch. The trail swings back into a young forest and crosses one last bridge before emerging at the parking area. Although this hike is not a spectacular one, it is quiet and peaceful, especially for being so close to three metropolitan areas. Often in midweek you'll have the trail to yourself and can hike in silence, hearing only the wind rustling the leaves or a flock of geese honking over the marsh.

11

Sandy Hook Nature Trail

Place: Tawas Point State Park
Total Distance: 1.5 miles
Hiking Time: 40 to 60 minutes
Rating: Easy
Highpoints: Scenic beaches, birding
Maps: USGS East Tawas; Tawas Point State Park map

Within the mitten that forms Michigan's Lower Peninsula is a sandy hook known as Tawas Point. This two-mile spit separates Tawas Bay from Lake Huron, and its tip is a jagged hook of sandy beaches and small dunes. The end of the peninsula is preserved within Tawas Point State Park, which some people have even referred to as the "Cape Cod of the Midwest." That designation might be stretching it a bit, but what isn't debatable is the point's unique sand dune ecosystem and its location as a major landfall for birds migrating across Saginaw Bay. Together, these features make Sandy Hook Nature Trail a short but extremely scenic trek and a major destination every fall and spring for birders.

During the migrations, the point is said to be "alive with birds." Often spotted along beaches or the small inland ponds are terns and gulls, including Bonaparte's gulls and Caspian terns, along with shorebirds such as red knots, whimbrels, and even the rare piping plover. The ponds also attract loons, flocks of mergansers, and a variety of other waterfowl species. The end of the

spit is practically treeless, but warblers, flycatchers, and hummingbirds feed among the willow thickets and shrubs such as sand cherry.

The trail is mainly a sandy path that connects a few stretches of boardwalk along the Lake Huron side of the spit. Its most obvious feature is neither birds nor beaches but a U.S. Coast Guard lighthouse that can be seen from different angles throughout much of the walk. At one time there were nineteen interpretive posts scattered along the trail, but only a handful remain and a copy of the accompanying brochure is almost as hard to find in the state park.

Access: The trailhead for this loop around the spit is located at the west end of the state park's day-use parking area. The 185-acre park is 3.5 miles from East Tawas or 42 miles from the I-75 and US 23 exit near Standish (exit 188). Follow US 23 northeast of East Tawas and turn east on Tawas Point Road. Signs point the way along Tawas Point Road to the state park entrance at the end.

Tawas Point State Park not only features the trail and a beautiful swimming beach 300-feet wide, but also a bathhouse, picnic shelter, and 210 modern campsites with a handful overlooking Tawas Bay. There is a fee for vehicles entering the park and an additional charge for camping overnight. Reservations are recommended throughout much of the summer, especially weekends, and can be obtained by writing to: Tawas Point State Park, 686 Tawas Beach Road, East Tawas, MI 48730; or by calling (517) 362-5041.

Trail: The trailhead is just off the beach parking area and is marked by a large display sign among some red pines. The trail quickly breaks out of the pines and passes the lighthouse and U.S. Coast Guard Station. The original lighthouse was built in 1853 and was located east of here, towards the park headquarters. This one was constructed in 1876, and the cement cribbing at its base is testimony to the two feet of water it stood in at the time it was built.

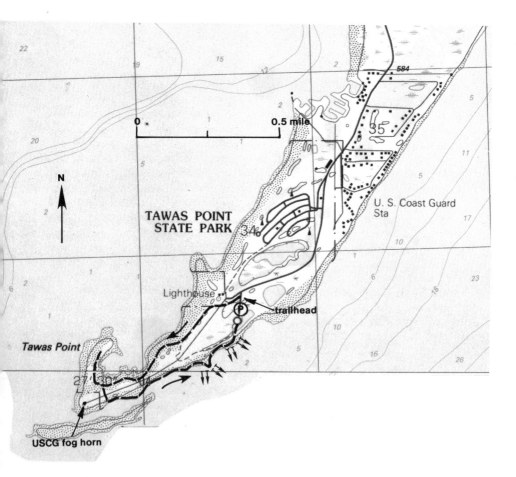

Lighthouse at Tawas Point

The lighthouse is still operated by the Coast Guard and closed to visitors.

Beyond the lighthouse, the trail enters the dune ecosystem and becomes a soft, sandy path along the crest of a low dune. To the west you can see the spit extending out and then curving back in its hook. Behind you is another view of the lighthouse. Post 6 is still around, and it points out the stages of plant succession, beginning with beach sand, which is so unfertile it is unable to support any visible plant life. As you move away from the bay and up the dunes, grasses appear, followed by wild strawberries and other low plants and then shrubs such as dogwood and sumac. Eventually, the point would be covered by a mature forest of white ash and red maple if left unmolested by man.

Within .3 mile of the parking area, the trail descends the dune via a stairway to the beach and crosses a bridge over a small creek. At this point, you follow the shoreline all the way out to the hook. A little more than a century ago, most of the point was under water, but the spit of land has been built up by the longshore currents sweeping along the Lake Huron coast. The currents keep sand moving in the shallow water parallel to the shoreline, until Tawas Bay is encountered. Upon reaching the bay, the currents spread out and slow down, depositing the sand in a long, narrow peninsula. The distinctive hook at the end has been formed by advancing waves, which bend and wrap around the end of the point. The most obvious evidence of the spit growing are the older hooks, each of which at one time marked the entrance to the bay. Eventually, geologists say, Tawas Point will extend completely across the bay, turning it into a lake in much the same way Tobico Marsh was formed (see Hike 10).

You can walk out onto the hook for 100 yards or so before heavy bush turns most people back. Keep an eye out both here and around the ponds for a variety of tracks of such species as cottontail rabbit, opossum, raccoon, and even mink and weasel. After backtracking from the hook, look for the "Nature Trail" sign posted inland from the beach. The trail resumes by cutting across the U.S. Coast Guard access road to their

fog horn, easily spotted from the path. Most of the time it's quiet, but you'll surely know when it isn't. The trail follows the road for the next .5 mile, where a "Bicycles and Other Vehicles Prohibited" sign directs you toward the Lake Huron shore. It's far more interesting, however, to head directly toward the Lake Huron shore after crossing the road and to continue along the beach. Here the bird life is prolific, for several sandy islands lie offshore and form a lagoon of calm water. Between the beach, the small islands, and Lake Huron's blue horizon, the view is worth taking an extended break.

At 1.2 miles into the hike, the trail swings away from the road and crosses a boardwalk along the crest of a low dune. You quickly come to a bench and deck where more views are obtained of Lake Huron to the east and the interdunal ponds with the lighthouse in the background to the west. A second viewing deck is reached in another .2 mile, and then the trail swings inland. Post 18 used to be erected somewhere near here and told of the ill-fated Kitty Reeves. The three-masted schooner sank some two thousand feet offshore in Lake Huron during a heavy November gale in 1870. She went to the bottom with $250,000 in precious copper ingots, which was never recovered.

Before returning to the parking area, the trail passes one of the three largest ponds in the park, where it is often possible to spot muskrats swimming by. Mallards and blue-winged teals nest here annually.

Rifle River

Place: Rifle River Recreation Area
Total Distance: 13 miles
Hiking Time: 7 to 8 hours
Rating: Challenging
Highpoints: Inland lakes, trout stream
Maps: USGS Rose City and Selkirk; Rifle River Recreation
*   Area map*

Hiking in the Rifle River Recreation Area can be as different as night and day or, perhaps more accurately, north and south. The park maintains a thirteen-mile network that basically forms a huge loop through the 4,329-acre unit located east of Rose City. In the northern half, the trail climbs steeply through old growth forests over several hills and ridges to provide scenic views of four inland lakes. In the southern half, the loop is as level a trail as you'll find in this corner of the state and passes through large grassy fields where the stumps of past logging days can be clearly seen.

Take your pick—north or south—or hike the entire loop described here. Unfortunately, backcountry camping is not allowed in the park, so if the thirteen-mile, seven-hour trek is too much for one day, consider a shorter loop that begins at post 4 and starts its return at post 11 for a six-mile day. This route winds through the rugged northern half of the park, tops off at the best views, and passes five of the six lakes seen along the loop. The hills that make this stretch such an intriguing walk also draw mountain bikers, but it's uncommon to see them south of Skunk Creek.

Still, the park, which draws 125,000 visitors annually, is large enough rarely to seem crowded during the summer. The recreation area was originally known as Grousehaven and was the private hunting and fishing retreat of H. M. Jewett, a pioneer auto manufacturer. In 1945, the tract was purchased by the then Department of Conservation and used as a field laboratory for fish and game research. The Parks Division acquired the area in 1963 and designated it the Rifle River Recreation Area.

The area is best known as the headwaters for the Rifle River, a state-designated scenic river, which is crossed twice on the trail loop. Just as impressive are the eleven inland lakes scattered throughout the park, including the most remote one, Lost lake, where a bog is forming around its shoreline. Wildlife is plentiful, especially along the southern half of the loop, where you will often spot a variety of upland gamebirds

such as ruffed grouse and woodcock as well as whitetail deer and even a growing trout fishery in the river.

Access: The park is located 4.7 miles east of Rose City on the south side of County Road F28 (Rose City Road). It's a three-hour drive from Detroit by departing I-75 at exit 202 and continuing north on MI 33 to that Ogemaw County town. There is a vehicle permit fee to enter the recreation area and an additional per night fee to stay in Grousehaven Campground, a modern campground, or in the park's three rustic campgrounds. The trail can be accessed either from the day-use area or from Grousehaven Campground. The state park also provides three frontier cabins that sleep eight each and can be reached by vehicle. For more information or reservations, contact the park headquarters of the Rifle River Recreation Area (517-473-2258).

Trail: The loop is marked by a series of twenty-five numbered posts that are keyed to the park map handed out at the contact station. These are in no way mileage posts. Distances vary between the posts, all but one interval being under a mile. Post 1 is located in the Grousehaven Lake Campground. From there, the trail skirts the north side of the lake, reaching a day-use area and beach in .5 mile, where post 3 is located. If just visiting the park for the day, this is the best place to start the trail since parking is limited in the campground.

The day-use area features a shelter, toilets, grills, and water. At the end of the parking area is post 4. From here, the trail climbs a low ridge and shortly comes to a junction, where a white boot points to the next post and the 2-mile loop east of Ridge Road. The loop climbs up a series of wooded ridges to

1060 feet, the highpoint along the trail, then makes a gradual descent to the west end of Grebe Lake before returning to where Ridge and Weir roads split. You can shorten the hike by heading right at the first junction to arrive directly at Weir Road. After completing the loop, the trail skirts a ridge between Weir and ridge briefly, then returns to Weir and follows the narrow road for .2 mile, passing Grousehaven and Lodge Lakes, whose accesses are located right across from each other. Lodge is a non-motorized lake with a maximum depth of thirteen feet, while Grousehaven is the second largest lake in the park at ninety-five acres and the deepest at fifty-four feet. There are picnic tables at the Grousehaven access, along with a nice view of the entire lake, including the campground at the west end.

The trail re-enters the woods at post 9, climbs a hill, descends to cross the wetlands between Lodge and Devoe lakes, and then climbs again—steeply this time. At the top, you are greeted with the best view of the day, as you can gaze over both lakes and the ridges around them through the fringe of trees on the crest. You descend and bottom out to a view of the observation tower on top of the ridge between Lodge and Grebe lakes. You can even hear people as they climb the tower's steps and marvel over the panorama. It was at that highpoint that the Jewett family maintained its Grousehaven Lodge in the 1930s, a luxurious hunter's camp that surely had an incredible view from its porch.

The trail skirts two ponds before arriving at post 10, .7 mile from Weir Road. In late July or early August, study the clearings around the ponds carefully, for this is raspberry country. At the junction, one trail heads west, reaching Devoe

Lake rustic campground in .8 mile, but this path goes south (left), where you quickly cross Ridge Road and skirt Scaup Lake, a six-acre lake with a depth of fifteen feet in the middle. Just beyond the lake, you break out into the first grassy clearing of the day and arrive at post 13 on the side of a dirt, two-track road. Head straight to reach post 11 and the return of a six-mile loop. But follow the road south (left) for another view of Scaup Lake and to pick up the posted trail to Lost Lake.

It's another .8 mile to post 14, traveling mostly through open areas where you can feast on more wild berries. At one point, you re-enter a sparse forest of young beech and a few old pines. The most noticeable sight, though, are all the old stumps, a reminder of the logging that took place at the turn of the century. The trail parallels Skunk Creek, but you don't see the sluggish stream until after passing the next marker. First you notice the sharpened stumps from beaver cuttings along the path, then the creek itself comes in view, a trickle that is almost hidden in places by beaver-felled trees. It's incredible what this animal can do.

The trail crosses a bridge over the creek 2.2 miles from Weir road. After the bridge, you cross a dirt road, not listed on park maps, then come to post 15. Beyond the marker, the trail is a level path that winds through a forest of young hardwoods and a few pines, reaching the next marker in .7 mile and post 17 in 1.2 miles, where a sign points out the side trail to Lost Lake. The lake is .5 mile away, with the last 100 yards a muddy and even spongy walk. No signs of mountain bikes here. If you're envisioning a pretty little lake, hidden in the woods, a place to soak tired feet or to wet a fishing line, Lost Lake will disappoint you. There is very little open water, for it is filled with what anglers commonly refer to as pencil reeds. Although it's not as scenic as the other lakes, it's still an interesting place. The lake is slowly converting into a bog, and the layer of plants and grasses around it where the spur ends actually bounces.

From post 17 to 19, the trail heads southwest through a young forest of predominately beech with a thick understory of ferns that can be waist high by midsummer. The marker is not on the banks of the stream, as park maps indicate, but is reached .7 mile from the Lost Lake junction or .3 mile before crossing the new bridge over the creek.

Mushroom seen on Rifle River Trail

The trail stays in the young forest, where you have your best chance of spotting deer, until breaking out at the Rifle River for the first time at post 20, 1.5 miles from the junction to Lost Lake.

Here you cross the park road to a large swing bridge over the river. The stonework you see below the bridge and downstream was put in by Trout Unlimited chapters and the Youth Conservation Corps to stabilize the river banks and create trout habitat. This massive project in 1988-1989 included digging diversion channels around warm water ponds in an effort to lower the temperature of the Rifle River and return it to its days as a wild trout fishery. The effort was a success, for the river's temperature has dropped six degrees. Don't be surprised, while standing on the bridge, to see those magical rings of rising trout.

On the west bank of the Rifle, the trail curves through the woods and crosses Clear Creek after .5 mile. The creek is well named, one of the many that feed cold, clear spring water into the Rifle, and along its muddy banks, you can usually see a profusion of deer tracks. Post 21 is on the banks of the creek, and the stretch to the next marker is a 1.4-mile walk through mostly ferns and huge, weathered stumps. Within .6 mile, the trail swings past the Rifle and heads right again before reaching post 22. The next leg is also a walk through an open field, with the trail skirting the river once

along the way. The marker (post 23) is at a bridge, and on the other side, you stand at the edge of Ranch Campground, a 25-site, rustic facility located mostly in an open field.

You follow an old two-track road away from the campground, spot Birch Cabin half hidden in the forest to the north, then re-enter the woods to cross Ranch Road, where post 24 is passed. Just up the trail, you emerge at Devoe Lake Campground, a rustic, 50-site facility on the shores of the park's largest lake at 130 acres. The trail resumes at the campground's boat launch, and along the way, you pass a hand pump for water. Post 12 and a trail sign mark the path, which departs into the woods that lies between the edge of the lake and the last loop of the campground. At one point, you pass an old post from before the trail loop was re-marked, but post 11 is just up the trail at the edge of Ridge Road. One path here crosses the dirt road on its way to post 13 in the open field, while the return trail heads east (left) towards post 10. Here you climb several hills that are heavily forested; thus, despite being so close to the lake, you are never rewarded with a view of the water for your uphill effort. Still, the terrain is a nice change for those who have just returned from the field west of the Rifle River. Within .5 mile, you reach post 10, where you turn north (left) to head directly to post 4 and the day-use parking area.

Reid Lake

Place: Reid Lake Foot Travel Area/Huron National Forest
Total Distance: 5.5 miles
Hiking Time: 3 to 4 hours, or two days
Rating: Easy
Highpoints: Backcountry camping, fishing
Maps: USGS Bucks Pond; U.S. Forest Service "Reid Lake
Foot Travel Area" map

Although best known for its cross-country skiing, Reid Lake Foot Travel Area also makes a fine destination for a day hike or even an overnight trip into the woods. Located in Huron National Forest, the three thousand-acre, non-motorized area contains a six-mile network of wide trails wrapped around its namesake lake.

Reid Lake was privately owned until 1966, and much of the surrounding land was farmed well into the early 1960s, as is evident by the open fields and even a small orchard. After the U.S. Forest Service purchased the land, the Youth Conservation Corps developed the trail system around the lake, and Reid Lake Foot Travel Area was opened in 1975. Its heaviest use is on weekends during the winter when skiers arrive to tackle a 2.5-mile loop from the trailhead to the lake and back.

During the rest of the year, the trickle of hikers, campers, and anglers that venture here discover a quiet spot with good fishing and scenic campsites. Foot travel is not hard around Reid Lake, for the trails are wide to accommodate

skiers, the junctions are marked with "You Are Here" maps, and the gently rolling terrain contains few climbs of any significance. All trails are in the well-forested, northern third of the area, which features the lake, a huge beaver pond, and many marshes and bogs.

Even though the trail winds around all these low-lying wet areas, it's surprisingly dry and can be walked in tennis shoes. But bring lots of bug repellent in June and July. An ideal time to visit Reid Lake is in mid- to late October, for the area contains some of the best stands of hardwoods in the Harrisville Ranger District of the Huron National Forest.

Pack in a tent or sleeping bag for a pleasant weekend retreat. Rustic campsites, featuring fire rings and benches, are set up around the lake, with many situated on a bluff overlooking the water. Located inland are vault toilets and a hand pump for water. Camping is free, and the sites are available on a first-come, first-use basis. The shortest trail to the lake is from the trailhead to post 7, a walk of less than a mile.

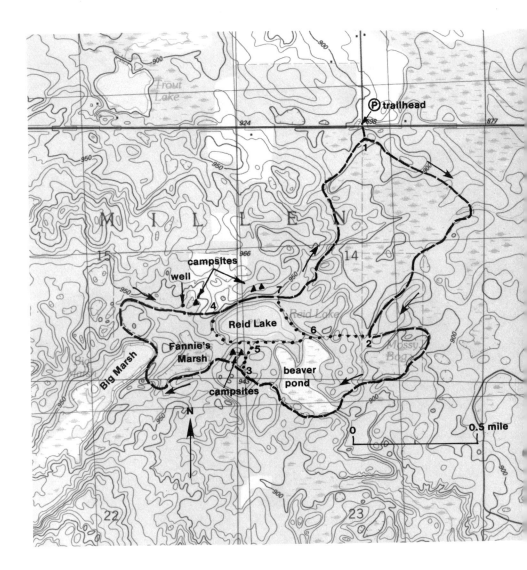

Campsites lie just to the west of here, on the north side of the lake, or .4 mile to the southeast along the shoreline trail to the south side. The trail described here, however, takes a longer route, in the order of the posts.

Keep in mind that mountain bikes and other types of bicycles are prohibited on the trails and that the area is open to hunting, including during firearm deer season from November 15–30. Back-country camping is permitted anywhere that is two hundred feet off the trails, though I don't know why anybody would want to set up anywhere but on a site.

Access: The foot travel area is reached from Harrisville by heading 19 miles west on MI 72 to its posted entrance. From Mio, head east on MI 72 21 miles to its junction with MI 65 near Curran, then continue along MI 72 for another 10 miles to the entrance on the

Anglers on a fishing pier

south (right) side of the state highway. There is a display board at the parking area with maps and a box where you can leave your intentions. There are U.S. Forest Service offices in both Mio (517-826-3252) and Harrisville (517-724-6471), where you can pick up maps or obtain more information. Sometimes the map box at the trailhead is empty.

Trail: Reid Lake is ideal for families. This route is a 5.5-mile hike that can easily be accomplished in an afternoon, and it can be shortened at almost every junction passed. To reach the first junction marked by post 2, head east (left) at the display board along a wide trail that follows the gently rolling terrain. At

.3 mile, you pass through the perfect rows of a red pine plantation. You quickly move into a hardwood forest, pass the first clearing of the day, and end up in an enchanting stand of paper birch. From here, the trail makes a long ascent to post 2, 1.3 miles from the start and marked by a "You Are Here" map sign on the edge of another open field. Reid Lake is only .3 mile to the west (right), but head east for a much more interesting route, especially in spring when the wildflowers are out.

The trail to post 3 quickly re-enters the woods and skirts one end of Mossy Bog. If the bugs allow it, these bogs and marshes make for interesting stops, especially for children who enjoy searching the banks and murky water for the abundant life that thrives here. The trail curves around the bog, ascends into a stand of paper birch, and 1.7 miles from the trailhead, passes an unnamed wet area—a green carpeted pond with a cemetery of standing dead trees in the middle.

After another .2 mile, you pass the rest of the bog, climb away from it along a low ridge, and drop down to the south end of Beaver Pond, marked by a dam that looks like Grandpa's woodpile. The trail actually crosses in front of the dam on planking and then skirts the rest of the pond itself, a body of water as big as Reid Lake. In the middle is a large lodge, while along the bank are fallen trees with the telltale signs of a beaver's handiwork—gnawed marks and wood chips around stumps.

From the pond, the trail moves into an open field, makes two sharp 90-degree turns that are well posted, then arrives at post 3. You can head straight north to reach Reid Lake, just one low ridge away, but to the west (left) is a scenic, 1.3-mile loop around two more marshes. Big Marsh Loop begins by descending to Fannies Marsh and skirting the south end of it. You climb over a low ridge, then around the east end of Big Marsh, which can be more like a small lake during a wet spring, only to resume climbing again. Eventually the trail descends towards post 4 at the northwest corner of Reid Lake. One hundred yards before the junction, the trail passes spurs to campsite 1, a pair of vault toilets, and the hand pump for water. The more scenic campsites, though, are numbers 2, 3, and 4. At the junction, head south (right) along the Lake Shore Loop to reach sites 3 and 4, a pair of shaded spots that sit on a bluff overlooking the lake and an old, rickety dock just below. Head east (left) at post 4 to reach campsite 2, which also sits above the lake and features a vault toilet nearby.

From the campsites, you can see all three docks on the lake, one on the south shore and two new ones on the north shore. Reid is stocked annually with rainbow trout but also holds good populations of panfish, especially bluegill, as well as largemouth bass and some perch. The trout and bass are most often caught by anglers who have hauled in a canoe, but the panfish can easily be landed from the docks on the north side. For either one, anglers usually turn to leaf worms rigged on a small hook and split shot to entice the fish into striking. Add a bobber if you're dock fishing for bluegill.

From the north shore campsites, the Lake Shore Loop quickly reaches post 7. The trail completely around Reid Lake is a .9-mile walk. To return to the trailhead, depart inland at post 7. This final leg appears like a road through the woods and, for the most part, gently descends for almost a mile to the trailhead.

14

Hoist Lakes West Loop

Place: Hoist Lakes Foot Travel Area/Huron National Forest
Total Distance: 7.8 miles
Hiking Time: 5 to 6 hours
Rating: Moderate to challenging
Highpoints: Scenic vistas, backcountry campsites
Maps: USGS Curran; Huron National Forest Hoist Lakes Foot
    Travel Area map

Hoist Lakes Foot Travel Area, set up in 1976 to provide a quiet sanctuary from the noise and rumble of our motorized society, offers outdoor opportunities found nowhere else on the east side of the Lower Peninsula. Encompassing 10,600 acres of the Huron National Forest, this foot travel area is large enough to provide lengthy backpacking trips, where people can sneak off into the woods for days at a time. With seven small lakes, the area offers walk-in, wilderness fishing adventures for anglers who like having a lake to themselves. And due to its rugged terrain, with many hills topping 1,200 feet, Hoist Lakes offers you the chance to climb a ridge, sit on its crest, and ponder the panorama at your feet.

Hoist Lakes Foot Travel Area is covered by forests of pine, aspen, and hardwoods that are broken up by small pothole lakes, numerous ponds, marshes, and beaver-flooded streams. There might also be a clearcut, for limited commercial logging is allowed to improve the vegetation for wildlife or to clear a ridgeline to improve the view.

Winding through the backcountry is a twenty-mile network of footpaths that forms two basic loops, sharing only a 1.5-mile stretch of trail. This description follows the West Loop, a 7.8-mile hike starting from the trailhead on De Jarlais Road. The East Loop, an 11-mile trek that begins from a trailhead off MI 65, is covered in this book as a separate hike (see Hike 15). From either loop, there are good opportunities to observe wildlife. Perhaps the most famous residents of the area are the least encountered ones: black bears. There are also red fox, mink, and coyotes, but more often than not the game hikers spot are wild turkeys, ruffed grouse, whitetail deer, beavers, porcupines, and a variety of waterfowl and birds.

Hoist Lakes is also a well-known cross country ski area, so trails tend to be wide and the hills and steep inclines have parallel paths to keep uphill and downhill skiers separate in the winter. In the summer, this parallel structure can be a bit confusing, but otherwise the

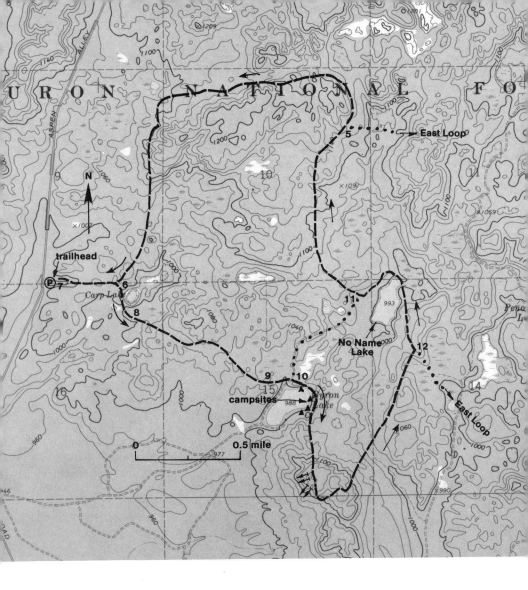

network is well marked with blue diamonds and "You Are Here" maps at most junctions.

U.S. Forest Service regulations prohibit camping or campfires within two hundred feet of an open body of water, swamp, or foot trail. Horses, motorized vehicles, including boats with outboard motors, and mountain bikes or other bicycles are not allowed in the area.

Groups must not be larger than ten persons, and you can't camp longer than sixteen days in one spot.

Some of the most beautiful backcountry campsites in the Lower Peninsula are located on this loop, on a bluff above Byron Lake. These are only 1.5 miles from the trailhead, leaving you with most of the hiking the second day. Good off-trail spots to pitch a tent are abundant in Hoist Lakes Foot Travel Area. Although there is a hand pump for water a mile from Byron Lake, it's good practice to always carry in water since the pump is not always working.

Access: The Hoist Lakes Foot Travel Area is east of Mio, 22 miles west of Harrisville or a good three-hour drive from Detroit. If heading north, take MI 65 through the town of Glennie, then in 5 miles, turn west onto Sunny Lake Road. Follow Sunny Lake for 5 miles, then turn north on Au Sable Road. The first junction is where De Jarlais (also known as Forest Service Road 32) splits off. Continue north (left) on De Jarlais, and in .5 mile the posted trailhead will appear.

If coming from Harrisville, keep in mind that there is a U.S. Forest Ranger office (517-724-5431) in town on US 23, open Monday through Friday from 8 A.M. to 5 P.M. Then continue west on MI 72, and just before reaching the town of Curran, head south on De Jarlais Road.

Trail: The parking area for the west trailhead contains a vault toilet and a large display board with maps and intention cards. From here, the trail departs into a forest of mixed pines and hardwoods and quickly comes to the first of many paralleling paths. Blue diamonds are well placed along one side, and in .5 mile, you climb over a small hill and gently descend to the first junction, post 6. The route will be described in a counterclockwise direction since many hikers arrive in the afternoon and hike only to Byron to spend the evening.

The yellow metal "You Are Here" maps are not always aligned with the actual trails, the first instance of this occurring at Carp Lake. South of the junction, the lake immediately appears to the east (left) of you, not west of the trail as

most maps indicate. The trail skirts the small, roundish lake from above, passes an unmarked vehicle track, then swings east to arrive at post 8 where the hand pump is located.

You continue east, with the trail passing through a stand of predominately maple that is magnificent in the fall, to climb a ridge and top out in paper birch. From here you begin a long but gradual descent back into hardwoods, finally bottoming out 1.8 miles from the start at post 9 at the north end of Byron Lake. One of the largest lakes in the area, Byron has panfish, perch, and a good population of smallmouth bass but is tough to fish from the shoreline. Since it's not an easy portage for hauling in a canoe, some anglers attempt to fish the lake with waders, while others hike in with a belly boat or float tube strapped to their backs.

An unmarked path follows the west bank, while the main trail heads around the north end soon to come to post 10, a junction with a map, and a "Campsites" sign. One trail veers north (left) to provide skiers an alternative to the steep hill that lies south of the lake. Follow the other to the east (right), quickly passing the first of three official campsites and many unofficial ones. Campsite 3 provides a tent pad, fire ring, and a bench, and a long stairway leads down the sandy bluff to the water. Here is one of the best spots to pitch a tent in the entire Lower Peninsula, for you can view all of Byron Lake along with forested ridges behind it.

The trail continues to follow the ridge along the east shore, passing a sandy beach at one point and then two more posted campsites. Eventually you descend past an unmarked vehicle track, climb a hill away from the lake, descend again, and begin climbing once more. This time it's a long haul up, but as you

Belly boat on the shore of Byron Lake

near the top, you catch a brief glimpse of your reward. At 2.4 miles from the trailhead, you top off at 1,140 feet at a clearing among the trees that, no doubt, has served as a scenic spot to pitch a tent. There is a 180-degree view, where you can see the miles of rugged terrain leading to the AuSable River. Ironically, the only thing you can't see is Byron Lake, which is hidden among the trees.

The trail skirts the top of the hill as it makes a sharp turn, then begins a .5-mile descent off it. You bottom out at a clearing, where you skirt a pond and marshy area (a good place to search for wildlife). You then follow a level route to post 12, where you turn left toward No Name Lake. This junction has been moved closer to No Name Lake since the maps on the trail were drawn. The shallow lake is quickly reached, and if it's a dry summer, the trail will skirt not water at its north end but an extensive mud flat before continuing to post 11.

This junction is a .6-mile walk from post 12 (not the quarter mile many maps indicate) and is formed by the easy cutoff spur from Byron Lake. The loop continues north (right), beginning with a gentle descent of .5 mile out of the forest and into an opening of saplings and young pines. As you cross this old clearcut, keep an eye out for deer, which are often spotted feeding among the young aspen in early evening. The trail climbs out of the clearing to return to a wooded setting and arrive at post 5, .8 mile from the last junction.

To the east (right) is the East Loop that goes to the trailhead off MI 65. To the north (left) is the route back to the western trailhead, a stretch that is rated "more difficult" for skiers. It's a difficult ski because the trail climbs from the junction at 1,140 feet to the top of a 1,200 foot hill, descends, then climbs another hill as it curves to the south. There's no spectacular views along this segment, other than the trees themselves. During the fall, the hardwoods take on a stunning array of color as the brilliant red of oak leaves contrast sharply with the golden ferns that form the undercover.

Within 1.2 miles of post 5, you pass a junction with an unmarked track that merges into the trail. The trees then open up briefly for a view of a ridgeline to the east. At this point, the trail veers to the east slightly in an poorly marked area, made even more confusing by a parallel skier's path. Just keep looking for the occasional blue diamond. The two paths climb a hill and begin the gradual descent to post 6, where you backtrack west (right) .5 mile to return to the parking area.

Hoist Lakes East Loop

Place: Hoist Lakes Foot Travel Area/Huron National Forest
Total Distance: 5 to 13.3 miles
Hiking Time: 3 to 8 hours
Rating: Easy to challenging
Highpoints: Inland lakes, backcountry campsites
Maps: USGS Curran, Bucks Pond; Huron National Forest,
  Hoist Lakes Foot Travel Area map

The twenty-mile network of trails in the Hoist Lakes Foot Travel Area basically forms a pair of loops. The longest is the East Loop, which winds 13.3 miles through the area before returning to a trailhead off of MI 72. At only 7.8 miles, the West Loop (see Hike 14) is a shorter and, most hikers feel, much more scenic trip due to the high vista that is climbed south of Byron Lake and the lack of clearcuts.

The U.S. Forest Service, in accordance with its policy of multiple use, allows logging in the foot travel area, and much of it is encountered along the East Loop, particularly in its northern half where the trees have been cut right to the edge of the trail in places. For those who cherish a quiet walk in the woods, it is rather dismal to enter suddenly a field of stumps, brush piles, and matchstick saplings. Although any section could be logged in the future, presently most of the clearcuts are passed between posts 5 and 3.

Without a doubt the most scenic sections of the East Loop lie in the southern half, and with a little backtracking you can put sections of the East Loop and the West Loop hikes described in this book together and avoid the signs of loggers entirely. The shortest hike would be a 5-mile round trip to North Hoist Lake, with a backtrack of less than .5 mile of trail. Or, from the small group of Hoist Lakes, you could continue west and follow a loop around No Name Lake, Byron Lake, and the high vista south of it before returning to the eastern trailhead. This walk would be almost 13 miles but would pass seven lakes and by far the most scenic tracts of the foot travel area while backtracking 3 miles of trail.

On either hike, there are opportunities for backcountry camping. You can pitch a tent anywhere in the area as long as you stay at least two hundred feet from a lake, stream, or foot trail; but campsites with fire rings, benches, and lakeshore views are encountered on the north side of South Hoist Lake and along Byron, making convenient stops halfway along the loops mentioned above. If planning to spend the night at either lake, bring a fishing pole and a

handful of Mepps lures or other small spinners. Byron has good populations of smallmouth bass, perch, and panfish, while South Hoist Lake is stocked annually with rainbow trout.

Like the West Loop, keep in mind that the trails were built for skiers as well as hikers. They tend to be wide and include parallel paths on many steep hills. There are also a large number of old vehicle tracks and present logging roads that cut through the area. But the trail system is extremely well marked with blue diamonds and "You Are Here" maps at every junction.

Access: The Hoist Lakes Foot Travel Area is 22 miles west of Harrisville or a good two-hour drive from Saginaw. To reach the eastern trailhead from I-75, exit onto US 23 near Standish and then, in 15 miles, head north on MI 65. Follow the state road as it curves east to cross the AuSable River and passes through the town of Glennie. Forty miles from US 23, the posted trailhead will appear just south of the junction with MI 72. The closest U.S. Forest Service office is the Harrisville Ranger District (517-724-5431) in town on US 23, open Monday through Friday from 8 A.M. to 5 P.M.

Trail: The East Loop can be hiked in any direction, and the posts are actually numbered in a counterclockwise direction. But since most visitors are traveling directly to either Hoist Lakes or Byron Lake, the route will be described in the opposite direction.

The parking area for the east trailhead contains a vault toilet and large display board with maps and intention cards. Next to the information board is a metal gate and three wide tracks departing into the woods, with one clearly marked as a logging road and the other two posted as trails. There are two routes to post 14. The lefthand trail to the south

quickly passes through an old clearcut, now a forest of saplings, and then swings west to meet the other route in 1.5 miles. By far the most scenic route, however, is to head north (right), following the wide path over a rolling terrain of lightly forested hills and through a pine plantation at one point. Within .7 mile you reach post 2 at a junction with a hand pump for water and two benches. There is also a yellow "You Are Here" map, but keep in mind that these metal maps are not always accurate, for the network has been re-routed slightly over the years. At this junction, a logging track appears from the south, while the trail is posted to the north and straight ahead to the west.

Head west for the Hoist Lakes, and the trail will immediately skirt two low-lying wet areas. The one to the north is an open marsh ringed by an impressive stand of paper birch. An occasional shotgun shell on the ground indicates that this area attracts a variety of wildlife, such as wild turkeys and grouse, and thus hunters in the fall and spring. The trail skirts this marsh from above and then ascends a hill to reach almost 1,153 feet. On the far side of the hill, you swing past a small lake partially covered by a mat of cattails and plants. Beavers are active in this area, for there are a pair of lodges in the open water and gnawed stumps along the trail.

Just beyond the pond is post 14, where the other trail from MI 72 merges from the left. A partial view of a valley and its surrounding ridges can be had through the trees to the west. In less than .5 mile, the trail comes to a posted junction not shown on the metal maps. One trail heads south (left) to follow a ridgeline around South Hoist Lake and then descends to post 13. The other, marked by a "Hoist Lakes Campsites" sign, departs to the west and within .3

Beaver Lodge

mile arrives at the lake's north shore. The campsites are located on a low bluff overlooking a bend in the lake. They feature a fire ring, benches, and an excellent view of the entire lake. A night here is well worth carrying in a tent and sleeping bag.

Just beyond the campsites, a short spur to the right (north) leads to North Hoist Lake, ending on another high bank where more than one backpacker has pitched a tent. The small, roundish lake contains evidence of beaver activity along the shoreline and two lodges, and often the beaver himself can be seen swimming across the lake in the early evening. Fish North Hoist for bluegill and sunfish and South Hoist for rainbow trout along with panfish. Most anglers fishing for the rainbows will use small garden worms and work the deep por-

tions in the middle of the lake. Also nearby is West Hoist Lake, but it's not seen from the main trail system. To reach it, you must follow one of a number of paths that heads west from the campsites trail.

The campsites trail continues around South Hoist Lake, where it quickly merges with the trail entering at post 13. The 2.5-mile leg from post 13 to 12 is a double path almost the entire way to help skiers negotiate the steep sections the trail covers. You cross an old logging track at .3 mile from post 13 and then begin climbing a hill to top off near 1,160 feet, the highest point you will reach in the entire east loop. From here the trail follows the crest of the ridge through a scenic section. You pass giant red pines along the way and are able to peer down into ravines where deer can often be seen in late spring and early summer. The stretch lasts for .5 mile, and then the trail begins to descend off the hill, passing at one point a "YCC 1980" post. The marker was left by a Youth Conservation Corps work party and explains why the route is so well posted.

Eventually the trail bottoms out, climbs a low hill, and then enters a clearing to cross Forest Road 4089, a well-graded dirt road that heads north to Penoyer Lake. On the other side of the road, the trail is marked and resumes northwest through an interesting marsh area. The path is surprisingly dry (most of the time) despite swamps on both sides and more beaver activity. Half a mile from the forest road, the trail ascends to post 12, a junction that has been moved since the metal maps were posted. The trail that heads due south (left) climbs to the best overview of the network (see Hoist Lakes West Loop), then curves north to reach the campsites on Byron Lake, a walk of 1.8 miles.

Head north, where the trail quickly descends to the edge of No Name Lake, a pretty body of water but a shallow one. By mid-summer, the north end often dries up. The beaver activity on this side is amazing. Soon you'll cross a sluggish stream on a pair of logs. Take time to investigate the creek, for an industrious beaver has dammed it several times and built a huge lodge in the middle of the flooded portion. The trail continues to follow the west side of the lake before swinging away to ascend to post 11, reached .6 mile from the last junction. To the south (left) is a .5-mile spur to Byron Lake, a much quicker and easier route (but not as scenic) to those back-country campsites than the one from post 12.

To the north, the east loop continues through a rolling stretch of woods be-

fore making its first encounter with the many areas of logging activity. Stumps are everywhere, and although it's hard to tell when the tract was cut, already there is a sapling forest of popples and other pioneering species covering the ground. Though many hikers might not be too crazy about the change in flora, deer love it, as is evidenced by their tracks in the sandy path. Eventually the trail re-enters the woods and descends to post 5, reached .8 mile from the last junction.

The west loop is the trail that heads north (left) to post 6. Stay on the east loop, which heads east toward post 4. The path quickly breaks out into another old clearcut. You cross it to re-enter the woods briefly, only to come out at a second, much larger logged tract. This one takes almost .5 mile to cross, and the trees have been cut right up to the edge of the trail. Not a tree has been left standing, and in many places the saplings have yet to take root. Despite the virtues of "multiple use forests," it's hard not to get dismayed at the sight of the stump-covered hills you pass through. You briefly re-enter the woods, pass through a third clearcut, and then, 1.8 miles from post 5, return to the forests, this time to stay there. The trail merges with an old logging road and takes a sharp swing south, where it skirts a scenic little ravine before arriving at post 4. The post is reached 2.2 miles from the last junction and is located at the side of a dirt road that heads north toward Forest Road 4089.

The trail continues across the road, and the next leg, a 1.8-mile walk to post 3, is a repeat of the last one. The trail begins by following a logging road, briefly paralleling another, and passing through another clearcut. At one point you enter an area that has been selectively cut—loggers have left a number of trees standing—but still it's hardly a "natural setting." This stretch has been shortened since the metal maps were posted and does not reach any high vistas. But it still crosses a very hilly terrain and is a good workout for most hikers.

Post 3 is in the woods and placed where an old logging road crosses the trail. The next segment is a 1.3-mile walk rather than the .7 mile listed on most maps and brochures, but it is a very pleasant hike over a series of forested hills. No scenic overviews or lakes are met here, but no logging activity is seen either. Eventually you ascend to the hand pump and benches at post 2. The trailhead and your car are now only .7 mile away to your left.

16

South Point

Place: Negwegon State Park
Total Distance: 5 miles
Hiking Time: 3 hours
Rating: Easy
Highpoints: Lake Huron beaches, shoreline views
Maps: USGS Black River and South Point

Perhaps the most unusual unit of the state park system in the Lower Peninsula is Negwegon on the Lake Huron shoreline. For most of its existence it was an undeveloped track that was hard to reach and visited only by those from the Harrisville and Alpena areas that knew about it. In recent years, more attention has been focused on the 1,800-acre state park as a controversy over its development—whether to leave it natural and rustic or to construct a modern campground—has raged.

The debate has allowed more people to find their way to the park, where they are usually amazed by what they find. Many believe that the most beautiful and possibly the most isolated beaches on Lake Huron lie in this park. Words like "paradise" have been used to describe Negwegon's 6.5 miles of shoreline. Many areas of this shoreline are lined by pine and cedar and feature wide, sugary beaches in remote bays closed in by rocky points and spits.

Acquired in 1962, this park was renamed from Alpena State Park in 1970 to honor an Ojibway Indian chief, who was loyal to the U.S. side during the War of 1812. Negwegon is presently undeveloped with the exception of a gravel parking lot, a well, and two trails marked by blue DNR pathway triangles. One trail heads south and makes a four-mile loop along the beach before swinging inland; it is occasionally referred to as the Beach Trail. The other trail is described here—an old two-track road that heads north from the parking area. After 2 miles, another old road veers off and ends at the tip of South Point for a view that's hard to match anywhere along Lake Huron.

No camping is allowed in the unit, and usage is light primarily due to the rough access road. The park entrance drive lies off Sand Hill Trail, a two-track dirt road that during the summer is often covered with drifting sand and deeply rutted. The Harrisville State Park staff, which administers Negwegon, says that "most two-wheel vehicles are apt to get stuck," but that might be overstated a bit. Definitely think twice about going in, though, if your car sits low to the ground or has worn tires.

Much will change in the future when the state decides how to develop this

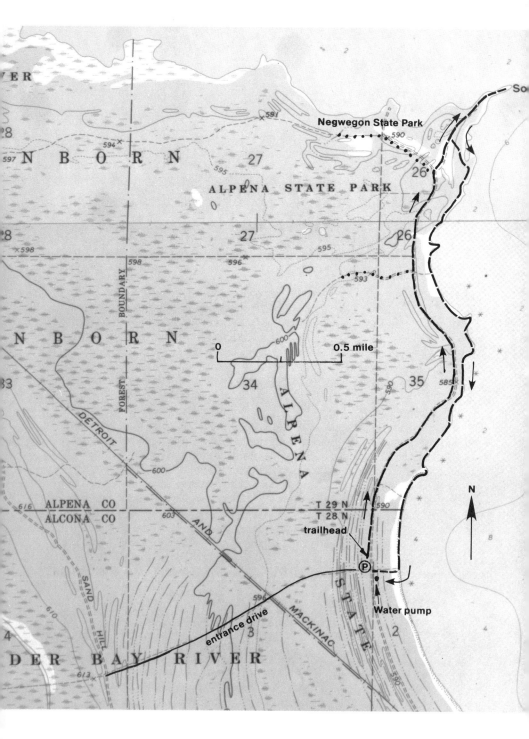

rare piece of Lake Huron real estate. In every master plan to date, however, the trail to South Point has remained a footpath and probably always will. Hopefully, those who cast the final votes about Negwegon's future will not push for conveniences such as electrical hook-ups for trailers, bathhouses, or refreshment stands that will bring crowds of people into the area. Crowded beaches are found anywhere in Michigan. Negwegon's greatest asset is not its beaches but the remoteness you feel while viewing Lake Huron from its shoreline.

Access: The park is almost halfway between Harrisville and Alpena off US 23. If coming from the south, stop by at Harrisville State Park (517-724-5126) for additional information or for an update on the condition of Sand Hill Trail.

Heading north from Harrisville, drive 12 miles on US 23 to Black River Road and turn east (right) for 1.5 miles. After passing the cemetery on the left, turn north (left) on unmarked Sand Hill Trail. It's the first road past Fontaine Road, which is posted, and appears as a sandy, four-wheel-drive track.

Be careful! You have to follow Sand Hill Trail for 2.5 miles before the park sign and a gravel road appear to the east (right). The entrance drive ends at a parking area in 1.2 miles, where a short path leads past a water spigot, the start of the Beach Trail, and finally to the park's largest bay.

Trail: The route to South Point begins at the north end of the parking lot where a yellow gate and an incredible off-road vehicle barrier, a mountain of sand and logs, block the entrance of the trail.

Rocky shoreline on the way out to South Point

Both testify to the growing problem of illegal off-road vehicle use in remote public land. The trail is a level forest road where a post stands almost every one hundred yards, a few with DNR pathway triangles on them (the others have been ripped off).

The old two-track path heads straight through a forest of beech, maple, and paper birch and can be wet in places. In .7 mile, you pass through one particularly nice stand of birch. Here the road swings east for a glimpse of Lake Huron. Side trails lead to a shoreline of rocks and pebbles where you can still see the main bay. The beautiful stretch of sand and surf to the south keeps most visitors from going elsewhere in the park.

Within 1.5 miles, you reach another spur that leads east to the next cove. This one is a sandy beach with no view beyond the rocky points at each end. Here, pines along the shore give way to beachgrass, which gives way to the radiant heat of the sand. It's very tempting to dive into the light blue water and enjoy your own private beach.

At 2 miles, another old two-track splits off to the northeast (right) and immediately enters the first grassy clearing of the walk. Follow this side trail, which eventually swings back into the woods and out onto South Point. Water appears on both sides of you, and eventually you break out of the trees at the gravel tip of the point .5 mile from the junction.

The view is unbelievable. To the north are miles of shoreline, along with two islands. The closest is Bird Island; further out is Scarecrow Island, preserved as Michigan Island National Refuge. If the day is clear, you'll be able to see across Thunder Bay to the water towers of Alpena. To the south is the jagged shoreline of this incredible state park. You can see all the way back to the first bay, whose golden sand almost hypnotized you into not hiking out here. It's a great view, but there's no place to bask in the sun's rays since, being a point, both sides are rocky.

You can actually continue further on the trail for an additional 1.2 miles past the junction to South Point. You would cross three wooden bridges and pass an old orchard along the way. After the second bridge, you can cut over to see the northernmost bay in the park. The trail eventually swings west to arrive at the edge of state land. Here, public land with its "No Wheeled Motor Vehicles" sign squares off with private land and its warning of "No Hunting or Trespassing Allowed."

Plans call for a loop to be set up to return you to the parking lot from South Point. As of 1991, that trail had not been laid out or marked. If you backtrack from the point, the hike totals 5 miles. I've never done that, though. Although the forests are fine, the beaches are beautiful and the shoreline spectacular. I've always returned by hiking along the edge of Lake Huron. That choice makes it a 6-mile day.

Heartland

17

Doane Lake

Place: Dr. T. K. Lawless County Park
Total Distance: 2 miles
Hiking Time: 1 hour
Rating: Easy
Highpoints: Inland lakes, birding
Maps: USGS Jones; Dr. T. K. Lawless County Park trail map

Dr. T. K. Lawless County Park is one of those little-known preserves in rural Michigan that many hikers would enjoy visiting—if they only knew it existed. Hidden in central Cass County, the park is a place that is enjoyed only by locals and the few lost travelers who stumble upon it accidentally. Of course, that's one of its attractions: a large park with lakes, ponds, and streams in a wooded tract that is lightly used and suffers few crowds other than an occasional family reunion.

Lawless is named after a Cass County doctor who was an avid conservationist. He owned much of this land until he gave it to the state. Known at one time as Cass County State Park, eventually the land was turned over to the Parks Division of the Cass County Road Commission in 1980, which re-named it and began developing a master plan for the area. At 640 acres, Lawless is one of the largest county parks in the state and presently supports a four-mile trail network. Eventually the park's trail system will be increased, with paths on the north side of the lakes as well as extending into the undeveloped, 180-acre

tract that lies on the south side of Monkey Run Road.

Other facilities will probably be added, but Lawless will never be a high development park. The county has decided that its real value is in "nature education and appreciation," and that the best way to enhance such is to develop only trails and a footbridge or two. The terrain is hilly, which attracts cross-country skiers and sledders in the winter, but a hike in Lawless is a short and easy trek that, if undertaken in early morning or dusk, often leads to numerous encounters with wildlife. The lakes and marshes attract a wide range of waterfowl and herons, while the woods are home to ruffed grouse and pheasants. You might also spot raccoons, cottontail rabbits, deer, or even a fox.

The hike described here is a two-mile loop from the parking area around Doane and Hogback lakes. An additional spur (Trail 5) that crosses a stream twice can be added to make a 3.2-mile walk, but some backtracking would be necessary.

Access: The park lies just off MI 60 between the towns of Jones and Van-

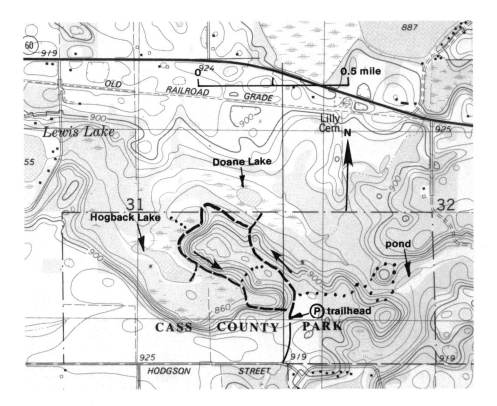

dalia, or about a thirty- to forty-minute drive south from Kalamazoo. Two miles west of Jones, the park is posted along MI 60 and is reached by turning south on Lewis Lake Road and then east (left) on Monkey Run Road. The entrance is less than a mile up Monkey Run Road, and the open fields around the trailhead include a picnic area, vault toilets, pavilion, grills, and during the winter, a designated tubing hill.

A small per-vehicle fee is charged to enter the park, and additional maps or information can be obtained by writing to the Cass County Road Commission, 340 North O'Keefe Street, Cassopolis, MI 49031; or calling (616) 445-8611.

Trail: Trails in Lawless are wide paths to accommodate skiers in the winter, and during the summer, they look like old, moss-covered roads. Departing from a display map, the trail is a gently rolling path through a young hardwood forest. You pass first a posted junction to the return of Loop 3 and then come to Loop 5. The latter 1.2-mile spur climbs a hill and crosses the stream from Doane Lake before doubling back. To reach Doane Lake, follow Trail 2/4 to the left here, and within .4 mile, you'll arrive at the spur to the right that descends to the water.

The small lake is encircled by cattails and other marsh plants, and if you approach carefully, you can often spot Canada geese, mallards, or even blue herons enjoying the quiet water. Any stomping of boots will send them off in a flurry of feathers. You get the feeling that this remote lake might be worth

fishing someday, for planking leads through the marsh to the water's edge while an old metal boat lies rusting away among the cattails. There are bass and bluegill, maybe even some big ones, but the best time to drop a line is through the ice during the winter. The mud is three- to four-feet thick around the edge of the lake, and wading in or pulling a boat to deep water would be a difficult task.

Trail 4, as it is marked on the map, proceeds to skirt the woods around Doane Lake's south shore and then the base of the hill that Trail 1 ascends. At this point, you pass some of the largest trees in the park—American beech whose white bark looks particularly ghostly in the spring when its limbs and branches are bare of leaves. Within a mile from the beginning, Hogback Lake pops into view, and a short spur leads past a picturesque duck hunter's blind to some planking at its edge. Hogback is slightly smaller than Doane, but its shoreline is also encircled by cattails. Most likely, the geese you chased off the first lake are now swimming here.

The trail continues to skirt the base of the hill and quickly comes to a junction. A shortcut that is closed in the winter heads left to ascend to Trail 2, which you hiked earlier. The fork to the right provides a more gentle climb to Trail 3, where you turn left to head back to the trailhead near the parking area.

Old boat in Lawless County Park

18

Long Lake Trail

Place: Yankee Springs Recreation Area
Total Distance: 4.2 miles end-to-end, 5.4 miles loop
Hiking Time: 2 to 3 hours
Rating: Moderate
Highpoints: Unusual geological formations
Maps: USGS Cloverdale, Bowens Mill, Middleville, Orangeville;
Yankee Springs Recreation Area map

The rugged terrain, inland lakes, interesting bogs, and unusual depressions known as Devil's Soup Bowls provide Yankee Springs Recreation Area with ideal hiking qualities. Its location, almost centered between the urban areas of Grand Rapids, Kalamazoo, and Battle Creek, makes it a popular park with everybody.

Actually, its popularity is the main drawback of its seventeen-mile network of trails. The trails are used for so many different recreational functions that the paths have become proliferated with directional arrows and colored diamonds. At times, you're actually confused as to which way to go. At one junction along the Long Lake Trail, there are signs for snowmobilers, skiers, hikers, and even an old post indicating a nonexistent bridle path. You half expect to see the golden arches of McDonalds as well. All this is to be expected, however, when a park draws more than 700,000 visitors annually as one of the five most popular units in the state park system.

During the summer, hikers don't have to worry about snowmobilers, skiers, or

horseback riders, who now have their own trail system in the southeastern corner of the park. Also, the vast majority of summer visitors are congregated around the Gun Lake campground and day-use area. But those on foot do have to share the trails with one other user group: mountain bikers, whose numbers in the park have increased steadily since the late 1980s.

Given these points, you're probably wondering why Long Lake Trail is included as one of southern Michigan's best walks. Despite its billboard-like appearance, Long Lake Trail is still one of the few extended routes in this area of the state and can be an extremely enjoyable outing if undertaken at the right time of the year. Avoid the park on weekends from mid-June to mid-August when the trails are busy with cyclists and other hikers. Springtime, especially from mid-April to early May, is best for viewing wildflowers and re-emerging plants. Since the five thousand-acre park is well forested with more than seventy species of native trees, mid-October to early November is also an

excellent time to wander through its woods.

Long Lake Trail is a 2.2-mile route that merges into Chief Noonday Trail just before you reach the soup bowls. It actually begins off the Sassafras Nature Trail, but this description picks it up at a nearby trailhead and parking area on Gun Lake Road. The hike around Long Lake to the glacial depressions and back along the same route would be a 5.2-mile afternoon. For the sake of diversity, though, this description returns along Chief Noonday Trail, which ends at a well-posted trailhead off Chief Noonday Road. This loop is shorter, only 4.2 miles, but you end up 1.2 miles up the road from where you left your car.

Although there is much climbing around the soup bowls, the trails are wide and can be easily hiked in tennis shoes. There are lots of wildflowers and trees to identify, but don't expect to encounter much wildlife in midsummer. With almost a million visitors a year, you

Boardwalk through a marsh

can bet that the residents of the woods remain well hidden during the day.

Access: The state park unit is a half hour drive from either Grand Rapids or Kalamazoo off of US 131. From the highway, depart at exit 61 and follow County Road A42 east for 7 miles to its junction with Gun Lake Road and turn right. From the east, head west on MI 37 from Hastings for 2 miles, then turn onto Gun Lake Road (also A42 at this point) to reach the park in 10 miles. The trailhead for Long Lake Trail is just .5 mile south of County Road A42 or just north of the park headquarters (616-795-9081), where information on the park or campground reservations can be obtained. The trail is marked at the side of the road by an orange diamond, where there is parking on the shoulder for one or two cars. A larger turnout is located up the road towards County Road A42.

Trail: Look for the orange diamond that marks the start of the trail, but once on the trail, focus on the yellow triangles that identify Long Lake Trail. Within .3 mile, the diamonds veer north (left), marking a snowmobile trail. Stay on the righthand fork, and within .5 mile from Gun Lake Road the trail arrives at a boardwalk. The planked section extends almost .4 mile as it winds through an interesting bog area that borders the north end of Long Lake. The wetland is drier than most people expect and most intriguing in spring when skunk cabbage, marsh marigolds, and fiddleheads by the bunches are pushing up through the ground.

There's no view of the lake from the boardwalk, but at its end, the trail swings southeast and climbs the side of a low ridge for the only glimpse of the lake it's named after. Eventually the trail merges into a wide sandy path, marked by all kinds of signs, including yellow triangles. This stretch is an old wagon road and heads south to pass a scenic marsh at one point. The road is believed to have been part of a stagecoach run from Kalamazoo to Grand Rapids, and in fact the name of the park comes from Yankee Bill Lewis, who arrived in 1836 and built an inn along the route here. The initial inn grew to become an odd assortment of log cabins that soon became known as Yankee Springs. Traffic could be heavy at times, for Lewis' inn was reputed to have put up one hundred travelers in a single night, while stabling sixty teams of stagecoach horses.

At 1.4 miles from the trailhead, the old wagon road arrives at a posted snowmobile crossing, where the yellow triangles of the Long Lake Trail direct you to swing left and cut through an open grassy area. The trail then ascends the first hills of the day, before descending to a dirt road that cuts across the interior of the park. A good climb awaits you on the other side of the road as you enter the hilly region around the Devil's Soup Bowls. At 1.8 miles, you pass a junction with yellow triangles going both directions, indicating a short spur to a park road. Take the lefthand fork to follow an electric line corridor briefly, pass by a second marked spur to the road, and cross a sandy path. On the other side of the path, you climb a hill forested in pines and soon come to the official end of Long Lake Trail at 2.2 miles.

Here is a well-posted junction on the Chief Noonday Trail, on which you head east (right) to continue to the soup bowls. Quickly the trail descends to within sight of the rough park road, which you would follow south briefly to reach the parking area for Graves Hill. The "peak" of this glacial moraine is just a few log steps above the turnaround, and from there, at 920 feet, it's possible to view the interior of the park and a portion of Gun Lake.

More impressive work by the glacier that scoured the land ten thousand years ago can be seen by continuing on Chief Noonday Trail. Named after an Ottawa Indian chief who resided in the area, the trail ends with a loop around the small soup bowl. By heading along the righthand fork, you soon traverse the narrow ridge that separates the two glacial depressions. To the south is the almost bottomless pit of the large Devil's Soup Bowl, to the north,

the smaller one, and both can be viewed with a mere twist of the head. From here it's a steep climb to the east side of the small bowl and the well-marked junction with the Deep Lake Trail, which continues east towards the rustic campground on the lake.

Stay on Chief Noonday, heading west and passing the northern edge of the small depression before backtracking to the posted junction of Long Lake Trail, where you continue on down Chief Noonday. At first Noonday is not as impressive a trail as Long Lake. It departs to the northwest, and for .5 mile winds through a clearing of brush piles and passes a former off-road vehicle scramble area. Eventually you ascend a sandy hill and then drop to the park road that was crossed earlier. On the other side of the road, you begin another steep climb before coming to the top of an 870-foot hill providing a view almost equal to that of Graves Hill. In the spring and fall, it's possible to see McDonald Lake to the north, and any time of the year you can span the forests and ridges for more than a mile.

The trail departs the hill with a rapid descent, and for the first time since leaving the junction with Long Lake Trail .7 miles earlier, you re-enter the woods. The trail levels out, and it's possible to catch a glimpse of Williams Lake before the path swings east for a good view of McDonald, where it would be easy to bushwhack to its shoreline and throw a line in the water. From here, the trail is a level walk past a pond and other low-lying areas until it breaks out of the trees at the parking area and trailhead just off Chief Noonday Road. Follow the road east (left), turning left again when you reach Gun Lake Road, to return to the Long Lake Trailhead, a walk of 1.2 miles.

Swan Creek Trail

Place: Allegan State Game Area
Total Distance: 5.2 miles
Hiking Time: 3 to 4 hours
Rating: Moderate
Highpoints: Birding opportunities
Maps: USGS Millgrove; Allegan State Game Area Foot Trails

Swan Creek Trail is best done during the off-season—either in early May when fiddleheads are popping through the forest floor and the flowering dogwood is in full bloom, or in the fall to witness one of the largest migratory gatherings of waterfowl in the state. In mid-July, you'll find the wildlife scarce, the fishing slow, and the mosquitoes and black flies ferocious.

The route described here, which encircles the creek and its impoundments, is part of a twenty-mile network of foot trails in Allegan State Game Area. This 45,000-acre wildlife preserve was created in 1946 by combining several tracts of public land. It includes parts of seven lakes, bogs and large marshes, open meadows, and oak, maple and pine forests that cover the sand plains of west-central Allegan County. It's managed primarily for waterfowl, and during the fall migration, seventy-five to one hundred thousand Canada geese alone stop in the game area to rest for a week or two before continuing their flight south. Peak migration traditionally occurs from November 1 to 15, when as many as thirty thousand geese may be

in the preserve at one time. It's an impressive sight and a lot of honking.

Other waterfowl spotted in spring or fall include wood ducks, mallards, even a growing population of mute swans, and the area is also known for its variety of warblers. But the most famous bird here is the wild turkey. After being hunted into extinction in this area, the state's Department of Natural Resources reintroduced the wild turkey in 1954. In November 1965, after establishment of a stable flock, the first, modern-day season in Michigan was held.

From late March to early May, the foot trails are popular with anglers who hike up Swan Creek to cast for spawning steelhead entering from the Kalamazoo River and for brown trout, which are stocked in the creek. South of the 118th Avenue dam is Swan Creek Pond, which holds good populations of warm-water species such as bass, bluegill, crappies, and northern pike.

The dam actually divides the Swan Creek Trail into two loops. To the north is a 4.5-mile loop along the creek and an impoundment to the Swan Creek Highbanks Unit, returning back down the other side. This stretch attracts steel-headers. For hikers, however, the much more scenic route is to the south, where a 5.2-mile trail skirts Swan Creek Pond to 116th Avenue, then returns on the pond's other side. Although the area is not hilly, both trails follow the base of a river bluff and contain a surprising amount of up-and-down hiking. They also pass a number of marshes and areas of stagnant water, which means the bugs can be thick here from late May through mid-August.

A woods road parallels much of the west side of the southern loop but is rarely noticed. The road, sandy, rutted, and rough, has little traffic and stays along the top of the bluff, while the trail stays close to the pond and creek. There seems to be little mountain bike activity here, nor, in fact, are there many man-made intrusions of any kind, a rare occurrence in this corner of the state. If 5.2 miles is too long, a well-marked foot-bridge crossing Swan Creek can be used to reduce the walk to 4 miles while

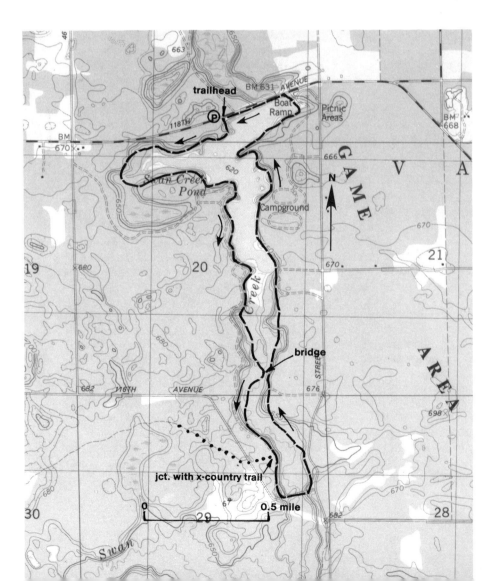

still covering the most interesting sections.

Access: The state game area lies just west of the town of Allegan, which is almost halfway between Grand Rapids and Kalamazoo. It is reached by departing US 131 onto MI 222 (exit 55) and heading west 10 miles. In Allegan, the state road merges with MI 89, which should be followed north to Monroe Road on the edge of town where there is a state game area directional sign.

Travel west on Monroe Road, a scenic drive that curves around Lake Allegan, for 7 miles. You then merge into 118th Avenue and reach the dam. On the east (near) side of the dam is a parking area and trail sign for the northern loop. Just up the hill on the west side of the dam is a parking area and trailhead for the southern loop, where you park for this trail. In another .25 mile is the state game area headquarters (616-673-2430), where additional information can be obtained.

Trail: From the parking area and trailhead on the south side of 118th Avenue, the trail quickly descends the bluff and reaches the edge of Swan Creek Pond. The main loop heads west (right) here, skirting the edge of the large impoundment. For the first .3 mile, you follow the shoreline of a long inlet on the pond's west side that is carpeted in lily pads. The flowers among the pads are impressive in midsummer, and on a still evening it's possible to see panfish and bass pick insects off the water's surface like trout. I was once here in mid-May and watched bluegill leap three or four inches completely out of the pond in an effort to feast on hatching mayflies.

The trail passes within sight of the guardrails along 118th Avenue, then swings away from the water and into the woods to skirt the marsh that surrounds the inlet at its west end. Within .6 mile of the trailhead, you cross a footbridge over a small creek, pass a few wood duck boxes (keep an eye out for the ducks themselves), and return to the water on the opposite side of the inlet. For the next .5 mile, the trail skirts the edge of the main portion of the pond for a very scenic stretch. Somewhere above you is the woods road, but it's rare to hear traffic on it and impossible, from this angle, to see any.

The trail climbs along the edge of the pond for a moderately hard walk, then at 1.4 miles from the trailhead arrives at a small knob. Here it's possible to view the pond to the north, and to the south to see Swan Creek slowly winding its way through a meadow of cattails. Right in front of you is where the creek empties into the impoundment, making this a pleasant spot for a break. The trail continues south from the knob, an even more invigorating walk than before as it weaves along the bluff. This segment might be confusing at times, for, although there are a few blue blazes on the trees, they are few and far between and very faded. But for the most part, the path stays close to the water.

Two miles from the start, the path becomes a very well-defined trail that swings sharply into the woods to a junction marked by DNR pathway triangles. Head east (left) here to reach the bridge and return trail that slices off 1.2 miles of the walk. For the full 5.2-mile hike, however, head right up the bluff and climb to the woods road, which the trail follows for the next .6 mile. The road is a four-wheel track that follows the edge of the bluff, providing views into the river valley below during early spring and fall. Occasionally you'll see a DNR pathway triangle in a tree, and within .4 mile, you come to a marked post that indicates the junction with the Cross Country Foot Trail. That path heads

Angler along Swan Creek

west three miles to Ely Lake Campground. Swan Creek Foot Trail, however, continues south to emerge shortly at 116th Avenue, a well-graded gravel road.

Cross the creek on the road, and on the east side look for where the trail leaves the road. The exit is marked by a "Hunting and Fishing Access Trail" sign. The return walk begins by paralleling 44th Street briefly and then climbing the bluff for a glimpse of the river below. You pass a turn-around at the end of a woods road, then descend sharply towards the creek. An old trail sign announces that the dam is 2 miles away; it might be an old sign, but it's right on the money.

The trail bottoms out in the valley at the bridge. DNR pathway triangles urge you to cross the bridge, but stay on the same shore and follow the trail that veers to the right. The trail begins climbing and doesn't quit until you reach the top of the bluff a mile from 116th Avenue. You then descend sharply to where

the creek flows into the pond, almost directly opposite the scenic knob enjoyed earlier. The trail skirts the pond for the next mile. Obviously, anglers like to cast their worms, bobbers, or small lures from the opening along the shoreline.

At one point, you are traveling below Pine Point Campground, but you can only tell by the beaten paths coming down the bluff or by the aroma of eggs and bacon drifting down in the morning. The campground features thirty-three sites and is reached from 44th Street just south of 118th Avenue. There is a nightly fee. The trail continues to stay close to the water for views of the pond and whatever waterfowl or wildlife the water attracts. Within 2 miles of 116th Avenue, you round Pine Point itself and, from its north side, can view the dam and 118th Avenue above it. The final leg of the loop consists of walking through the beach of the day-use area and past the boat launch, then climbing up to the paved road. Your car is now .4 mile west (left) on 118th Avenue.

Grand River Trail

Place: Grand River Park and Riverbend Natural Area
Total Distance: 3.7 miles
Hiking Time: 2 hours
Rating: Moderate
Highpoints: Riverbend views
Maps: USGS Aurelius; Grand River Park and Riverbend
  Natural Area Trail Guide

This hike is best done in the fall when the hardwood trees that border the Grand River take on their orange and red hues, the old farm fields become waves of golden grass, and the deer blend in so well with the forest that they're spotted only when they flag their tails. This stroll takes you through Michigan farm country as well as along the state's longest river. You pass crumbling stone fences, old fields, and the classic red barn of a bordering farm. A slow-moving Grand River, woods of towering oaks and maples, farm fields and barns — what else would you expect in the heartland of Michigan?

This trail is one of the most scenic of the handful of paths developed along the banks of the Grand River, a waterway that has played a prominent role in Michigan's history. The first inhabitants located along the river are thought to have been mound-building Hopewell Indians, here between 150 B.C. to A.D. 300, who were responsible for more than forty-six mounds along the Grand in what is now the heart of Grand Rapids. Ottawa tribes also had major vil-lages on the river's banks, from Portland all the way to Grand Haven, and by the early 1800s, fur traders were setting up outposts on the Grand. Indians called the waterway "Owashtenong." They eventually were forced to cede and sell most of the land after signing treaties in 1836 and 1841, and the first white set-tlers referred to the waterway as "La Grande Riviere."

This 3.7-mile trail loop extends along the river through two connecting parks, Grand River Park and Riverbend Natural Area, administered by the Ingham County Parks Department. Together, the two units make up a preserve of 540 acres that includes a five-mile network of trails and a variety of terrain — high river bluffs, low-lying floodplains, mature for-ests, and fields in various stages of suc-cession. Wildlife is not abundant, for you are only a few miles south of Lansing, but deer have been spotted in increas-ing numbers in recent years along with a variety of birds.

The loop is marked in blue dots and triangles and served by two trailheads, with the main one in Grand River Park.

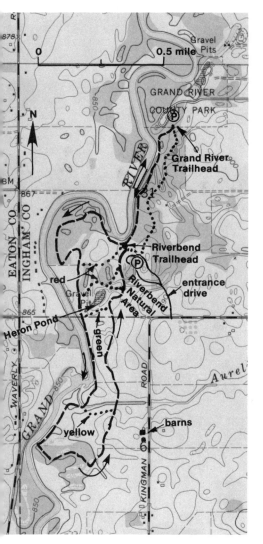

October when fall colors are at their peak.

Access: The two adjoining parks are just south of Lansing and can be reached by departing I-96 onto south MI 99 (exit 101). Quickly turn due south (left) on Waverly Road, then east (left) onto Holt Road for 1 mile. At the corner of Grovenburg Road, the park is posted. Here you head south (right) for 2 miles to the entrance of Grand River Park, or 3 miles to Riverbend Natural Area at the west (right) end of Nichols Road.

The parks are open from 8 A.M. to dusk year-round, and there is a small vehicle permit fee to enter Grand River. For more information, contact Ingham County Parks Department, 301 Bush Street, Mason, MI 48854; or call (517) 676-2233.

Trail: The trailhead in Grand River Park is posted by a large map sign and located near an intriguing toboggan run. From here, two trails depart into the woods and parallel the river to the natural area. They are so close to each other that from one, you can see the people on the other. They were built primarily to keep skiers from running into each other, something hikers rarely worry about. With that in mind, the best path is the one that lies closest to the Grand River, where you wind through the older hardwood forest and view the waterway from its high bluffs. Spurs depart to the edge of the bluff, and eventually the trail passes an old nature center, presently boarded up. It arrives at the Riverbend trailhead in .5 mile.

This trailhead features a second map display, along with a split rail fence along the bluff and benches on which to sit and enjoy this scenic bend in the river. There is also a canoe launch and an observation platform that put you closer to the water. The Grand River is Michigan's longest river at 260 miles,

That park is developed with picnic shelters, tables, canoe rental in the summer, and ski rental in the winter. The other trailhead is in Riverbend Natural Area, but don't start there just to save the vehicle entry fee that is charged at the other park. The stretch along the water in Grand River Park is the most scenic of the loop, especially from mid- to late

The farm seen along Grand River Trail

with the second largest watershed (the first being the Saginaw River system). The waterway begins in Hillsdale County, empties into Lake Michigan at Grand Haven, and passes through eighteen counties. This far east, the Grand is for the most part a slow, sluggish river (especially during the summer), and a stick thrown upstream takes most of the afternoon to pass you on its way downstream. Or so it seems.

From the display sign, the trail along the river quickly descends off the bluff, passes the observation platform, and enters the wooded floodplains by way of a long boardwalk. You continue to skirt the river for a short way, then swing into the middle of this low-lying area where the understory is an amazing growth of horsetails, whose numbers in July are exceeded only by the swarms of mosquitoes attracted to you. Within 1.2 miles from the beginning, you depart the woods and enter an open field, soon to pass the posted junctions of three spurs. At this point, the trail becomes a mowed strip that lies between an old farm field and the wooded banks of the river.

You're close to the water, but you can't get a clear view of it without bashing through the brush. Be patient; within .6 mile, just past the posted junction with the Yellow cutoff, the main loop returns to the wooded floodplains and the edge of the Grand River. You follow the banks briefly, then come to a bridge blocked off by a "Trail Closed" gate. The last section of the loop is usually under water from spring through most of the summer and is only opened to skiers during the winter. Hikers swing east, climb out of the floodplain, and return to the open fields.

You walk through old farm country here. The grass is usually knee high and in shades of mustard, gold, and brown in the fall. Just up the hill is a classic red barn surrounded by a silo and other faded farm buildings. Although the trail along this back stretch is not wild or in the woods, it's very picturesque in its own way and very much heartland Michigan, . . . right down to the electric cow fence the trail briefly skirts. You cut across these old farm fields for .7 mile, until you reach the posted junction with the Green cutoff. Just beyond the junction, before you reach Heron Pond, the blue posts marking the main loop swing to the east. Most people continue marching straight here for a close look at the small body of water. There's a dock at this end, and from it you can stare into the crystal clear water and see small panfish dart among the aquatic weeds. There must be some larger fish as well, because enough anglers have hiked in for the county to post a sign warning them about bank erosion and trash.

You can backtrack from the pond and relocate the last blue marker, or you can just keep skirting the pond's east end and hook up with the Red Trail. There is also an old road that cuts across here. Regardless what route you follow north, they all climb away from the pond, pass another field, and return to the Riverbend trailhead. The last leg back to the main trailhead actually begins on the side of the parking lot, but that route is not nearly as pleasant as the path you first hiked that departs north from the benches.

The Ledges Trail

Place: Fitzgerald County Park and Island Park
Total Distance: 1.1 miles one-way
Hiking Time: 30 to 40 minutes
Rating: Easy
Highpoints: Sedimentary cliffs, rock climbers
Maps: USGS Eagle and Wacousta; Fitzgerald Park Trail Guide

Rock climbers know that the only natural place to practice their sport in Michigan (as opposed to climbing buildings) is in a town appropriately named Grand Ledge. Located just west of Lansing in Eaton County, the community is named after "The Ledges" that border the Grand River. The towering faces of sheer rock are ancient sedimentary outcroppings that have become popular with not only climbers but hikers as well.

The Ledges border both sides of the river west of town, but rock climbers gather at Oak Park at the end of West Front Street on the north side to inch their way up and rappel down one particularly steep face. Hikers head to the south side where the Ledges Trail skirts the base of the cliffs, linking Fitzgerald County Park with Island Park. Except for the initial descent to the river, this point-to-point path is a level and easy stroll that provides both a close view of this unique geological formation and a good vantage point from which to watch those daredevil climbers across the river.

This hike is short, even if you backtrack to the starting point, but is surely one of the most unusual walks in south-ern Michigan. The Ledges have attracted people to the area throughout history, beginning with Chief Okemos, a legendary Indian who led his tribe to the river of the "Big Rocks" each spring to hunt and tap trees for maple syrup. Later the area was known as Robbers Caves, since the many caves at the base of the ledges were supposedly used by thieves to stable stolen horses while they awaited sale. Other legends tell of fugitive slaves using the caves as part of the Underground Railway in their flight to freedom in Canada.

By 1894 the beauty of the Ledges had attracted a religious group who established the Grand Ledge Spiritualist Camp Association. Within Fitzgerald Park, they constructed a large pavilion and organized a camp that brought thousands here at the turn of the century for "summer encampments." The pavilion that the spiritualists originally used for séances was later used for a factory, roller-skating rink, and basketball court, successively. Today, it's the big red barn in the park and serves as the home of the Spotlight Theater.

Access: You can hike the trail from

either end, but the best place to start and end is Fitzgerald Park, an Eaton County park located 1.5 miles west of Grand Ledge at 3808 Grand Ledge Highway. From Lansing, head west on MI 43 and, 4 miles past I-96, it becomes Grand Ledges Highway. Or depart I-96 at exit 93. The 78-acre unit borders the Grand River and features six picnic sites, nature trails, a fish ladder, and a small nature center that is open May through October, 1-5 P.M. on Wednesday, Saturday, and Sunday. On the other side of the park, just east of the barn theater, is the start of the Ledges Trail, marked by a box with interpretive brochures.

The other trailhead is located in Island Park, whose entrance is just a block southwest of where Bridge Street crosses the Grand River in downtown Grand Ledge. There is no fee to enter or use the facilities in Island Park, whereas Fitzgerald has a vehicle entry fee.

Trail: The western half of the trail lies in Fitzgerald Park and has eleven numbered posts that correspond with the interpretive brochure. From the historic barn, you quickly descend a stairway to the edge of the Grand River and cross a bridge over Sandstone Creek. On the other side is interpretive post 5 and the first set of ledges. The impressive rock cliffs were created when most of Michigan was covered by an ocean 270 million years ago and sediments (sand, silt, and clay) were carried by water and deposited in layers. Time and pressure compacted the layers into sandstone before the Grand River sculptured the cliffs through years of erosion.

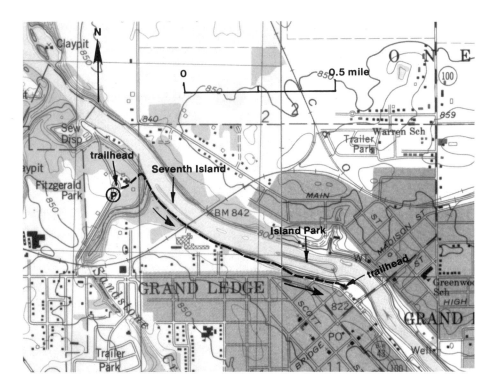

Overlooking Grand River from the top of the ledges

In the middle of the Grand River is The Seventh Island, the final island used by The Seven Islands Resort. In the early 1900s, the resort attracted thousands of tourists who came to Grand Ledge for steamboat rides and mineral baths. Island Park was the second island within the resort. Most people arrived by the Detroit-Grand Rapids and Western Railroad, which in 1888 built the railroad trestle that the trail passes underneath .5 mile from the start.

The trestle marks the boundary of Fitzgerald Park. From here, the trail crosses private property, and a couple of houses will pop into view high above you. But most of the time the level trail is a secluded walk among hemlocks, with the Grand River lapping on one side and the stone cliffs hovering above you on the other side. After passing the trestle, you'll arrive at a clearing in the trees where you can see the steepest ledges across the river. These tower 70 feet above the north bank. Bring a pair of binoculars, and you can sit and watch climbers slowly inch their way up the rock face.

The trail ends at Island Park, where an old iron bridge crosses the river to the narrow island. This interesting park features benches, picnic tables, and small docks along the shoreline as well as a flock of resident ducks eager for a handout of bread or crackers.

Wildwood Pathway

Place: Deerfield County Park
Total Distance: 3 miles
Hiking Time: 2 hours
Rating: Easy
Highpoints: Covered bridge, backcountry camping
Maps: USGS Winn; Deerfield County Park brochure

Deerfield County Park is a little-known gem for hikers, hidden in the heart of Michigan. Established in 1973 by Isabella County Parks and Recreation, the park is a collage of land owned by the county, Deerfield Township, the Mt. Pleasant School District, and the local Boy Scouts. Together the parcels create a 640-acre tract forested in hardwoods, populated by deer, and split in the middle by three miles of the Chippewa River. This far upstream, the Chippewa is a small but scenic river that gently flows and swirls over a gravel bottom.

Near its north entrance, Deerfield features the usual park amenities: swimming area and beach, shelters, tables, grills, and a short interpretive path. But by crossing the Chippewa on a swingbridge, you can leave behind the picnic area and enter a quiet woodland. Travel is by foot or skis in the winter along a 7.5-mile network of trails that pass some surprising sights, such as a wooden covered bridge, an old water wheel, scenic vistas above the river, and even a pleasant set of backcountry campsites along the banks of the Chippewa.

This area is also a haven for wildlife, especially whitetail deer, which are often sighted in early spring or mid-September. You might also encounter wild turkeys in the park, along with a number of other species including ruffed grouse and cottontail rabbits. The Chippewa supports a good fishery, and anglers do well tossing spinners around for smallmouth bass and northern pikes or bouncing leadhead jigs through the pools of the river for walleye.

The main loop within the park is the Wildwood Pathway, a 2.6-mile route that is a designated National Recreational Trail within the National Trails system. What is described here is the most scenic walk the park offers and begins with River Loop, which borders the Chippewa, before merging into the eastern half of the pathway. This outing is a 3-mile hike that can be turned into an overnight adventure by carrying in equipment to the walk-in campsites.

Access: Deerfield is west of Mt. Pleasant or about an hour's drive from Lansing on US 27. There are two entrances to the park, with this trailhead on the main one off of MI 20 (Remus

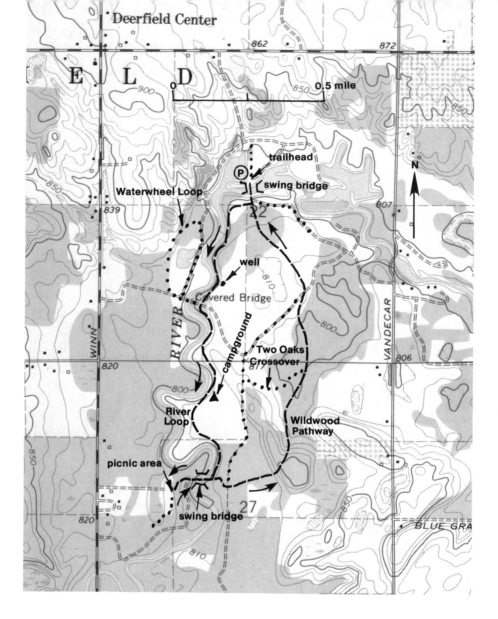

Road). Exit onto Business US 27 through Mt. Pleasant, then head west on Remus Road. The park entrance is posted 6.5 miles west of the university town on MI 20. The trail network can also be reached from the west entrance, which is reached from MI 20 by heading south 1.6 miles on Winn Road.

There is a vehicle entry fee to visit the park as well as a nightly fee to camp at the walk-in campsites. More information can be obtained by calling Deerfield County Park at (517) 772-2879.

Trail: The trailhead is posted at the parking area near the river, where a wide, wood chip path heads south to arrive shortly at the impressive swingbridge over the Chippewa River.

From the middle of the bridge there is a nice view of the river. Just across the bridge, River Loop is posted, departing from Wildwood Pathway to the west (right). Turn onto River Loop, following a low bluff above the river. In late fall, when the leaves have fallen, the trail provides a view of the river's gentle current almost every step of the way. Within .7 mile of the trailhead you come to an artesian well where the cold, clear water spills down the bank. Fill up the canteen; this water is safe to drink. There is also a bench nearby with a pleasant view of the covered bridge over the Chippewa.

It's a quick walk along the bluff to the bridge itself. This is not a turn-of-the-century structure; rather, it was built in 1973 by a businessman who purchased a railroad trestle from the Coleman to Mt. Pleasant line so he could construct his own covered bridge. The crossing is the only covered bridge in Michigan that has to be reached on foot and is listed with the International Covered Bridge Society. "We're known worldwide," park officials will tell you.

On the other side of the bridge is a picnic table, a grill, and a spur known as the Water Wheel Loop that, if you decide to walk it, will add a mile to your hike. A portion of this side trail is not well marked (though that might change in the future), but it's easy to follow as it travels along the west bank of the river. You soon pass what appears to be a dried-up pond. This is a walleye rearing pond used by the state's Department of Natural Resources. Biologists fill the basin each spring and for two months raise walleye fry into fingerlings before

Wooden covered bridge on the Wildwood Pathway

releasing them in a number of places, including the Chippewa. The small water wheel is just beyond the pond on the bank of the river.

Cross back over the covered bridge, turn right, and continue down River Loop. The trail stays along the top of the bluff and quickly comes to the best view of the day. From this point, you overlook a bend in the Chippewa in one direction and the bridge in the other. With a bench located here, its hard not to take a break, even though you're less than a mile from the trailhead. The path continues along the bluff, eventually descends to the water, and at 1.1 miles arrives at the campground. There are ten sites here; not all of them are numbered, but most provide a great view of the river and its forested banks from the door of your tent. Facilities include fire rings, vault toilets, and a hand pump for water. Since the campground can only be reached on foot or by canoe, it's rarely filled.

The River Loop continues along the bluff beyond the campground, passes another viewing point, and then swings inland where, in 1.5 miles from the trailhead, it comes to a posted junction to the second swingbridge. The short spur to the bridge leads to a scenic picnic area (tables, grills, and vault toilets) on the west banks of the Chippewa in the Memorial Forest Recreation Area. Just beyond the spur junction, the River Loop merges with the south end of the Wildwood Pathway.

You can return on either segment of the Wildwood loop, but the western (left) half seems to be an old vehicle track while to the east the pathway is a true footpath that winds over a more interesting terrain. The latter route begins in hardwoods, moves into a pine plantation, then passes through the grayish white trunks of a young beech forest. Unlike the River Loop, this leg of the Wildwood Pathway climbs over a series of rolling hills for a very pleasant but certainly not strenuous walk. The rolling terrain ends in .6 mile when you pass the posted junction of the Two Oaks Cross Over. In the last stretch to the first swingbridge, the trail becomes a level walk through the forest. Right before reaching the bridge, you pass the posted junction of Scenic Walk, a short, one-way spur that overlooks an oxbow in the Chippewa River.

North Country Trail—Baldwin Segment

Place: Manistee National Forest
Total Distance: 11 miles
Hiking Time: 6 to 7 hours
Rating: Challenging
Highpoints: Numerous small lakes, backcountry camping
Maps: USGS Big Star Lake and Walkup Lake; North Country
  Trail Baldwin Segment map from the U.S. Forest Service

When completed, the North Country Trail will be America's longest foot trail, spanning 3,246 miles from Crown Point in upper New York to Lake Sakakawea on the Missouri River in North Dakota. It will pass through seven states and treat the walker to a diversity of landscapes—from the grandeur of the Adirondack Mountains and the Finger Lakes of New York to the simple beauty of rural Ohio and the vast plains of North Dakota. But clearly the crowning jewel of this national trail is Michigan.

The Great Lakes State will contain more of the North Country Trail, 872 miles, than any other state. The segments in the Ottawa National Forest in the western half of the Upper Peninsula are the wildest, most remote stretches of the entire route, while such natural treasures as Tahquamenon Falls, the Lake Superior shoreline, and Pictured Rocks provide some the most dramatic scenery. Eventually the trail reaches the Mackinac Bridge, crosses the Straits of Mackinac to the Lower Peninsula, and heads south for Ohio. A portion of this stretch, which totals more than one hun-

dred miles, will pass through the Manistee National Forest. The first section to be built and dedicated was the eleven-mile Baldwin Segment, officially opened in November 1986. Since then more than seventy miles have been designated, but trail planners chose this stretch first because of its superb setting. Passing from Lake County into Newaygo County, this portion of the North Country Trail begins in hardwood forests, skirts around Sterling Marsh, and ends by traversing rolling hills for excellent views of several small and undeveloped lakes.

If the entire 11-mile hike is too much, the southern half of the hike, beginning at 16 Mile Road east of Walkers Corners, is by far the most scenic stretch and makes for a pleasant 5-mile hike to Walkup Lake. If transportation on a point-to-point trail is a problem, plan to begin at the southern trailhead off Cleveland Road and hike to Condon Lake and back for a round-trip of 6 miles.

Condon and other lakes in the southern half also provide a picturesque setting for those interested in backcountry camping. Camping is permitted anywhere along the trail, but hikers should plan on setting up camp at least three hundred feet from the path. Pack in water and pack out trash. You might also want to carry in a fishing rod, for Condon, Leaf, and Highbank lakes offer some good angling possibilities.

Best of all, the North Country Trail is designated exclusively for hiking, with all vehicular traffic prohibited. Although the number of walkers increases annually, usage of the Baldwin Segment is still relatively light, even on the nicest summer weekends. In mid-week, you can have the trail and the surrounding woods practically to yourself.

Access: The Baldwin Segment's northern trailhead, where this description starts, is located in the southern half of Lake County, a ninety-minute drive from Grand Rapids. At Baldwin, head south on MI 37 for 3 miles, then west on Big Star Lake Road. In 2.5 miles, the North Country Trail crosses the road at a posted junction right before Jenks Road. To leave a car or to hike the alternate round trip from the south end of the trail, from Baldwin head 8.5 miles south on MI 37 to the village of Lilly, then follow Bingham Road west and south to the village of Bitely. In Bitely, head west for 3 miles on Cleveland Road to the posted trailhead on the south (left) side of the road at Nichols Lake access site.

Maps and information on the trail can be obtained in Baldwin at the Manistee National Forest Ranger office (616-745-4631), located right off MI 37 at the south end of town. The office is open Monday through Friday, 8 A.M. to 5 P.M., and has an information display outside. For more information on other parts of the national trail, write to North Country Trail Association, P.O. Box 311, White Cloud, MI 49349.

Trail: From its start on Big Star Lake Road, the North Country Trail departs south in a mix of hardwoods and pine, traveling above Jenks Creek, until it breaks out on Jenks Road. It follows the dirt road briefly to cross the small stream before returning to the woods to the right. Within a mile, the trail arrives at Sterling Marsh. Depending on the rainfall, the marsh is mostly a sea of cattails and grasses, with an occasional patch of open water that attracts a variety of waterfowl and, given the prints in the sandy soil, deer.

The trail skirts the scenic marsh (picturesque if there aren't mosquitoes buzzing around your head) for the next .6 mile and ends up on its west side. White and blue diamonds and an occasional ribbon mark the path, which in the fall is often covered by leaves and needles. You leave the swamp, pass through an impressive stand of hardwoods, and, 2 miles from the start, come to the edge of private land. The enjoyable hike now becomes an eyesore for the next .4 mile, for the owner has hung "No Trespassing" signs, ribbons, and wire all along his wooded property. It's a sad sign for society when one of the greatest boreal forests in the country can be sold, posted, and treated like your neighbor's backyard.

At 2.3 miles, the trail emerges at a dirt track, crosses it, then parallels it for a short way before heading southwest into a stand of red pine. The perfect rows tip you off that this is a pine plantation, looking about as natural here as the golden arches of a McDonald's would. Take heart, within .2 mile you enter an old hardwood forest where giant oaks and maples spread their canopies. The trail eventually swings due south, crosses another vehicle track, and

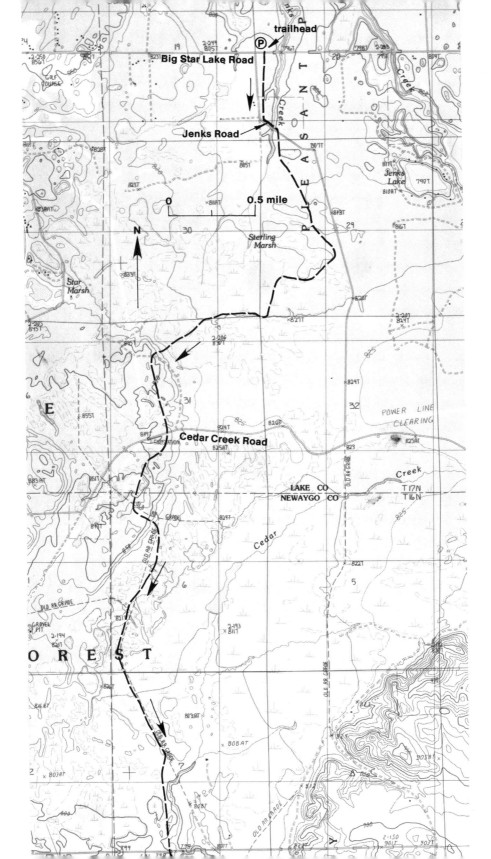

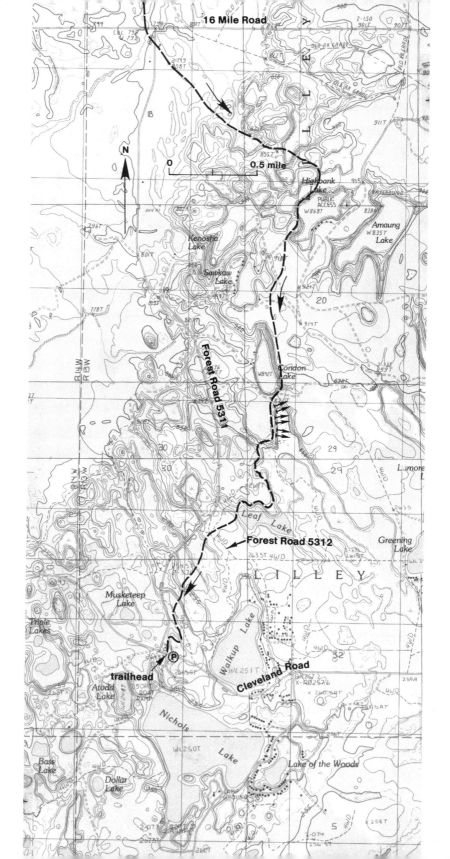

makes its first climb of the day—forty feet to some impressive hardwoods on the ridge top.

From here, it's a quick walk to Cedar Creek Road, a wide, well-graded dirt road reached 3.4 miles from the northern trailhead. For those planning to start hiking from here, note that the trail can be hard to spot from the road. The only sign is on the north side of the road, twenty feet back and partially hidden among the trees. The next stretch, from Cedar Creek Road to 16 Mile Road, can be the most confusing to follow. The trail soon crosses an electric line corridor, cuts through a stump field and passes a swamp. Keep an eye out for the white diamonds, for the trail passes through a low-lying area and is hard to see at times. If all goes well, you should reach a vehicle track (really an old railroad grade), cross it, then come to it a second time .8 mile from Cedar Creek Road. You return to the hardwoods for a pleasant stroll until encountering the railroad grade a third time, where a "Hiker Trail" sign has been posted 1.2 miles from Cedar Creek Road. This spot is confusing due to the other logging roads in the area, but again, the white diamonds will lead you down the grade, which is straight as an arrow.

The old railroad line is an interesting stretch since it runs through a low-lying area of cedar and spruce and even passes a cattail marsh at one point. Your boots remain dry for the most part, though it can be buggy in the summer to say the least. At 1.7 miles from Cedar Creek Road, you enter a wide, grassy meadow, with the trail a tree-lined avenue through its middle. Watch for the white diamonds since the trail shortly swings away from the railroad grade, emerging at 16 Mile Road .5 mile later and never crossing Cedar Creek. If you follow the grade instead, you end up crossing the creek on a log and emerging at a rustic log cabin before reaching the road. If you find yourself there, head west (right) .2 mile on 16 Mile Road, where you'll find "Hiker's Trail" signs on both roadsides.

The hike from the northern trailhead to here is 6 miles, but the best portion is yet to come; therefore, 16 Mile Road is an ideal place to begin if you need to shorten the hike. From here, a logging road leads to a footbridge over Cedar Creek, arriving at Forest Road 5311 in .2 mile. On the other side of the road, the trail cuts through a dark stand of pine, passes into well-spread hardwoods, and, .8 mile from 16 Mile Road, begins a steady climb along the side of a ridge. You top off, climb again, and break out at a rough dirt road.

On the other side of the road, the trail quickly descends to the first lake of the day, a small, unnamed, round lake hemmed in by hardwoods. It's a pretty sight as you stand above it and perhaps ponder that ultimate question—I wonder if there're big bass in there? From here, the trail soon crosses the crest of a ridge to a bluff above Highbank Lake, where a few cottages and the U.S. Forest campground can be seen below. The trail levels out somewhat, crosses a road 1.7 miles from 16 Mile Road, and then curves around a small pond connected to Sawkaw Lake, though it's hard to spot either body of water through the trees.

It's easy to spot Condon Lake, however, which is reached 2.1 miles from 16 Mile Road or 8.2 miles from the northern trailhead. The trail skirts the east side of the lake on a high bank, which allows you to look down through the trees to the water below. This spot and the unnamed pond before Highbank Lake are the best places to pitch your tent on this hike. The bluff above

Small pond seen from the North Country Trail—Baldwin Segment

Condon is level and as isolated as anywhere along the trail. The trail arrives at a vehicle track to the lake and skirts its south end, though you never view the water from here.

Eventually the trail climbs to the edge of a bluff that borders an open meadow and marshy area. This is intriguing hiking. You remain hidden in the foliage yet are able to look down and spot any wildlife attracted to the area, especially the deer that often cut through here at dusk. The trail descends to cross a vehicle track, then returns to its ridge to skirt the lower half of the marshy area, which features more open water and waterfowl.

The trail swings west and quickly emerges above Leaf Lake, reached 3.5 miles from 16 Mile Road. You skirt the lake for more than .5 mile and end up descending to its west end for another scenic stretch of trail. From here, you are rewarded with a clear view of the length of the lake, a good spot for an extended break or lunch. You climb away from the lake and quickly cross Forest Road 5312, which is posted.

The last leg of this trail drops into an interesting meadow and crosses the middle of it. Ringed by hardwoods, this spot can be stunning in the fall, with the golden grass flowing in the wind and framed by the brilliant autumn colors. You climb out of the meadow, merge with an old logging road, and, .5 mile from the end, catch your only glimpse of Walkup Lake. From here, you cross another vehicle track before skirting a meadow and emerging at the pavement of Cleveland Road. Across the road is the posted access site for Nichols Lake.

Lake Michigan

24

Great Warren Dune

Place: Warren Dunes State Park
Total Distance: 4 miles
Hiking Time: 2 to 3 hours
Rating: Moderate
Highpoints: Sand dunes, beach walking
Maps: USGS Bridgman; Warren Dunes State Park map

Some people come to Warren Dunes State Park to hang glide; others arrive to study the plant succession; and most come to lie on the beach or play in the Lake Michigan surf. Ultimately, though, there's one main attraction drawing people to this corner of the state—sand. The two miles of Lake Michigan beach and the wind-blown dunes that tower 230 feet above the water attract a variety of visitors, from thrill seekers and sunbathers to university botany classes and even hikers.

This 1,507-acre park offers to hikers a four-mile loop that includes a bit of everything: a stroll along Lake Michigan, stretches through forests, knee-bending climbs up mountains of sand. You'll even get a good look at how life gets started. It's possible during this hike to stand on a small ridge of sand looking at nothing but bare beach and water to the west, at the first clumps of well-scattered grasses at your feet, at the next stages of succession to the east—shrubs emerging from grasses, poplars and other short-lived trees replacing shrubs—and finally the well-shaded canopy of an oak and hickory forest covering the ridge of a dune. Life, from sand to trees, in one sweeping view.

Others are intrigued by the geology of the area and come to identify the different types of dunes: parallel dunes, blowouts, and parabolic dunes (parallel dunes that have been carved by a series of wind-blown indentations). To help visitors understand the unique natural aspects of the area, the park staff erected interpretive posts along much of the trail in 1990. The numbered posts correspond with a brochure available at the park office.

Even if you have little interest in ecology or geology, Warren Dunes is simply a pleasant place to take a hike . . . most of the year. Because of its location close to several major urban areas, including Chicago, Warren Dunes traditionally receives the second highest number of visitors of any state park. Almost 1.5 million people pass through its entrance gate each year, with the vast majority being out-of-staters arriving from June to September. If you hike to sneak away from crowds and other signs of humanity, Warren Dunes is not the place to go on the Fourth of July.

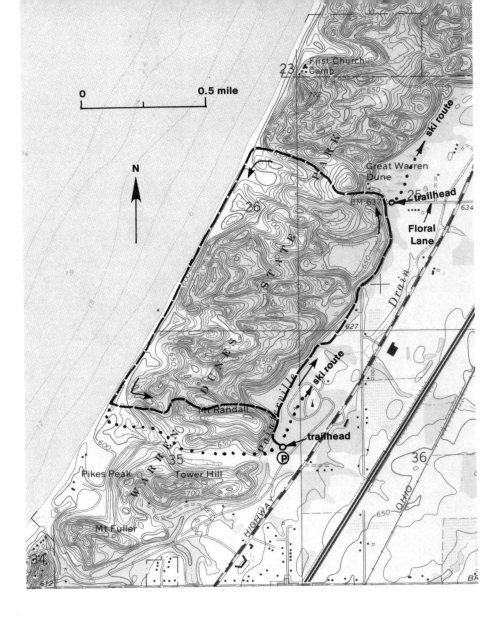

The best time to venture into the park is when the wildflowers bloom in April, or in mid- to late October when the leaves of the hardwood forests are touched with brilliant hues of oranges and reds. Arrive in mid-week during these off-season months and the crowds will be gone, the campground prac-tically empty, and often you'll be the only one on a stretch of beach.

If you are planning to arrive during the summer, the best days are Mondays and Tuesdays, the lull between the weekend crowds. By Wednesday the campground is filling up again, and Sat-urday there often are so many people at

Warren Dunes that parking is impossible. If this is the case, avoid the main entrance and begin the loop off Floral Lane. Better yet, head north and explore Grand Mere State Park, saving this hike for another day.

Boots are not necessary for the trail; it can easily be done in tennis shoes. Keep in mind that a portion of the route over open sand is not marked and that there are quite a few dunes to climb during the outing. Children under the age of six and others with weak knees might require more time than what is listed above.

Access: The state park is just off I-94, 15 miles north of the Michigan/Indiana border. From the interstate, depart at exit 16 and head south on Red Arrow Highway. In a little more than .5 mile, you pass Floral Lane, at the end of which is a parking area and a posted trailhead that you can start at if the park is crowded. The main entrance is 1.5 miles further south on Red Arrow Highway. The south end of the park contains a 197-site campground and a day-use area, featuring picnic grounds and three bathhouses along Lake Michigan. From the contact station, head north (right) along the park drive, passing the headquarters (stop here to pick up a map) and arriving at a small parking area and main trailhead just before entering the campground. Within the parking area are vault toilets, picnic tables, and a water pump.

Those who plan to camp at Warren Dunes during the summer would do well to make reservations in advance. Write to Warren Dunes State Park, Red Arrow Highway, Sawyer, MI 49125; or call (616) 426-4016.

Trail: Two trails depart north from near the trail sign. One heads into the campground as part of the park's ski run. The other trail starts on the west side of Painterville Creek and is marked by a blue DNR pathway triangle. The latter immediately heads into the forest and parallels the base of Mt. Randall. This migrating dune rises 220 feet above the lake and is literally pouring sand down between the trees, determined to bury the trail someday.

Within .2 mile, you arrive at a junction with a trail that heads west (left) and skirts Mt. Randall to end up at the northern edge of the day-use area. Continue north. Nearby, a footbridge crosses the creek to the campground, while the main trail passes through a low-lying area. This area once held a pond, which was drained off by farmers in the early 1900s. Even though the interdunal ponds are gone, in the spring this stretch can still be wet and muddy.

More reminders of unsuccessful farming efforts are met just to the north when the trail passes a small, grassy meadow. The farmer's failure has turned out to be the hiker's gain seventy years later though. Unable to grow a crop in the sandy soil, farm families let their eighty-acre plots revert to the state rather than pay a twenty-five dollar tax on land. That allowed Edward Warren, a merchant and conservationist from Three Oaks, to purchase the duneland for next to nothing, preserving it from future development.

Painterville Creek swings out of sight, along with the campers on its east side. In .8 mile from the trailhead, you come to an old farmhouse foundation and what appears to be the end of a road. The park's organization camp is nearby. The trail continues along the former road, pavement popping up now and then. After traveling along the old road for .5 mile, you arrive at the end of Floral Lane where a ski map has been posted.

The trail tops off at a spot many be-

Hiker along the trail

lieve to be Mt. Randall (although it isn't), comes within view of the back side of a blowout that was crossed earlier, and .6 mile from the parking lot, arrives at a bootprint marker. The sign directs you down a log staircase, then more boots keep you descending a steep trench between Mt. Randall and the next dune. Just when you think the trail is going to head into a low-lying wet area, it skirts Mt. Randall and breaks out near the footbridge to the park's campground. Backtrack south (right) along the trail to return to the parking area and trailhead.

If open sand is more to your liking, take the other route from the day-use area back to the trailhead. Head due east from the back of the third parking area. There is no trail, but taking a straight course will take you over two dunes and past a pair of bowls that the

wind has carved out of sand. Eventually the grass returns, and a path emerges to lead you back to the trailhead and parking area.

Along this latter route, you pass beneath Tower Hill to the south, the tallest dune in the park at 230 feet above the lake. The dune is famous as one of the best spots for hang gliding in the Midwest. What makes this dune so attractive for gliders, especially those just learning the sport, are the smooth winds that come off the lake and the soft and forgiving sand. At one point in the mid-1970s, the heyday of the sport, there could be almost one hundred hang gliders on the dune on a windy weekend and twenty more in the air. Accidents were so numerous that the park had to clamp down on unqualified flyers and institute a permit system. It's still possible to see the colorful gliders, although the best time to catch them is on weekends from late September through October when there might be two or three soaring into the wind.

The ski route is a well-marked trail that heads north. To continue the loop and venture onto Great Warren Dune, head west (left) along an obvious trail with log barriers at its entrance. The hike to Lake Michigan begins in the woods but quickly climbs to the edge of a two hundred-foot, open dune. A path leads to the top, but the trail actually skirts it along its south side. For the first time on the hike, you leave the forest and view the park's interior, a section dedicated by the state as the Great Warren Dune Natural Area. The panorama includes dunes all around you, some forested, others covered with grass, and a few just bare sand. On the horizon is Lake Michigan, and straight ahead is the sandy avenue that makes up the trail.

There are no trail markers out here, and numerous paths depart in every direction where hikers have wandered off to explore the park's backcountry. It's hard to get turned around, however. Just keep heading west, and within .6 mile from Floral Lane, you will reach a low, sandy bluff above the beach. The

first thing most people notice is the wind. What seems like a gentle breeze in the forest can be gale-like by the Great Lake. Don't forget to pack a jacket.

The loop continues by heading south along the beach 1.2 miles until it reaches the edge of the third parking lot and bathhouse in the day-use area. Walking along the beach is pleasant, especially during the off-season, but the more adventurous skirt the edge of the wooded dunes that drop towards the waterline. There are paths along these dunes most of the way, and halfway back to the bathhouse you can cut across two fascinating blowouts that beckon you to climb their sandy slopes for a better view of the area.

From the day-use area, there are two ways to complete the loop. From the northwest corner of the parking lot, a "Foot Trail" sign can be seen on the edge of a wooded dune. This marks a well-developed trail around Mt. Randall and begins with an immediate climb into the hickory-oak forest. In early spring and late fall, you never lose sight of Lake Michigan in the first half mile, and you can usually hear the surf anytime of the year.

Warren Woods

Place: Warren Woods Natural Area
Total Distance: 2 miles
Hiking Time: 1 hour
Rating: Easy
Highpoints: Virgin beech trees, birding
Maps: USGS New Buffalo East and Three Oaks; "Warren
  Woods Natural Area" map from the Department of Natural
  Resources

The story of Edward K. Warren, conservationist and visionary, is almost as intriguing as the stand of primeval beech-maple trees enjoyed today along the two-mile loop through the Warren Woods Natural Area. In the 1870s, Warren was a partner of a general store in Three Oaks, Michigan, barely making a living. When he decided to purchase a two hundred-acre tract of virgin forest around the Galien River, townspeople wondered about his sanity.

He purchased Warren Woods in 1879, only seven years after the country's first park, Yellowstone National Park, was established. The conservationist knew that the woods represented one of the last surviving stands of virgin beech-maple left in the state. Everything else had been logged. He held onto the area, despite financial problems that in 1883 forced him to beg from his neighbors to clothe his family.

But things have a way of coming around. Eventually, Warren developed a process that substituted turkey wing feathers for the increasingly scarce whalebone in women's corsets. He set up the Warren Featherbone Company and made a fortune at the turn of the century. He promptly used much of his profits to buy duneland along Lake Michigan, which bankrupt farmers were letting go to the state for back taxes of less than twenty-five dollars. While others shook their heads at him, Warren deeply believed that someday "these lands would be of great value to thousands of people as a place of recreation."

The vision of this general store merchant was incredible. Today the dunes that were worthless in the early 1900s are part of Michigan's "Gold Coast." The only thing he misjudged was the number of people who would enjoy his dunes. Thousands? More like 1.5 million visitors a year arrive at Warren Dunes State Park from across the country (see Hike 24).

That state park also manages the Warren Woods Natural Area. Located seven miles inland, this wooded tract is a complete contrast to the rest of the

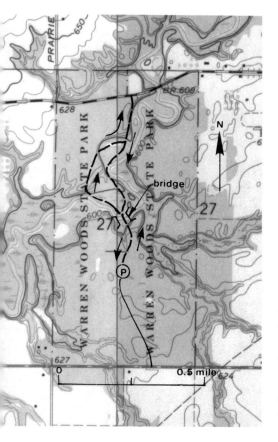

and makes an ideal family outing. But beware, the Galien is a sluggish river, and during the summer mosquitoes can terrorize young hikers. Bring plenty of protection for insects then.

Access: The natural area can be reached from I-94 by departing at Union Pier (exit 6) and heading east on Union Pier Road, which quickly becomes Elm Valley Road, for 2.5 miles to an un-marked entrance that resembles a dirt road. There is also a posted trailhead on Warren Woods Road, 7 miles east of Warren Dunes State Park, but the south-ern entrance is the best place to begin the hike. From Elm Valley Road, it's a .25-mile drive to a parking area with vault toilets, tables, and a large display map.

Continue north along I-94 to exit 16, then head south on Red Arrow Highway to reach Warren Dunes State Park (616-426-4013). The park headquarters or contact station at the entrance can supply a map to the natural area that is more than adequate for this hike. To en-ter either unit, you need either a daily vehicle entry permit or an annual state park pass.

Trail: From the Elm Valley Road park-ing area, the trail begins as a wide, wood chip path just east of the display map. It skirts a wooded ridge, and in .3 mile, you come to a pair of benches that sit on a bluff and overlook the Gal-ien River and a wooden suspension bridge across it. Steps descend to the bridge, and on the other side, the trail splits.

Head west (left), so that the blue DNR pathway triangles face you. The trail fol-lows the bank of the river for a short spell, then ascends a bluff for an over-view of the water. These stretches along the river are where birders look for war-blers and thrushes. During the spring migration, the birds move through the

unit on Lake Michigan; no towering dunes, but also no crowds, overflowing parking lots, and filled-to-capacity camp-grounds. Amazingly, the natural area can be a quiet spot even at the height of the summer season when rangers are turning away visitors at the state park.

The natural area is open daily from 8 A.M. until dusk year-round, but the best time to come is late September through mid-November when the leaves take on their autumn colors. Birders arrive in the spring, however, to look for warblers and other song birds, while skiers enjoy the trails during the winter when there is sufficient snow. The trail is easy to follow

Suspension bridge

woods and often can be seen in the sycamores along the banks. This area is one of the best in Michigan to see a yellow-throated warbler, a small, gray bird with a distinct yellow bib. Other birds regularly spotted in the area are pileated woodpeckers during the summer and redheaded woodpeckers in fall and winter.

At .5 mile from the start, the trail takes a sharp swing north and enters for the first time the rare stand of virgin hardwoods. If the size of the trees doesn't overwhelm you, consider that as far as historians can verify, this portion of Warren Woods has never been deliberately disturbed by man. Warren purchased it in 1879 because it had not been logged, and since then the area has not experienced selective or any other type of cutting. When the huge trees fall, the deadwood is not even removed by state park officials.

At .7 mile, you arrive at the junction with the return trail to the bridge. But don't skip the .25 mile to the trailhead at Warren Woods Road, for here is where the largest trees are seen. It's mind-boggling that at one time all of southern Michigan was covered by a forest like this. Most trees are so large two people can't link their arms around them. Sadly, some people feel compelled to carve their initials into these virgin beech and maples.

The return trail is a level walk that follows a ridge from the junction and in .2 mile comes to a view of the Galien River, which most of the year, especially in the summer, is a slow-moving and muddy waterway. Eventually the trail descends off the low bluff and hugs the riverbank for .3 mile before arriving at the bridge, which is crossed to return to the parking area.

Baldtop

Place: Grand Mere State Park
Total Distance: 2 miles
Hiking Time: 2 hours
Rating: Moderate
Highpoints: Scenic vistas, sand dunes, Lake Michigan beach
Maps: USGS Stevensville and Bridgman

Since Grand Mere State Park was established in 1973, the vast majority of users have either been locals strolling along Lake Michigan or educational groups and college botany classes intrigued by the area's many rare and endangered plants. Hikers in this almost one thousand-acre tract of woods, towering dunes, and wide, sandy shorelines have been few. And it's no wonder. For years the only park signs were on the beach, not near the I-94 exit, while the trails were unmarked and the maps published by the state's Department of Natural Resources misleading.

All this will change in the 1990s as the Department of Natural Resources moves ahead with developing the park. Within the first year of the new decade, the main entrance drive and parking area were paved and a half-mile, hand-icapped accessible trail was built around the South Lake. Eventually a trail network will be posted that most likely will include the 2-mile route described here around the park's tallest dune, often called Baldtop. It's not only a natural loop, it's the most scenic walk in the park.

The unique land formations and flora that attract naturalists to the park are the reasons Grand Mere was designated a National Natural Landmark. The glaciers that scooped out the Great Lakes ten thousand years ago also carved out a number of smaller depressions along the western edge of the state, which evolved into interdunal lakes, ponds, and wetlands. At one time, Grand Mere contained five such lakes that were protected ecologically by a line of wind-blown sand dunes between them and Lake Michigan. Now there remain only three, a result of aquatic succession. Today Grand Mere is a textbook example of the various stages of succession. Beginning at North Lake, you can see how each lake is progressively disappearing, with open water turning into marsh, and, eventually, woodland, the fate of the former two lakes.

Dunes not only protect the lakes and wetlands surrounding them but create a cooler environment for plants that are not found elsewhere in southern Michigan. Hemlock and white pine give Grand Mere the traces of a boreal forest normally seen only in northern Michigan, while the profusion of wildflowers includes the rare starflower. The park also attracts a number of birders, for it lies on a major migration flyway. Almost 250 species of birds have been sighted here, and during the spring and fall large numbers of hawks can be seen migrating on the east winds, along with common loons, cormorants, and a variety of waterfowl and herons.

Even for those not into rare plants, aquatic succession, or birds, Grand Mere makes an excellent destination for a hike. The trails are not extensive, but this 2-mile walk can be a workout because of the steep climb to Baldtop's ex-

cellent views and because of stretches through the soft sand of open dunes. The beach is wide and semi-private, even though you can view summer cottages at each end. The only drawback is the presence of insects, especially deerflies from mid-July through mid-August. Given the natural wetlands, such pests are expectable, but, at times, the deerflies are as ferocious as any I have encountered in Michigan. The only blessing is that they diminish in number the closer you are to Lake Michigan.

Access: The park is south of St. Joseph. From I-94, head west on John Beers Road (exit 22), immediately com-

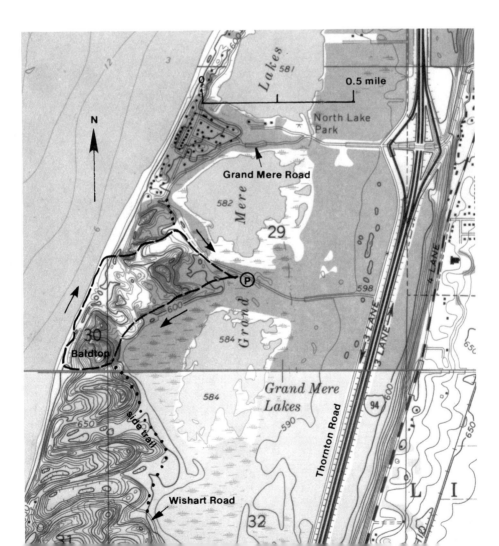

The view from Baldtop

ing to the junction of Thornton and Grand Mere roads. Three roads lead into the park, but the official entrance that was paved in 1990 is off Thornton Drive, .5 south of Grand Mere Road. You can also access the trail by continuing west on Grand Mere Road, where a trail sign and parking for a half dozen cars lies at its end. The third access point is the end of Wishart Road, reached by following Thornton south and Willow Road west (right).

Camping is not allowed in the park, and a daily vehicle permit or annual state park pass is required to enter it. Grand Mere is managed by Warren

Dunes State Park (616-426-4013), which can be reached from exit 15 on I-94 (see Hike 24).

Trail: It's .5 mile from Thornton Road to the park's parking lot, where you also find a pair of vault toilets and a picnic shelter. The trailhead is near the shelter, and the hike begins along a handicapped-access, paved trail. You skirt South Lake, though it's almost impossible to see it through the trees, and within .3 mile pass the side of an open dune. In another quarter mile, you reach a V-junction in the trail and get your first glimpse of South Lake. Turn onto the route to the right. The path to the southeast (left) continues west of the lake and in a mile reaches the end of Wishart Road at the park border. Actually, this trail used to be Wishart Road, which curved around South Lake and ended at what is now the park entrance drive.

The right path at the junction makes a steep climb and heads toward Baldtop. You climb the wooded base of a dune but soon break out in a sandy pass, with Baldtop to the north and a wooded dune to the south. Visible straight ahead is Lake Michigan. True to its name, Baldtop is free of trees at its 760-foot peak. The top is a one hundred-foot climb from here and a heart-pounding effort for most people. But from the high perch of the open dune you can see all of South Lake, including the vast wetland area that surrounds it. To the west is the wide beach along Lake Michigan, and to the south is the distinct dome of Cook's nuclear power plant.

Descend back to the sandy pass and follow it west, the easiest and most common route to Lake Michigan. You head downhill to the wide beach. Posted here is a "Grand Mere State Park" sign that lists the hours the park is open. It seems strange to me that the sign is posted here, but so be it. The west side of Baldtop is a huge blowout, and from the beach, it looks like half the dune was scooped out by a giant kid with a sand bucket and shovel.

The beach is wide, thirty to forty yards at this point depending on the current level of Lake Michigan, and the water is shallow. You can hike south to view the towering wooded bluffs that border the shoreline, but in .3 mile you'll come to state land border signs. Head north from Baldtop, and in .3 mile you'll hike around the dune's forested north side and arrive at another blowout area, not nearly as impressive. Another Grand Mere park sign has been posted here.

Hike inland and climb to the edge of the dune, where you'll see South Lake again to the southeast while due east is the wooded fringe of the open area with trails wandering through the trees. By heading northeast, you can pick up a wide path through the beachgrass that climbs around a distinct wooded dune and then enters more open sand on the other side. From here you can view all of Middle Lake, which has considerably more open water than South Lake. These two lakes show how someday both will fill in and become woodland. Hike down to the lake and find the sandy path skirting it through the low brush and grass. By heading east (right) you will return to the parking area, passing some great blackberry patches along the way. If you head north here, and you'll end up at the Grand Mere Road trailhead.

North Trails

Place: Saugatuck State Park
Total Distance: 2.5 miles
Hiking Time: 1.5 to 2 hours
Rating: Moderate
Highpoints: Sand dunes, scenic vistas
Maps: USGS Saugatuck; Saugatuck State Park map

As strange as it may seem, to reach one of the more remote parks on Lake Michigan, you must head towards a minimum security prison. Saugatuck State Park is a 844-acre preserve that includes two miles of Lake Michigan shoreline, wind-blown dunes, scenic vistas, and, right in the middle of this seemingly undeveloped wooded tract, the Michigan Dunes Correctional Facility. Strange but true.

The park was a trade-off after the St. Augustinian Seminary sold the land and its thirty-year-old school to the state. When word leaked out that it was going to be converted into a four hundred-bed correctional facility, environmentalists and residents from Holland and Saugatuck protested loudly in what one writer called "a well-organized but belated opposition." Crime won out, but to calm its citizens, the governor's office declared all but fifty acres of the tract Michigan's newest state park. Today hikers pass by barbed wire and bullhorns on their way to sand dunes and shoreline.

There's no campground at Saugatuck, nor any other facilities beyond vault toilets and picnic tables, though the park will be further developed as its master plan is slowly implemented. There's also no quick way to reach Lake Michigan, for the nearest stretch of beach is almost a mile walk from the parking area. But the lack of developed facilities, drive-in beach, and, undoubtedly, the sight of a prison keeps the number of annual visitors low, only 43,000 (which is what Holland State Park just to the north receives on a holiday weekend). Add to that fact that the majority of park users are skiers who arrive from December through February, and you have Saugatuck's most charming aspect: beaches without crowds and trails that still possess a little solitude even at the height of the summer season.

The Saugatuck's fourteen-mile network of footpaths is divided into three basic loops referred to on park maps as North Trails, Center Trails, and South Trails. All are wide paths and well marked with "You Are Here" maps at almost every junction. The South Trails is a 5.5-mile loop that extends into the designated natural area in the bottom half of the park and offers skiers and hikers the

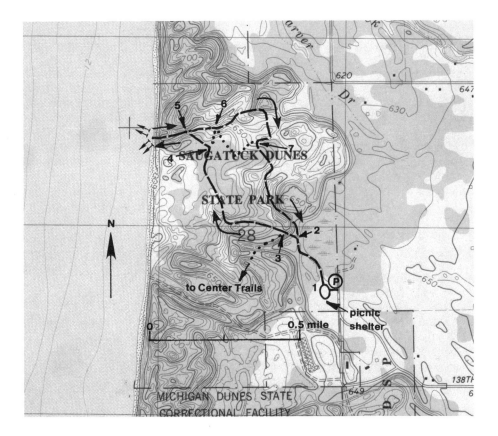

most level terrain. The Center Trails is a 2.5-mile trek that includes a segment of the North Trails. This is the most popular stretch during the summer since Lake Michigan lies less than a mile down it, along a route that appears more like a dirt road than a trail in the woods.

The loop described here uses the North Trails, which offers hikers a pleasant mix of open dunes, stands of pine and hardwoods, and an impressive overview of Lake Michigan from a high, sandy bluff. The loop is a 2.5-mile trek but can be extended into a 4.5-mile day by first hiking the Center Trails and then continuing on the North Trails at post 3.

A mid-day hike on a summer weekend results in encounters only with the kind of wildlife that wears bathing suits and carries in beach towels and suntan lotion. If you take to the paths early in the morning or during the early evening though, it's possible to spot a variety of woodland animals including whitetail deer, woodchucks, chipmunks, rabbits, and raccoons. Experienced birders find the park rich in species, including the common tern (which is not such a common sight in Michigan anymore). You're more likely to spot brown thrashers, grosbeaks, pileated woodpeckers, tufted titmouses, and even great horned owls and turkey vultures.

Access: The park is reached from I-196, just north of the town of Saugatuck. Depart at exit 41 and go west on Blue Star Memorial Highway. You immediately turn right onto 64th Street, just west of the overpass. Head north for 1 mile and turn west (left) onto 138th Avenue, where a sign points the way to "Dunes Correctional Facility." Follow this road to the posted park entrance and day-use area, which includes parking area, tables, grills, vault toilets, a shelter, and a display board. From here, two trails depart into the woods.

Generally, the contact station at the park's entrance is closed, but a box on the outside is usually stocked with park maps. For more information on this unit, contact Holland State Park, 2215 Ottawa Beach Rd., Holland, MI 49424 or call (616) 399–9390.

Trail: The trailhead for the Center and South trails is easy to spot from the south end of the parking area. The trailhead for the North Trails is a little more obscured and begins at the north end of the parking lot. It is marked by a pole and blue pathway triangle. The trail quickly enters the woods and appears as the typical wide path built to accommodate skiers in the winter. The beginning section travels beside a wooded dune ridge to the west and a marsh on the right. The birds should be plentiful around the marsh, as will be wildflowers in spring and early summer when at times it's even possible to spot pink ladyslipper orchids.

Eventually the trail climbs away from the marsh and arrives at post 2, .3 mile from the trailhead. The next post is reached by following the fork that curves sharply west (left) and climbs into a stand of red pine and mixed hardwoods of oak, beech, and maple. Post 3 is reached in .4 mile from the trailhead and marks the junction where hikers from the Center Trails join this loop. At this point, the North Trails be-

comes a soft, sandy path that makes a steady descent through an old pine plantation. After bottoming out, the trail continues as a pleasant, needle-covered path through the pines right to post 4, reached .8 mile from the trailhead.

Swing northwest (left), soon to reach post 5. There head due west (left) for a view of Lake Michigan. The spur will quickly break out of the trees and become a soft, sandy path that climbs to

Pokery Hoard flowers

the edge of a steep bluff high above the lake. It's a superb overlook. To the south the shoreline bulges out slightly and you can see much of the park's beach, including any swimmers and sunbathers out that day. To the north a hill cuts short your view, but due west you can span the endless waters of Lake Michigan.

Return to post 5 and continue straight to post 6, where for the first time in the trek you encounter a strip of wind-blown and grass-covered dunes. Choose the outer loop (left) and begin ascending one of these dunes. This segment is more difficult hiking than the inner loop since you have to trudge through soft sand. But the trail is much more scenic, and the open terrain provides a good prospective of the ruggedness of this park. After traveling .3 mile along the outer loop, you come to a post that directs you to leave what appears to be the main trail and veer off to the right. You quickly come to a four-way junction with another unofficial path. The main trail lies straight ahead, but it's hard for most hikers to resist scrambling up the path to the top of the dune on their right. From this perch you have a 360-degree view of the hilly topography you've been trekking through. Forested ridges lie in one direction, wind-blown dunes in another. And just to the north is a steep drop and the next trail marker.

At 1.8 miles from the parking area, the trail arrives at a bright yellow sign warning skiers to slow down to avoid going over the edge. The reason for the warning is clear. The trail takes a sharp 90-degree turn here and descends down a grassy dune. It bottoms out at a marker that directs you to take a second sharp turn, and quickly you ascend to post 7 on the edge of the forest.

If the sun is out and the sand is hot, the forest marks a pleasant change in scenery. You turn left at post 7, leaving the open dune area and descending into the cool shadows of a predominately oak forest. The trail makes several wide turns before arriving at the edge of the marsh enjoyed earlier in the hike. Post 2 is quickly reached, and the loop is completed by backtracking the first .3-mile leg.

Trail marker and dunes

Homestead Trail

Place: P. J. Hoffmaster State Park
Total Distance: 3.5 miles
Hiking Time: 2 to 3 hours
Rating: Moderate
Highpoints: Lake Michigan overlook, sand dunes
Maps: USGS Muskegon West; P. J. Hoffmaster State Park
 map

Sand dunes, contrary to most people's first impressions, are more than just big hills of sand that are fun to run down. The dunes found along the Lake Michigan shoreline are actually part of a complex ecosystem that is made up of many different zones, including beaches, wetlands, climax forests, and lastly, open dunes where plants struggle to gain a foothold against shifting sands and a scarcity of nutrients. Dunes are also one of nature's most beautiful formations, a delicate work of art where gentle breezes carve windswept sculptures from the sands of the Great Lakes.

In Michigan, we are blessed with a shoreline that showcases 275,000 acres of sand dune formations, the largest display of freshwater dunes in the world. They stretch from the tip of the state's thumb off Saginaw Bay to the giant perched dunes above Lake Superior and include the country's most famous dunes, the Sleeping Bear Dunes, off Lake Michigan. Perhaps the best place to learn and study about these truly remarkable formations is at P. J. Hoffmaster State Park, where you can combine

a visit to Gillette Nature Center, Michigan's Sand Dune Interpretive Center, with a hike through the various life zones of a dune along the Homestead Trail.

The Gillette Nature Center was built in 1976 as a bicentennial project to serve as an interpretive center to the state's most noted natural treasure. The two-story center is literally overshadowed by a huge, wind-blown dune that can be viewed from a glass wall on the west side of the lobby. The center features a hall entitled "From a Grain of Sand" in which the wildlife, plants, and trees of each dunal zone are displayed in a three-dimensional exhibit, complete with the sounds of waves and birds in the background.

There is also an eighty-two-seat theater that uses a nine-projector, multi-image slide show to explain further the dunes' delicate nature and the reason the state has moved to protect them from overdevelopment. Finally, check out the three-dimensional relief map to see the type of terrain you'll be covering in the next two to three hours. The

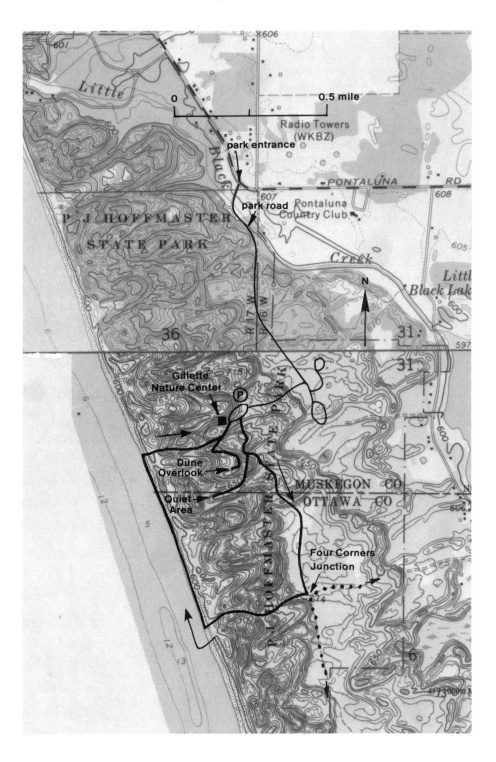

Homestead Trail circuit may look rugged, but the climbs are moderate and the route can be handled by children as young as five or six if you schedule in an extended swim or lunch break on the Lake Michigan beach.

Most of the trail passes through a designated Natural Area and includes possible sides trips to a "Quiet Area," the park's most remote corner. You also climb up a long stairway to magnificent views from the Dune Overlook Platform. Summer is an ideal time for this hike, when you can stop for a swim in the Great Lake, but it's also the park's busiest season. Many like to come here in spring or fall when the crowds are gone and there's nothing on the beaches but sand, driftwood, and a bootprint or two.

Access: The 1,043-acre park is located just south of Muskegon and can be reached from I-96 by departing at Fruitport (exit 4). Head south on 148th Avenue and immediately turn west (right) onto Pontaluna Road for 6 miles, until it dead-ends at the park entrance. From US 31, depart onto Pontaluna Road, halfway between Muskegon and Grand Haven, and head west for 3 miles.

The nature center (616-798-3573) is open year-round Tuesday through Sunday. In the summer, the hours are 9 A.M. to 6 P.M. and the rest of the year the center is open from 1 to 5 P.M. Tuesday through Friday, and 10 A.M. to 5 P.M. Saturday and Sunday. There is no fee to visit the interpretive center, but there is a vehicle fee to enter the park. For more information on campground reservations or fees, call the park headquarters at (616) 798-3711.

Trail: The circuit should be walked in a clockwise direction, therefore you start by heading south from the trailhead off the parking area and end at the trailhead behind the interpretive center.

Those who hike it in the other direction often miss where the trail leaves the beach. The parking lot trailhead is posted "Homestead Trail/Quiet Area," and the trail begins by climbing a wooded dune to reach a bench and the marked junction to the Quiet Area in .2 mile. This special area, reached by following the one-way spur .3 mile to its end, sports a deep ravine surrounded by wooded dunes that form a quiet escape for hikers.

The main trail continues south to descend through woods and to pass a posted junction with a trail that veers off north to a picnic area and shelter. Orange bootprints lead you along the Homestead Trail as it passes through a stand of young trees and then a large, grassy meadow. After crossing the meadow, you re-enter the woods and, 1 mile from the trailhead, reach a well-posted, four-way junction. Here the hiking trail merges with a ski run and bridle path.

Head east (right) along the Homestead Trail and enter the park's Natural Area along a wide path that also accommodates skiers in the winter. The trail begins with a gentle climb as it skirts the base of a dune forested in oak and maple. The trees found here and elsewhere away from the beach stabilize the dunes and protect them from wind erosion — sometimes. Within .2 mile of the four-way junction, you pass a spot where the dune has begun migrating across the trail.

In another .2 mile, you break out onto the Lake Michigan beach. If it's summer, this spot can seem a striking contrast after spending most of the first 1.5 miles (or 2.1 miles if you visited the Quiet Area) in the cool, shaded dune forest. If it's a blistering ninety degrees Fahrenheit out, you won't be able to run fast enough into Lake Michigan.

The staircase climb to the dune overlook platform

For the next .5 mile, you follow the beach north along a natural path formed between the waves rolling in from the west and the sandy bluffs that box you in on the east. Occasionally you pass a blowout, a U-shaped depression of loose sand, but most of the time the beach meets an eroding bluff lined at the edge by trees, many of them tumbling toward the lake. After a good storm, the beach can be an impressive sight, with whitecapped waves pounding the shoreline and washing up everything from helpless fish, a spare tire, or somebody's tennis shoe to a plank with rusty bolts in it and whole trunks of trees.

Eventually you reach a "Nature Center" sign mounted in a small hill of sand that directs you back inland, where you quickly come to a boardwalk. The planked trail leads you into foredunes, and soon you ascend to a large interpretive sign. The display marks an excellent spot to compare the different zone communities of dunes. You just departed the "beach zone," an area of seasonal and even daily extremes that has few permanent residents, sunbathers included. You are now in the "foredunes," areas of loose sand that are battered by wind and hikers and held into place only by clinging vegetation such as dune grass, sand cherry, and riverbank grape. But the sign is near a trough, a depression between dunes. These low-lying areas result in "interdunal wetlands" of shallow ponds and pools that in wet periods support a variety of insects, shorebirds, and other plants. Finally, you are about to climb into a zone of "backdunes," and the display points out that these dunes are secured by oaks, maples, and towering white pine. Unless marred by fire or so-called "development," the backdune is the climax of this chain of succession and the symbol of a stable area.

From the interpretive sign, you begin a quick climb up a sandy path that turns into another stretch of boardwalk. When it tops out, you'll be in a well-shaded area, looking at a forested gully between two huge dunes. On the far side, it looks as if the sand is pouring down between the trees. Shortly, you reach the stairway that leads to the Dune Overlook Platform.

You're only a short way from the nature center and parking area, but don't pass up the climb to the scenic overlook. Reaching the platform is no easy task, for it is 165 steps to the top. But the stairway puts you 190 feet above Lake Michigan. From here, the panorama is of the Great Lake, its sandy shoreline, and, most of all, the dunes that are almost everywhere you look, whether wind blown or well forested. The sight of these dunes is a fitting end to a day spent hiking through them.

Silver Lake Sand Dunes

Place: Silver Lake State Park
Total Distance: 3.6 miles
Hiking Time: 2 to 3 hours
Rating: Moderate
Highpoints: Sand dunes, Lake Michigan beach
Maps: USGS Little Point Sable; Silver Lake State Park map

This book actually covers the best forty-nine trails in southern Michigan, because the pedestrian area of Silver Lake State Park is technically a trailless tract. It is located in a mile-wide strip that separates Silver Lake from Lake Michigan and features some of the barest dunes found anywhere in the state. Many of them are steep hills without even a blade of grass, and there is no way to maintain a trail in these shifting sands. That's no reason not to explore the area on foot, however. Even without a beaten path or trail signs, it's hard to get turned around in Michigan's version of the Sahara Desert.

Silver Lake State Park contains 2,800 acres, with 1,800 of them located in the backcountry between the two lakes. The strip of dunes is divided into three areas. Small sections at the north end are designated for off-road vehicles, and the south end is reserved for a dune-ride concession. But most of the acreage lies in the pedestrian area, where hikers follow the ridges of open sand out to Lake Michigan and then back again. The state park contains almost four miles of Great Lake shoreline,

a wide sandy beach that is rarely crowded, and a just reward for the hike out.

The rest of the park, however, attracts more than its share of users. Silver Lake draws more than 600,000 visitors a year, and the east side of the lake is a tourist mecca—a bumper-to-bumper row of motels, ice cream shops, go-cart tracks, and souvenir shops. The state park campground, featuring 249 modern sites, is also located here, and the demand for sites is heavy to say the least.

All this activity contrasts with the dunes themselves, where much of the crowds and noise of the Lake Michigan tourist season is lost among the ridges and valleys of the wind-blown sand. The dunes run east to west for the most part, and some tower more than 130 feet above Silver Lake. From the crest of many of them, you are rewarded with good views of this unusual area, with the inland lake on one side and Lake Michigan's blue horizon on the other. Although the strip is a mile wide, most hikers end up walking 1.8 miles by the time they reach the lakeshore.

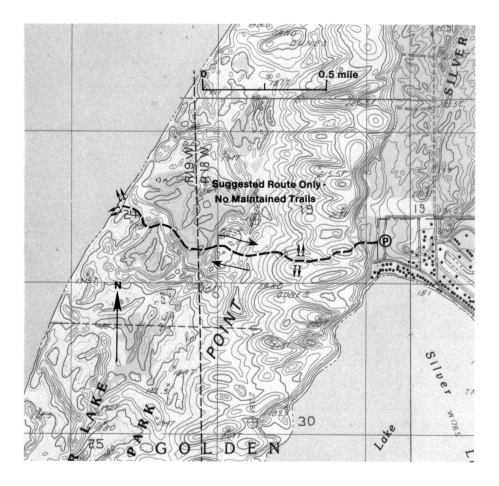

This hike can be done in tennis shoes; in fact, that's the preferred footwear since it's easier to dump the sand out of them. Don't forget a hat, sun screen, and a water bottle, for in midsummer trekking through the sand can be hot work.

Access: The state park is south of Ludington and can be reached from US 31 by exiting at Shelby Road and heading west 6 miles to County Road B15 (18th Avenue). Head north (right) for 5 miles. Just before reaching the lake, you pass the park headquarters (616-873-3083), where additional information can be obtained. County Road B15 swings around the east side of the lake, goes past the state park campground entrance, then heads east toward Mears. Where County Road B15 merges with Hazel Road, turn west (left) onto Hazel Road and follow the "ORV Access Area" signs. These will lead you to the dune pedestrian parking area, well posted and located right next to the huge lot where off-road vehicle users park their trailers and rigs. Along with parking, the trailhead area contains vault toilets, picnic tables, grills, and a hand pump whose cold, clear water will taste like champagne after your return.

Trail: A short trail marked in the parking area by a "Dune Access Stairway" sign will lead to the open dunes. Before reaching the dunes, you climb two sets of stairs through an oak/maple stand. From the top step, you leave the shady and cool forest and, in a single stride, enter the world of rippled sand and brilliant sunlight. It's a striking contrast.

The view from the top step reveals towering ridges of sand that extend east to west, while to the north you can hear and see the ORV riders in their own area. Any doubts that the dunes are migrating east are quickly settled by the trail sign at the top of the stairs that is now almost completely buried in sand. At this point, many families with children head south to follow the treeline for a fifteen-minute walk to Silver Lake. This walk is a considerably easier trek through the sand along the western shore of Silver Lake, and children can run down the steep dunes right into the refreshing waters of the lake.

To reach the Great Lake, select one of the ridges and begin scaling it. By climbing the one to the north (right) you will be able to watch the ORV daredevils race along dunes of their own in a variety of vehicles—trucks with oversized tires, four-wheelers, VW "bugs," and homemade dune buggies. But the dune ridge straight ahead is visibly higher than those around it, and from its sandy peak you are rewarded with the best view in the park, overlooking both Lake Michigan and Silver Lake.

Here the sand is pure, sugarlike, and there's not a plant around, not even dune grass. The sides of the dune,

Family returning from Silver Lake

sculptured by the wind, form steep slopes with an incline of 45 degrees or more, while the surface at the top has a rippled wave-effect to it. If there is a wind, sand will be visibly moving across the dune, making many hikers hesitant to pull out their cameras.

After trudging along the crest of the dune, you descend to the section where grass has taken root, within .7 mile from the trailhead. Although the area is trail-less, several routes are visible through the grass and lead into the strip of oak and jack pine. Depending on where you're cutting across, several interdunal ponds can also be seen. Although these ponds may vanish completely during a dry spell, early in the summer they are a haven for a variety of wildflowers, grasses, and animals.

It's about a .5-mile walk through the sparse forest, where unofficial trails criss-cross in every direction. Either put your trust in one or simply continue heading west. Eventually you depart the lightly forested strip, undertake another short climb through wind-blown and grass-covered dunes, and end up on the edge of a sandy bluff looking down at the Lake Michigan beach. Now here is a true beach!' The Lake Michigan shoreline is more than thirty yards wide and nothing but sand, with the exception of an occasional piece of driftwood. If you have undertaken this trek in the middle of the week, you might well have a good stretch of this beach all to yourself.

To return, simply retrace your steps east. The ORV fence to the north will be the sign that you're wandering too far to the north.

Ridge and Island Trails

Place: Ludington State Park
Total Distance: 5.2 miles
Hiking Time: 4 to 5 hours
Rating: Moderate
Highpoints: Scenic views, sand dunes
Maps: USGS Hamlin Lake; Ludington State Park trail map

Ludington State Park can be a busy place. The largest unit along Lake Michigan and second largest in the Lower Peninsula at 5,200 acres, it attracts more than 700,000 visitors a year, with the vast majority arriving between Memorial Day and Labor Day. At that time, the beaches are popular, the campgrounds often filled, and the paved pathways that skirt the Big Sable River between Hamlin Lake and Lake Michigan crowded with families riding bicycles to their campsites.

But don't let this discourage you from visiting this state park. With its extensive acreage, hikers can easily escape the summer heat and the crowds by following a foot trail into the wooded dunes to the north. The park's developed area, and the focus for most visitors, is concentrated along the Big Sable River, where three campgrounds contain a total of almost four hundred sites, and where you can find a concession store, nature center, picnic area, and park headquarters.

To the north is Ludington's backcountry, featuring a terrain that ranges from open dunes and protected marshes along Hamlin Lake to towering pines or miles of undeveloped Lake Michigan shoreline, complete with a historic lighthouse. A twenty-mile network of trails provides foot access into this area, ending at the edge of the park's Wilderness Natural Area, a trailless, 1,700-acre section of mostly forested dunes. This unique "dune wilderness" continues beyond the state park border, for to the north of Ludington is Nordhouse Dunes, the only federally designated wilderness in the Lower Peninsula (see Hike 32).

A popular hike in the park is to follow an access road out to Point Sable Lighthouse, then circle back along Lighthouse and Logging trails for a five-mile trek (Hike 31). Just as scenic a circuit, however, is formed by Ridge and Island trails, which lead you to the edge of the wilderness area and past the fascinating perched dunes above Hamlin Lake. This circuit makes for a pleasant day hike, where lunch can be enjoyed deep in the park at a rustic CCC shelter overlooking the inland lake.

In summer, bring a quart of water per person, a hat, and sun screen, for some stretches of the walk are through open

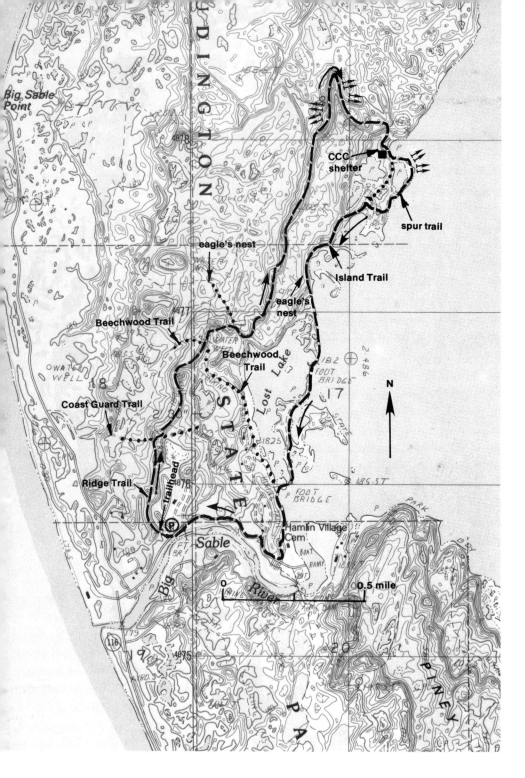

Big Sable
Point

CCC
shelter

spur trail

eagle's nest

eagle's
nest

Island Trail

Beechwood Trail

Beechwood
Trail

Lost Lake

182
FOOT
BRIDGE

2.486

N

Coast Guard Trail

WATER
WELL

18

1825

185.ST

FOOT
BRIDGE

Ridge Trail

trailhead

Sable

River

Hamlin Village
Cem

BOAT
RAMP

PARK

PINEY

0   0.5 mile

116

dunes. But the vast majority of the day will be spent in the cool shade of the forest, away from beach blankets, beach balls, and the crowds that congregate along the park's designated beaches.

Access: The park is located 8.5 miles north of the city of Ludington at the end of MI 116. From US-31, head west on US-10 through the heart of the city to the waterfront where it merges into M-116. Just before crossing the Big Sable River, you pass a campsite reservation center where arrangements are made to obtain a site. Keep in mind that the campgrounds are heavily booked from early July through Labor Day and advance reservations are strongly recommended. They can be made by contacting Ludington State Park, P.O. Box 709, Ludington, MI 49431, (616) 843-8671.

Trail: The Ridge Trail begins behind the park store (open daily in the summer 8 A.M. to 9 P.M.), where there is ample parking and where a last-minute snack can be purchased. There is also a hand pump nearby, so don't forget to fill up your water bottle.

The trail is posted "Ridge Trail/Logging Trail" and is marked in maroon bootprints. It begins with an immediate climb up a ridge, which it skirts to the north. The climb might leave you puffing, but the change in ambiance is well worth it. On the ridge is a quiet forest, and you're left looking down on the bustling park. You follow the ridge above Cedar Campground for a spell, where numerous unofficial paths cross the main trail. It's hard to get turned around, though, if you just keep heading north and look for the next bootprint post.

The trail swings away from the campground, continues along the ridge, then reaches a junction with the Coast Guard Trail after a U-shaped curve. Reached .6 mile from the trailhead, the junction is on a hillside forested in maple, oak, and a few pine. Black bootprints mark the Coast Guard Trail, which heads west to a scenic overlook on Lake Michigan and east to the Hamlin Lake day-use area. Ridge Trail continues to climb up the hill, topping off to follow a ridgeline. For the next half mile, there are steep ravines on either side of the ridge, heavily forested in an old stand of maple and beech. The trees are so thick that the forest floor is almost devoid of any undergrowth.

Eventually you come to the junction with the Beechwood Trail, reached 1 mile from the trailhead. This trail heads northwest, eventually to end at the Lighthouse Trail, and southeast, where it quickly descends to a bench overlooking a small lake. It's even possible to get glimpses of that lake through the trees from the Ridge Trail.

The maroon boots continue to lead you north along a ridge to a highpoint of ninety-three feet above Lake Michigan, then takes a sharp but well-marked 90-degree turn and descends to Eagle's Nest Trail, marked in green. This is a major junction, with five trails departing from the area, but a display map and a rainbow of bootprints help you decipher how to continue on the Ridge Trail. The Ridge Trail continues north by ascending another ridge, quickly passing a vault toilet to the left, and then coming to the stone foundation of a shelter that once stood here. Look carefully through the foliage, and to the southeast you can view Lost Lake. A decade ago, the view must have been better, for just up the trail is a pair of benches angled towards the lake. Ecological succession has resulted in saplings replacing bushes, thus blocking out the view.

Continuing along the trail north, you descend slightly, pass a pond, then return to a ridgeline via an easy climb. At

1.9 miles, the trail passes a second set of benches with the same problem: trees have obscured most of the view. The trail continues along this ridge, where at times you get a glimpse of Lake Michigan to the west. Just when you are getting frustrated with the leaves that are denying you your hard-earned panorama, the trail ascends and, 2.1 miles from the beginning, comes to a clearing.

To the west are the open and grass-covered dunes of the park, with Lake Michigan on the horizon. The trail quickly climbs to its highest point of 128 feet above the lake, where under the shade of a large oak tree you are re-warded with an unobstructed view of the dunes and the Great Lake to the west and a portion of Hamlin Lake to the east. More panoramic views follow for the next .3 mile as you traverse what is basically a migrating sand dune. On its west side is open sand being inched along by the winds off Lake Michigan. On the east side is a scattering of trees trying valiantly to keep this moving mountain in place.

At 2.5 miles, the trail makes a sharp curve and descends off the ridge. To the east, you get a full view of the open and grass-covered dunes that surround Hamlin Lake, a sight equally spectacular to the views of Lake Michigan. Within another .2 mile, a maroon boot directs you to descend into a shaded beech forest, but it's easy here to scramble fifty yards to the top of a sand dune to the east for the best vantage point for see-ing Hamlin Lake and the dunes perched above it on its northwest shoreline.

The trail, meanwhile, descends rapidly through the forest, swings east (left), and bottoms out at the edge of a pond. Just on the other side is the picturesque stone shelter on the shores of Hamlin

that marks the start of Island Trail, the second half of this trek. The shelter, like many of the structures in state parks, was built by the CCC in the early 1930s under the direction of the National Park Service. When Ludington State Park offi-cially opened on August 1, 1934, Corps members served as trail guides to visi-tors from sixteen states and Canada.

Island Trail is marked by blue boot-prints and departs from the shelter to head south along a strip between a pond and Hamlin Lake. You soon come to another pond on the east side (left side) of the trail, and here the main route heads due south. A somewhat ob-scured path veers off here to the east and hugs the shoreline, and by taking it you can get an excellent view of the steep dunes that make up Hamlin Lake's west shore. On the right side of this spur trail is the pond, with lily pads and cattails protruding from the water.

Within .3 mile, the trails merge and Is-land Trail continues south by skirting the edge of a marshy bay. Tree-studded is-lets separate this lagoon from the rest of the lake and make for calm water that attracts a variety of waterfowl, often seen resting among the cattails. The trail skirts so close to the shoreline that sometimes the path is flooded out by high water, but planking has been set here and there to provide dry footing most of the way.

Eventually you round the lagoons and return to the open lake, .6 mile from the shelter, while passing a small inland pond to the west. Hamlin was originally dammed by loggers in the 1880s to cre-ate a large holding area for trees felled up the Big Sable River. The trees were milled in the village of Hamlin, which was located within the state park, then taken to Lake Michigan by mules. In 1888, the dam burst and the resultant

Stone hut on the Ridge Trail

flood swept away the mill, forty homes in Hamlin, and more than a million board feet of lumber.

Today the state maintains the dam, which regulates the water level of the 4,490-acre lake. The lake is known by anglers for its excellent bluegill, northern pike, and muskellunge fishing since many of the inlets and bayous, including Lost Lake, serve as pike and muskie spawning grounds. The north end of Lost Lake is seen after you're almost a mile from the shelter, at the junction with the east end of Eagle's Nest Trail. Island Trail continues south as it cuts along a scenic spit, with Lost Lake on one side and Hamlin on the other.

At 1.2 miles from the shelter, you cross an impressive bridge and hike across an island, passing well-protected coves on Hamlin Lake that often attract waterfowl and other birds. Within .3 mile, the trail arrives at the south end of the island. You can spot the campers on the other side of Lost Lake just before you arrive at a boardwalk and bridge to the mainland. On the other side is a junction, where you can ascend the ridge to intersect Beechwood Trail or swing south (left) to reach the day-use area and beach on Hamlin Lake. From the beach parking lot, it is a .5-mile walk along the Sable River Trail, a route marked by red posts, back to the concession store and trailhead for the Ridge Trail.

31

Lighthouse Trail

Place: Ludington State Park
Total Distance: 4.8 miles
Hiking Time: 3 hours
Rating: Moderate
Highpoints: Historic lighthouse, Lake Michigan beach
Maps: USGS Hamlin Lake; Ludington State Park trail map

Within Ludington State Park, one of most popular units in Michigan, Big Point Sable Lighthouse is without question the most popular destination for walkers and hikers. Most visitors simply follow the access road out to the historic lighthouse, snap a few pictures, then turn around and head back along the same, sandy road. But the more intriguing way to reach Big Point Sable is to hike the park's Logging Trail, which winds through the woods and around interesting ponds, then to head west on the Lighthouse Trail through open dune country. You can then return by hiking the Lake Michigan shoreline, where some of the best beachcombing this side of the state can be enjoyed. This is paradise for lovers of weather-beaten, gray-faded driftwood. The loop covers 4.8 miles and is of moderate difficulty, but the only time you see the access road is when you cross it.

Although in summer the park is busy, too busy for some people, the crowds taper off dramatically once you leave the campground and hike north. The first half of the route can be buggy, but the bugs are almost nonexistent in the

open dunes or along the beach. You'll see more people here than on the Ridge/Island Trail loop (see Hike 30), but the almost two-mile stroll down Lake Michigan in August is great, especially if it's early evening and the sun is beginning to melt on the horizon.

Sturdy tennis shoes are adequate for this trip, and there are two stone shelters in the first half in case of a sudden downpour. If you're packing a lunch, the best place to feast is on the small dunes overlooking the lighthouse and Point Sable — dining with a true view.

Access: The park is located 8.5 miles north of the city of Ludington at the end of MI 116. From US 31, head west on US 10 through the heart of the city to the waterfront, where US 10 merges into MI 116. After crossing Big Sable River, you pass the contact station. Straight ahead is a parking lot with a fish-cleaning station. The trailhead is in Pines Campground, but this is the best place to leave the vehicle if you don't have a site.

A daily vehicle permit or annual state park pass is required to enter the park, and during the summer, advance reser-

Big Sable Point Lighthouse

beginning of the Logging Trail. The path looks like the old logging road that it once was. It immediately climbs a ridge forested in pines and hardwoods. On the other side of the ridge, you descend to a small wetland and the junction with the Coast Guard Trail, a path marked by black arrows. The Logging Trail, marked by dark green arrows, keeps heading north and winds around several more ponds and marshes before arriving at the first of two major junctions, .7 mile from the campground.

Here you'll find a stone shelter built in the 1930s by Civilian Conservation Corps members and trails leading off in every direction. The roof of the shelter is new and provides effective escape from the rain. The trails were recently re-marked, so it's awfully hard to get turned around. The Logging Trail continues north over small hills and in another .6 mile reaches a major junction of three trails (Logging, Eagle Nest, and Ridge), where there's another stone shelter, hexagonal in shape and a most interesting structure. The Logging Trail continues almost due north and winds through the woods, where you have the best chance on this hike of spotting a deer. In .6 mile from the hexagonal shelter, you reach the posted junction with the Lighthouse Trail.

Heading west (left) here with the brown arrows, you hike through a mixed forest of oak, maple, and pines. You soon break out at a small pond, then pass another, and another, until you have passed almost a half-dozen low-lying wet areas. Even on a windy day, these small openings in the trees are smooth and calm oases with not a ripple among the lily pads and cattails covering them. Eventually the Lighthouse Trail climbs out of the lowlands and up a dune, which is forested at first but "bald" on top. The panorama from the top is

vations are strongly recommended if you want to camp. They can be made by contacting Ludington State Park, P.O. Box 709, Ludington, MI 49431; or call (616) 843-8671.

Trail: Follow the access road into Pines Campground, where, at the very back next to site 53, a post marks the superb; you gaze out over rolling dunes that stretch out to Lake Michigan, crowned by the top of the lighthouse.

The trail descends sharply and re-enters the lightly forested area. In the final .5 mile, the Lighthouse Trail leaves the trees for good and winds around interdunal ponds and over dunes. It's not really a trail, but more like a series of footprints in the sand. It's hard to get turned around, though. Halfway across the open space, the tower appears, showing you the way just like the guiding light it was built to be for sailors on the Great Lakes.

The trail ends at the Big Point Sable Lighthouse. The classic structure was authorized by President James Buchanan in 1858 after the barge *Neptune* sank off the point and thirty-seven people drowned. Actual construction didn't begin until President Andrew Johnson ordered it done in 1866, and on November 1, 1867, the light was illuminated by Burr Caswell, the first resident of Mason County and the first lighthouse keeper.

The light used a third-order Fresnel lens that was shipped in from Paris and cost one thousand dollars. The signal was fixed white, and the lamp used 179 gallons of "refined lard wick oil" during each shipping season from April to May. A Lifesaving Station was also established here in 1875 but was discontinued in 1921. Forty-seven years later, the light was automated by the Coast Guard.

Since 1940, government agencies have taken several steps to protect the lighthouse from the rough weather on the point and to renovate the structure. The light was placed on the National Register of Historical Sites in 1983 and, in 1990, received a grant for shore protection from Michigan's Historic Preservation Office. Today, the Big Sable Point Lighthouse Keeper's Association has the task of completing the renovation. Although you can't enter the structure, except during special tours offered by the association during the summer, the light and the lightkeeper's house make for a scenic place to break for lunch or an extended rest stop.

There are two ways to return to the trailhead. Most people follow the access road back to the campground. The road is closed to all traffic except park workers and runs between the edge of the forest and the open dunes to the west. It travels 1.8 miles back to the campground, and along the way, you pass a number of ponds and wetlands.

The road is a level and easy walk, but it has always amazed me that most people return on it when a far more interesting route is to follow the beach. The shoreline is wide and sandy, and driftwood is scattered from one end to the other. You can stroll along the hard sand near the water, with Lake Michigan's surf pounding on one side and the low, rolling dunes on the other. Within 1.5 miles, you'll approach a depression between two dunes where a trail post with a black arrow has been placed. This is the west end of the Coast Guard Trail, and you can follow that path for .6 mile to its junction with the Logging Trail you passed earlier. Or, if you find the beach intriguing, you can continue along it for almost another mile, until you reach the large bathhouse where you cut inland to the fish-cleaning station and parking lot. Of course, if you really enjoy beach walking, you can always swim across the mouth of the Big Sable River and follow it almost the whole way to Ludington.

Michigan Trail

Place: Nordhouse Dunes Wilderness Area
Total Distance: 6 miles
Hiking Time: 4 to 5 hours
Rating: Challenging
Highpoints: Sand dunes, scenic overlooks
Maps: USGS Manistee; Nordhouse Dunes Wilderness map
* from the Manistee National Forest*

"Wilderness" is such a subjective concept. To many, the only true wilderness in Michigan is on Isle Royale National Park, an island in the northwest corner of Lake Superior that is free of roads, vehicles, or, except for a handful of buildings around the ferry docks, any other man-made intrusions. To others, wilderness is anywhere without a McDonalds.

With the Michigan Wilderness Act of 1987, the federal government declared the Nordhouse Dunes area of the Manistee National Forest a wilderness, the only area designated as such in the Lower Peninsula. To some purists, this designation is debatable. Nordhouse Dunes is not a large tract—only 3,450 acres—nor is it a pristine setting. The area is criss-crossed in places by old logging tracks and Forest Service roads.

True wilderness or not, though, there is no question that this niche of wind-blown dunes, wetlands, and rolling hills of hardwoods and conifers is a unique spot for southern Michigan and even for the western side of the state, which is famous for having the world's most ex-

tensive set of freshwater dunes. The most striking feature of this area is its undeveloped nature, most notably along the four miles of Lake Michigan shoreline where you won't find a single bathhouse, ice cream stand, or paved parking lot. Paralleling the shoreline are open dunes and forested bluffs, and skirting the edge of these is the Michigan Trail.

Although the future for Nordhouse Dunes calls for moving away from signs, markings, and even names for trails, this path is worthy of its title. Lying like a thread between the roar of the Lake Michigan surf and the quiet interior of the forests, this route is not only one of the most scenic hikes in Michigan but possibly also in the Midwest. The actual trail stretches 1.9 miles above the shoreline between the southern observation platform in the Lake Michigan Recreation Area to a stretch of open dunes. You then return to the campground by following what is known as the Nordhouse Dune Trail and the Nipissing Trail to complete a trek of 6 miles. Alternatively, by departing the shoreline ear-

lier, you can shorten the hike to 2.4 miles by returning along the Middle Trail, or to 5.5 miles via the Algoma Ridge Trail.

Any of these return routes takes you away from the Great Lake and into the heart of this small wilderness, where solitude and encounters with wildlife will be enjoyed. The interior trails traverse numerous ridges and hills (old dunes, really) and are the most physically challenging to hike, but there are rewards for the effort. A quiet walker, especially at dusk, might sight a variety of wildlife including whitetail deer, raccoons, porcupines, numerous squirrels harvesting nuts, maybe even a fox or coyote.

Encounters with people are also likely, especially during July and August or on trails near the Lake Michigan Recreation Area. During the firearm deer season, November 15–30, hunters will often be seen along the interior trails. But Nordhouse Dunes can be something of a "wilderness experience" for those who come equipped with a backpack, tent, and sleeping bag or for those who venture onto the remote open dune area at the southern end of the tract. Due to its fragile nature, campfires and camping are discouraged in the open dunes, but nearby are pockets of conifers or hardwoods that are excellent places to set up camp for a night among the dunes. Carry in all your water and a backpacker's stove to make life easy in the woods, and carry out your trash. The backpacking effort will seem well worth it in that magic moment when the sun begins to sink into Lake Michigan, people disappear, wildlife peek out, and the "wilderness" of the Nordhouse Dunes settles in.

Access: The Lake Michigan Recreation Area is at the northern edge of the federal wilderness and located almost halfway between Manistee to the north

and Ludington to the south. From MI 55 in Manistee, head south on US 31 for 10 miles and then turn west (right) on Lake Michigan Road for 8 miles to its end. From US-10 turn north on US-31 at Scottville, 7 miles east of Ludington. Lake Michigan Road is reached in 11.5 miles.

The recreation area features one hundred rustic and wooded campsites well spaced along four loops. There are hand pumps for water, fire rings, and picnic tables, but no electricity or showers. The area is open year-round and managed from mid-May to mid-October. There is a nightly campsite fee, and advance reservations are possible for an additional charge by calling 1-800-283-2267. There is no charge for day use of the area or to hike the trails.

The tract's ten-mile network of trails is also accessible from a trailhead at the west end of Nurnberg Road. From US 31, head west on Lake Michigan Recreation Road for 3 miles, then head south (left) on Quarterline Road for a little over a mile to reach Nurnberg Road. Three trails marked by U.S. Forest Service signs and one with a display map depart from here: Nipissing, Algoma, and Nordhouse Dunes trails. Make sure you have water before you arrive, for the trailhead contains only a parking area for your vehicle. More information or maps can be obtained at the Manistee Ranger Station, 1658 Manistee Highway, south of the town of Manistee, or by calling (616) 723-2211.

Trail: At the recreation area, the hike begins with a scramble up 122 steps to the southern observation platform, where the view was probably stunning at one time but now is partially blocked by treetops. Right behind the platform is a red trail post and map sign for the Arrowheads Trail, the start of the network. The left path heads inland, but most hikers head right, for the views of Lake Michigan entice them onto the shoreline portion. The trail actually follows a dune ridge high above the shoreline and is surprisingly level and easy walking for the first mile. On one side are dunes forested in hardwoods, pines, and an occasional paper birch. On the other side is a steep drop, a strip of white, sandy beach, and the blue horizon of Lake Michigan. The contrast between the shade of the woods and the sun on the sand is remarkable.

Within .3 mile of the platform, you come to the junction of the Arrowhead Trail, the first cutoff along the way. The observation platform is .5 mile down this trail to the left. Continue south, however, for more of this enchanting walk along Lake Michigan. The forest is composed mostly of northern hardwoods such as maple, beech, and white and red oak, with hemlock and red and white pines mixed in. At 1.1 miles, however, you pass through a scenic stand of paper birch, after which you arrive at the junction of the Middle Trail.

This cutoff is a .7-mile walk to the Nipissing Trail. The Michigan Trail continues south and becomes considerably harder to hike, beginning with an immediate ascent along a embankment stairway that quickly passes the junction with the Algoma Ridge Trail. You climb several more humps over shoreline dunes on the Michigan Trail before descending to the posted junction with the Dunes Edge Trail, reached 1.6 miles from the observation platform. For the first time in the hike, the open beach and Lake Michigan surf are only a few steps away.

Continuing straight ahead, the trail returns to the edge of the forest briefly, then breaks out where a tongue of wind-blown sand dunes extends inland. In the remote southern portion of the tract, trails are only minimally posted; this is, after all, a designated wilderness. Most likely, however, footprints will lead across the open sand to a distinctive path in the woods on the other side of the open area. The trail then emerges at a second band of open dunes, wider and a little more confusing than the first. Cut across them and hike between the trees and the open shoreline, soon coming to a wide, sandy path that is posted with a "You Are Here" map.

You sure are. You've now reached the southern edge of the trail network and what lies beyond is an area of wind-blown dunes, slopes of beachgrass, and woody patches and islets often populated by juniper and stunted jack pine and surrounded by open sand. All the dunes were formed within the last thirteen thousand years, after the glaciers receded and the level of Lake Michigan fluctuated between a high of 640 feet and the present 580 feet. During low water levels, the prevailing winds from the west pushed the exposed lakebottom sand into dunes onshore. The dunes stand 140-feet high in some places and are a textbook display of natural plant succession. Beginning with just sand and water at the edge of Lake Michigan, you can follow this path of succession: mosses, lichen, and grasses first appearing, only to be replaced by larger shrubs such as sand cherry, jack pine, and aspen saplings, which are finally eclipsed by a hardwood climax forest.

This open area of the Nordhouse Dunes is trailless, but adventurous hikers can continue southwest by following the beach. In a little over 2 miles, you would leave the federal tract and enter Ludington State Park's Wilderness Natural Area, a 1,699-acre extension of this undeveloped segment of Lake Michigan shoreline. Backpackers will want to retreat to the trail and set up camp in the edge of the forest along the bluffs. The open dunes close to the beach make perfect front row seats for the nightly performance of a fiery sun melting into the Great Lake.

At the posted map, the wide and sandy path heading due south into the forest is the Nordhouse Dunes Trail. Within .3 mile, the route arrives at another map marking the junction of the Dunes Edge Trail. Stay on Nordhouse Dunes Trail to the right, shortly passing a few small marshes surrounded by hemlock. An unposted old track that climbs steeply up a hill appears shortly as a V-junction. The main trail veers right here as a sandy path and begins a long ascent of its own. This is followed by an equally long descent, after which the trail curves around a large marsh with an open pond in the middle. From the trail, you can look down into the entire wetland, an excellent place to look for deer early in the morning.

The 1.4-mile Nordhouse Dune Trail ends by swinging noticeably to the east and descending gently to the trailhead and parking area off Nurnberg Road. Pick up the next route, the Nipissing Trail, by crossing the parking area to the north to the path marked by a "No Motorized Vehicles" sign. Although a map might suggest otherwise, this trail is surprisingly scenic, for you straddle the crest of a line of wooded dunes almost all the way back to the campground.

Avoid the unmarked, wide trail that soon drops off the ridge sharply to the east, and within .5 mile from the parking area, you will come into view of Nordhouse Lake. From above, the lake appears as a main body of water surrounded by several smaller ones. Rangers report that there is little chance of catching a fish in any of them, but the water is a scenic sight. More views are obtained .5 mile after the trail moves away from the lake. You climb a seven hundred-foot knob and, to the southeast, see the interior of the wilderness tract and more forested ridges on the horizon.

The trail continues to traverse this line of forested dunes, and 2.1 miles from the Nurnberg Road area, you arrive at where the Middle Trail ascends the ridge to merge with your path back to the campground. A gray water tower looking totally out of place quickly pops up, the only sign that you have officially left the federally designated wilderness. You're now actually above the campground. Before you reach the observation deck in another .25 mile, the trail will pass two stairways, the first leading down to the sites along the Oak Loop and the second to the Hemlock Loop.

Sleeping Bear Dunes

Old Indian Trail

Place: Sleeping Bear Dunes National Lakeshore
Total Distance: 3 miles
Hiking Time: 1 to 2 hours
Rating: Easy
Highpoints: Lake Michigan beach
Maps: USGS Frankfort; Old Indian Hiking Trail map from
  National Park Service

Compared with such spectacular walks in Sleeping Bear Dunes National Lakeshore as Empire Bluff, the Dunes Trail, or Pyramid Point, Old Indian Trail falls short in the steal-your-breath panoramas that climax the other routes. But if it was located anywhere else in southern Michigan, Old Indian would be considered an outstanding walk and would undoubtedly draw a great deal more users than it does now. The trail winds mostly through a forest of pine and hardwoods, but does climb through some low shoreline dunes along Lake Michigan and allows you to spend an afternoon on a somewhat isolated beach. It's a wide path and easy to follow. The hills might trouble a few novice skiers during the winter, but they rarely trouble a hiker during the summer, not even children.

Since it is located on the southern end of the national lakeshore and a good distance from the visitors center and the major attractions of the area, Old Indian probably draws less attention than any other foot trail in the area. Although you can't run naked on its beach, you can often escape the summer crowds here

that are encountered elsewhere in this popular park.

Access: The heart of Sleeping Bear Dunes National Lakeshore is Empire, a small, scenic town located 22 miles from Traverse City or 74 miles from I-75 and Grayling at the west end of MI 72. From the National Park Service Visitor Center (616-326-5134) in Empire, head south on MI 22 for 12 miles and look for the entrance to the trailhead parking lot, which is posted on the north (right) side of the road. If heading north from Frankfort, follow MI 22 and look for the posted entrance just beyond Sutter Road. Within the parking area is a display sign and map box along with a vault toilet. Camping is not allowed here.

Trail: The hike begins along a level trail that immediately enters the woods. You soon pass the posted junction with the first route west (left). Proceed straight to get to the next junction, reached in .3 mile. Continue straight at this junction also. This route is by far the most interesting and is hilly enough to be marked by black triangles indicating an "Advanced" trail for skiers. For the

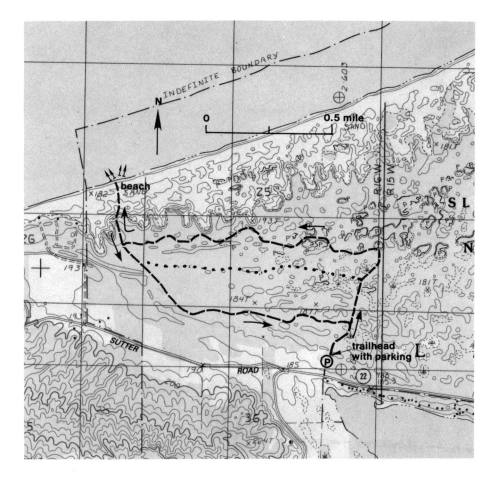

next mile, you hike over a series of low dunes, forested in mixed hardwoods (maple, beech, oak) and pines. You remain in the woods except when the trail descends to a marsh or pond.

In 1.2 miles from the trailhead, you pass a spot where open dunes are migrating south into the forest, sand pouring down between the trees. From here it's .3 mile to the posted junction to the beach. At the junction, head north (right) toward Lake Michigan. You quickly break out of the trees to enter an area of open dunes, where you trudge through the sand for .2 mile to reach the lakeshore.

This is a scenic spot, even though a couple of cottages are visible to the west. To the east you view nothing but the wide expanse of low beach dunes along Platte Bay, while off in the distance is the famous Sleeping Bear Dune. Out in Lake Michigan, you can see North and South Manitou islands (see Hikes 38 and 39). South Manitou's perched dunes along its west side are clearly visible. The beach is usually twenty- to thirty-feet wide, depending on the lake level, and you can walk it the length of Platte Bay.

To return, backtrack to the junction where you turned toward the beach.

Hiking toward Lake Michigan through open dunes

Head southeast (the right trail) along a level route that quickly passes the "middle" trail. Continue southeast to take the southernmost spur, reached .3 mile after the beach junction. Green "Easy" triangles mark our route east (left), while another unmarked trail continues its course south. The Old Indian Trail picks up its name from this route to the beach, for part of it follows an old Indian path that was established by early tribes traveling the coastline between camps and fishing spots.

This return leg is .75-mile long and relatively flat. It traverses ancient beach dunes that mark the former location of the Lake Michigan shoreline, when the water level was considerably higher in the early postglacial era. At one point, you pass through an impressive stand of beech, with one huge tree right next to the trail. Eventually you arrive at the first junction you passed from the trailhead. Head south (right), and you'll be back at the parking lot in minutes.

Platte Plains Trail

Place: Sleeping Bear Dunes National Lakeshore
Total Distance: 7 miles
Hiking Time: 3 to 5 hours
Rating: Easy
Highpoints: Lake Michigan shoreline, backcountry camping
Maps: USGS Beulah; Platte Plains Hiking Trail map from the
  National Park Service

On the mainland, there are two walk-in campgrounds within Sleeping Bear Dunes National Lakeshore. One is Valley View, a lightly used facility north of Glen Arbor. Those forested sites are at the end of a 1.5-mile trail, with neither dunes nor Lake Michigan nearby. The other is White Pine Campground, reached on foot from the Platte Plains Trail. This backcountry campground is a gem. Located in a ravine between two forested dunes, the facility is an escape from the noise and bustle of the park's busy tourist season in midsummer; yet the campground still lies near the three main attractions of Sleeping Bear Dunes. Within a short walk of your tent are wind-blown dunes, panoramas of the rugged shoreline and the Manitou Islands, and isolated stretches of Lake Michigan beach. And, the only price to stay at this get-away is the short walk in from MI 22.

Platte Plains Trail is actually a fifteen-mile network of trails with three official trailheads. The shortest route to White Pine Campground begins at Trail's End Road and winds 1.8 miles over a series of hills. But the most scenic route and the one described here begins at Platte River Campground and is commonly referred to as the 6 Mile Loop. The hike actually measures closer to 7 miles, with White Pine Campground reached after a 3-mile hike. What makes this loop so interesting is the variety of terrain you pass through, including open dunes with views of Lake Michigan, steep forested ridges, and an old railroad grade where the path is a wide and level route.

If planning to spend a night in the backcountry, pack in water along with your food, tent, sleeping bag, and other equipment. There's a community fire ring in the campground, but cooking is best done on a backpacker's stove. And don't forget the bathing suit, for the swimming is excellent in Platte Bay.

The hiking season runs through the typical spring to fall period, with heavy demand for the limited number of sites in July and August, especially on the weekends. These summer months are popular for those who like to romp across hot dunes to cool off in the surf of Lake Michigan. October brings in the spectacular fall colors, while by late December or early January a good base of snow has formed and cross-country skiers begin arriving. Winter camping anyone?

Access: Begin the trip in Empire (see Hike 33) at the National Park Service headquarters on the corner of MI 72 and MI 22, or 22 miles west of Traverse City. Open from 9 A.M. to 5 P.M. daily, and often later in the summer, the visitors center (616-326-5134) has nautical and natural displays on the Sleeping Bear Dunes as well as information on other trails and activities within the park. The most important thing to obtain is a backcountry permit, needed to spend a night at White Pine Campground.

From the headquarters, head south

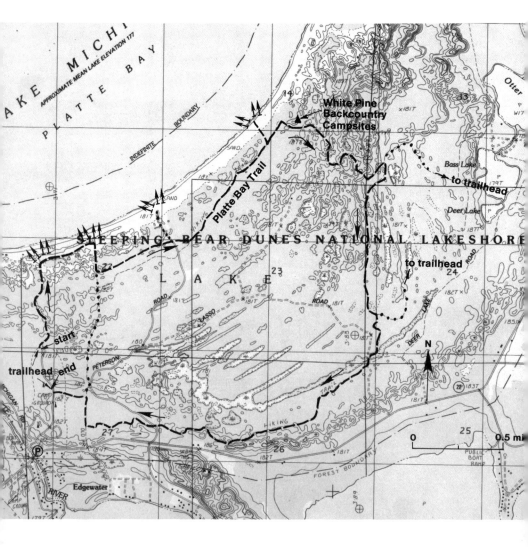

on MI 22 and in 9.5 miles you reach Platte River Campground, a rustic facility that also features a picnic area, water, vault toilets, and a contact station with a map box. There are actually two trailheads in the campground. One, marked by green "Easy" triangles, is located halfway through the campground and provides access to the Old Railroad Grade. The second trailhead, where this hike begins, is found on the loop at the end of the campground road and is marked by blue "Intermediate" triangles. It leads directly to the scenic stretch along Lake Michigan.

Alternative trailheads to the Platte Plains include Otter Creek, reached 4 miles out of Empire and west on Esch Road, and Otter Lake Trailhead, 6 miles south of Empire at the west end of Trail's End Road.

Trail: The trail from the back of the campground departs into the pine forest and winds along a hilly terrain. The route is easy to follow and is well marked by blue triangles. Within .5 mile, you break out of the trees and enter the low dunes along the Lake Michigan shoreline. At first you walk on planking, but when the planks end, many discover how tiring hiking on soft sand can be. You arrive shortly at a locator map, where straight ahead are the cool breezes off the Great Lake and a scenic view of the beach.

To the east (right) is the soft, sandy path to the junction with the railroad gauge. You hike over open dunes and through patches of beachgrass. Here and there an odd pine or cottonwood is thriving, but for the most part you are in the heat of the sun for the next .4 mile until you reach the next junction and "You Are Here" map. To the north (left) is another scenic view of Platte Bay and the shoreline that extends north. To the south (right), the trail quickly merges into the railroad gauge. You don't have to be a train buff to envision a line running along the wide and level path. The narrow gauge line was built in the nineteenth century between a logging town on the west end of Platte Lake called Edgewater to docks on Lake Michigan, where ships carried the cut lumber to cities like Chicago. The railroad bed is a level path, because workers filled in every dip and flattened every rise of sand before laying the tracks.

The old grade heads south to MI 22, but those planning to spend the night at White Pine Campground quickly depart at another posted junction. Here the trail east (left) is marked by green "Easy" triangles. The next .5 mile is yet another change in scenery, as you enter a forest that provides more solid footing than the dunes but remains a level walk. Eventually you break out in a grassy clearing and arrive at Peterson Road, where the trail is marked on both sides by green triangles. A short walk down the road to the left is a parking area, vault toilet, more beach, and sweeping views of the bay.

East of Peterson Road, the trail remains in the lightly forested area for almost .5 mile. You then move into a thicker stand of oak and pine, where you stay until reaching the posted junction of a scenic lookout to Lake Michigan, 2.4 miles from Platte River Campground. The path to the lookout heads out of the woods and into windblown dunes, where you can view the entire bay along with the famous Sleeping Bear Dunes to the north and South Manitou Island in Lake Michigan. The main trail leaves the junction and follows a gently rolling terrain. In less than a mile, you arrive at White Pine Campground.

White Pine is located in a narrow ravine, with wooded ridges running along

Young backpackers on Platte Plains

both sides of the secluded sites. The campground offers a vault toilet, a community fire ring, and only six sites, which explains why this area is a quiet section of the park even during the busiest weekend of the summer. There is no view of the lake from the campground, but from site 6 a path wanders west through the woods and quickly breaks out into an area of wind-blown dunes. From the high perch of the dunes, you are rewarded with an immense view of the Sleeping Bear Dunes and South Manitou Island. The Lake Michigan beach, with it clear waters and sandy bottom, is just a dune or two away. Return in the evening and sit on the last dune before the beach to watch the sun melt into Lake Michigan. What more could you ask for in a campsite?

For those spending the night at White Pine, the second day involves a little over 4 miles of walking or a two- to

three-hour trek. In other words, there is no reason not to spend the morning on the beach.

From the campground, the loop continues due east. The triangles change color, from green to black, for "Advanced." It's rated primarily for skiers, but hikers will also notice that the walking is a little more strenuous. The approaching ridges and hills are ancient shoreline sand dunes and mark the position of Lake Michigan after each glacial ice melt. The steepest climb is at the beginning, and after topping off, the trail follows the crest of the ridge around a pond filled by cattails. You descend, climb again to skirt another pond, and then drop quickly to the base of that dune. The trail levels out somewhat to wind through an impressive stand of pines, and .8 mile from the campground, comes to a posted junction.

To the north (left) is the 1-mile spur to

Viewing Platte Bay and Sleeping Bear Dunes

a trailhead at Trail's End Road, but the main loop continues south (right) along a level stretch that is marked by green triangles. Here's another interesting change of scenery, as on one side of the path tower pines, with their thick understory of ferns, while on the other you pass one cattail marsh after another. The largest marsh is seen .4 mile from the last junction, and often in June wild iris can be spotted from the trail. Other marshes follow for almost the entire 1.1-mile length of this stretch.

At the junction with the second trail to Trail's End Road, head right. The next leg is a level path rated "Easy." In .3 mile, you come to Lasso Road. Turn left on the road and watch for where the trail continues on the right, marked by a locator map. The terrain remains level and is forested for a mile, then the trail begins skirting more of those ancient

lakeshore sand dunes. At one point, there are forested ridges towering over you on both sides of the path. The interesting topography suddenly ends .5 mile from Lasso Road when you pass an old rubbish heap. The trash here indicates two things: that the trail has swung close to MI 22 at this point, and that the garbage problem is so great in our society it has people dumping refuse in our national parks.

Eventually the trail climbs a ridge to skirt more marshy areas, which are visible until you drop back down into the forest and cross Peterson Road for the second time. On the other side of the road, the trail swings north and, in .3 mile, meets the old railroad gauge. Turn right here and follow the old line. Soon a posted spur will appear on the left that leads .2 mile west back to the campground.

Empire Bluff Trail

Place: Sleeping Bear Dunes National Lakeshore
Total Distance: 2 miles
Hiking Time: 1 hour
Rating: Moderate
Highpoints: Scenic vistas
Maps: USGS Empire; Empire Bluff Self-Guiding Hiking Trail
  brochure

Empire Bluff Trail is one of the shortest routes in this book but hardly lacking in outstanding hiking qualities. Few trails in Michigan and none in the southern half of the state lead to a more spectacular view at the end as does this short path to the edge of Empire Bluffs, which rise more than four hundred feet above the sandy shoreline of Lake Michigan. Add six interpretive posts and an accompanying brochure that explains the natural and geological history of the area, and you have one of the best short hikes in the state.

The National Park Service says the round trip is 1.5 miles, but I measured it as closer to 2 miles and rated it moderate due to the amount of climbing involved. You also have to keep an eye out for poison ivy, commonly seen in the open areas along the way, and should refrain from descending the sandy bluffs at the end since it will hasten erosion.

Despite the poison ivy and having to talk children out of jumping off the bluffs, this hike is still an excellent choice for families and can be done by most people in under an hour. Pack along a lunch and enjoy your peanut butter and jelly sandwiches with a view that would rival any overlook at the finest restaurants in the world. Better yet, bring a flashlight and arrive at near dusk on a clear evening for a sunset second to none.

Access: Begin at the National Park Service Visitor Center on the corner of MI 22 and MI 72 in Empire (See Old Indian Trail for access directions to Empire). The park headquarters (616-326-5134) has interesting displays and information on all the trails in the area, including the interpretive brochure for Empire Bluffs. From the visitor's center, head south on MI 22 for 1.7 miles and then west (right) on Wilco Road. The trailhead is to the left, a mile down Wilco Road. There is a small parking area with a display sign here, map box, vault toilet, and a lone picnic table next to an old stone fence.

Trail: The trail begins with an immediate uphill climb, and post 1, next to an out-of-place boulder, explains why. Glaciers that picked up rocks and soil in

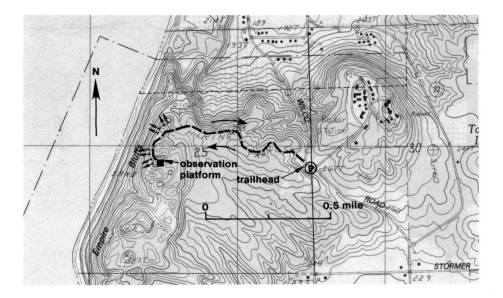

Canada and the Upper Peninsula retreated from here 11,800 years ago, leaving the debris behind as bluffs, hills, and out-of-place boulders. You move from the open fields of an old farm mentioned in post 2 to the cool shade of a beech-maple climax forest, where in May the common trillium is often seen in full bloom.

The trail levels out momentarily. As you approach post 4, which marks the location of an old orchard, you begin following the hilly terrain of perched dunes. Glimpses of the magnificent view are seen between the trees here, teasing you with what lies ahead. Eventually you descend to post 5 and then climb to 6, where you break out of the forest to witness a spectacular panorama.

It's a breathtaking sight for most hikers, many who never envisioned such a reward at the end of such a short walk. You are more than four hundred feet above the lake and can view Platte Bay to the south and the Sleeping Bear Bluffs to the north, with the famous Sleeping Bear Dune itself appearing as a small hill on top of the high, sandy ridge. Seven miles out on the horizon is South Manitou Island, and this entire picture is framed by dune grass and weathered trees.

At this point, the trail swings south and follows a boardwalk along the bluffs for 500 feet to an observation platform. Here is a hiker's bench with a view unmatched anywhere else in Michigan. You could rest here for hours. Along the boardwalk, you passed a "North Boundary Hang Gliding" sign, and it's easy to understand why this spot is such an excellent one for the sport. Between the gentle winds off Lake Michigan, the straight drop of the bluffs, and the view below, you almost feel like taking up hang gliding—almost.

Boardwalk and standing dead trees at the end of Empire Bluff Trail

Dunes Hiking Trail

Place: Sleeping Bear Dunes National Lakeshore
Total Distance: 4.5 miles (round trip)
Hiking Time: 3 to 4 hours
Rating: Challenging
Highpoints: Sand dunes, Lake Michigan shoreline
*Maps: USGS Glen Haven; The Dunes Hiking Trail map from
 the National Park Service*

This trail is undoubtedly the most popular and famous hike in Sleeping Bear Dunes National Lakeshore; or, at least, the beginning is. The Dune Climb, at the start of the park's Dunes Hiking Trail, attracts people from all around the country, who arrive to struggle up the steep slope of open sand only to then turn around and gleefully romp down it. After reaching the top of the slope, though, many do continue on toward the Lake Michigan shoreline along the route marked by blue-tipped posts.

Unfortunately, a large number of these hikers start out shirtless, hatless, and, worst of all, shoeless, and never reach beautiful Lake Michigan at the trail's end. They soon discover that trudging through soft sand up steep dunes in the hot sun is not the same as walking down a beach. This hike is challenging, and, although the park service claims its distance is 1.5 miles one way from the top of the Dune Climb to the lake, I've measured it a number of times and discovered that a round trip from the parking lot is much closer to a 4.5-mile day.

But for those who come prepared with walking shoes, sunglasses, a wide-brimmed hat, sun screen, and water, the Dunes Hiking Trail can be a most unusual trek during the summer. The rolling dunes are beautiful and vary in cover from open sand or patches of beachgrass and wildflowers to a lone cottonwood here and there. The hike is a workout for many people, but the isolated beach along Lake Michigan and its refreshing surf is a great place to recuperate before heading back along the same route.

On windy days, blowing sand makes the hike a less desirable outing, and at times the flies along the beach can be particularly ferocious. But overall this is one of the most scenic walks on the lakeshore, and by packing along a bathing suit and a beach towel you can turn this into a full-day affair. Don't forget to take along a camera. There are panoramas of Glen Lake at the beginning and the famous shoreline of the Sleeping Bear Dunes at the end.

Access: At the corner of MI 72 and MI 22 in Empire, or 22 miles west of Traverse City, is the National Park Ser-

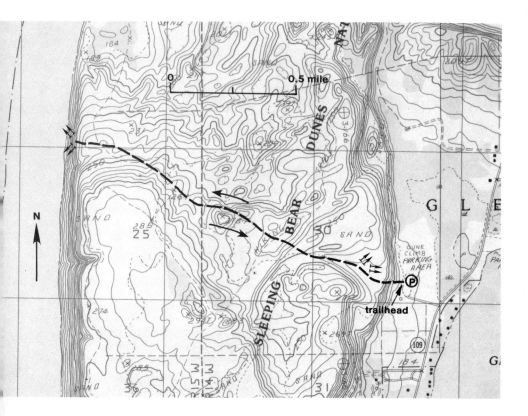

vice Visitor Center, a nautical-looking building. The center (616-326-5134) is open 9 A.M. to 5 P.M. daily and features historical and nature exhibits, a slide program, and a wallfull of free handouts on the park, including one on "The Dunes Hiking Trail." From the visitors center, head north on MI 22, veer left onto MI 109 and in about 6 miles reach "The Dune Climb."

Trail: The steep slope of the Dune Climb is only a few yards from the parking lot, store, and restrooms. It's a knee-bending ascent up the famous Dune Climb, a sandy slope of 50 or 60 degrees that rises 130 feet above the picnic area. Take your time, and remember that you are supposed to feel winded on

the way up. At the top, catch your breath and enjoy the spectacular view of Glen Lake and the rolling farmland that surrounds it.

Most people then climb the slope to the southwest, which reaches to about 890 feet and on which are benches that sit in the shade of some cottonwood trees. But a sign posted "Dunes Trail" clearly points the way across a sandy plain, where the first blue-tipped marker appears. Soon you're faced with a second dune but not nearly as steep as the Dune Climb. At the top you get your first view of the Great Lake. A sign here says, "1 mile to Lake Michigan," and many believe they are only ten or fifteen minutes from the beach. Although it might be just a mile to the lakeshore as the crow flies, it certainly is more than that as hikers walk. You're still almost 2 miles and several dunes from the water.

From this high point, you descend quickly, only to climb another dune. From here you get a much better view of what lies ahead, a rolling terrain of dunes covered with sparse beachgrass. This entire area is part of a four-square-mile tract of perched dunes on Sleeping Bear Plateau, perhaps the most impressive set within this national lakeshore that is famous for its dunes. For the next mile, you follow the posts, climbing up and down hills of sand. The trail is little more than a path of soft sand, and here is where most bare-footed and bare-chested hikers give up and turn around.

Eventually you scale a dune and are greeted with the best view of South Manitou Island, on Lake Michigan's horizon. You can even see the island's historic, one hundred-foot-high lighthouse, built in 1871 to mark the entrance of Manitou Passage. At this point, the trail descends, makes one more short climb, and then crosses a somewhat level area for .5 mile. Throughout much of June, this area is colored with wildflowers ranging from the bright yellows of hoary puccoon to the distinct oranges of wood lilies.

You don't see the beach until you're almost in the surf, but near the end of the trail the breeze becomes cooler and the sound of the surf is more distinguishable. Suddenly you're on a low bluff, looking straight down at the water and the wide band of sand making up the beach. Most people flop down on the beach right at the end of the trail, but if you walk in either direction, you should soon have a stretch all your own. To return, backtrack to the last blue-tipped post and retrace your steps.

Climbing the Dune Climb

Pyramid Point Trail

Place: Sleeping Bear Dunes National Lakeshore
Total Distance: 2.8 miles
Hiking Time: 1.5 to 2 hours
Rating: Moderate
Highpoints: Lake Michigan overlook, sand dunes
Maps: USGS Glen Arbor; Pyramid Point trail map from
  National Park Service Visitor Center

If you're lucky, while hiking Pyramid Point Trail, you'll see a hang glider strapped onto his colorful glider on the edge of a steep dune, 260 feet above Lake Michigan. With one short leap, the pilot will begin a silent journey, soaring over the light blue waters of the Manitou Passage—beautiful.

But even without a daredevil in the air, the panorama from the launching site is breathtaking and reason enough to endure the uphill climb to it. Another reason to hike this 2.8-mile loop is the diversity of terrain—grassy meadows and beech-maple forests to rolling hills and wind-blown sand dunes.

And if that isn't enough, Pyramid Point is as much off the beaten path as any spot in Sleeping Bear Dunes National Lakeshore, with the exception of the Manitou islands. While the famous "Dune Climb" is crawling with people at the height of the summer season, it's still possible to escape the crowds in this corner of the park.

The access road to the trailhead is Basch Road, a winding, dirt road that isn't plowed during the winter in this area where snowstorms sweep across Lake Michigan. But the wildflowers abound in the spring, summer is great for climbing dunes in bare feet, and autumn is brilliant with the reds of maples and yellows of beech trees. Even November has its own advantages, for the fallen leaves allow additional views from ridge tops.

Access: On the corner of MI 72 and MI 22 in Empire is the National Park Visitor Center (616-326-5134). Open daily during the summer from 9 A.M. to 8 P.M., the center has interpretive displays, brochures, and information about the entire park. From the center, head north on MI 22, and the resort town of Glen Arbor will be reached in 8 miles. Continue for another 5 miles, and when MI 22 curves to the east, look for the posted Port Oneida Road. Turn north (left) on it for 2 miles, then go east (right) on Basch Road. The dirt road climbs steadily for .3 mile until it levels out at the trailhead parking area, where there is a vault toilet, display board, and map box.

Trail: The walk begins in a grassy

meadow along an old two-track road that heads straight for a line of forested hills. Unlike other parts of the park, these are not forested dunes but are actually glacial moraines, the handiwork of Michigan's ice age ten thousand years ago. Within .2 mile, the trail begins to ascend into the hills through a beautiful stand of paper birch. You reach the first posted junction in another .2 mile.

Continue north (left) for .2 mile to reach the hang glider launch site. It's a steady march up to the 840-foot high-point, but in the end, you break out onto the sandy edge of a dune and overlook Lake Michigan. Due north is North Manitou Island, off to the east is South Manitou Island, and straight down is the Lake Michigan shoreline.

The area is posted for hang gliders, for at one time a steady stream of pilots hiked in here with their flyers. Using the wind currents that came up the side of the steep dune, the gliders flew for hours, landing in the meadow the trail crosses to the east. Their numbers are greatly reduced today since many gliders prefer flying inland, where they are towed into the air by a vehicle. Still, every once in a while a pilot can be seen getting ready for a flight or soaring in the winds off the lake.

From the viewpoint, backtrack to the posted junction and then head east. This trail begins a quick descent through a beech-maple forest and drops 130 feet before it bottoms out at the edge of the hardwoods. Just to the north, clearly visible through the trees, is a migrating dune, slowly spilling its sand into the woods. This is a perch dune, sitting on top of the Lake Michigan bluff and being pushed inland by the constant winds off the water. For many people, it's too tempting at this point not to kick off their boots and scramble up the

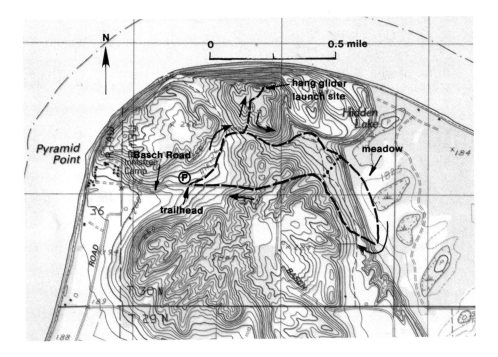

Overlook on a perched dune

slope of warm sand to see the view from the top.

But the trail swings away from the advancing dune to arrive shortly at a posted junction. The path to the west (right) is a cutoff spur, but the meadow is reached by continuing south. Another rapid drop must be negotiated before the trail bottoms out and enters the meadow, an open area created when farmers arrived here after the Civil War. The last farm was gone by the 1930s. Today the meadow is a beautiful spot, a grassy area hemmed in by forested dunes on one side and framed by birch and beech on the other. Blue standards lead you through the length of the meadow and re-direct you back into the woods at its south end.

The trail now regains all the elevation lost on the previous leg. But the .4-mile ascent is a scenic one if the leaves have already dropped, for you can view the entire meadow along with the Lake Michigan shoreline. At the posted junction, you head west (left) for the final leg to Basch Road. This stretch holds the steepest climb of the day, with a deep ravine running along the south side of the trail. Within .3 mile of the last junction, you break out at the dirt road, where a triangle directs you to head west (right). It's a downhill walk along Basch Road for .4 mile to the trailhead parking area.

North Manitou Island

Place: Sleeping Bear Dunes National Lakeshore
Total Distance: 15 miles
Hiking Time: 3 days
Rating: Moderate to challenging
Highpoints: Lake Michigan shoreline, dunes, backcountry
  camping
Maps: USGS North Manitou Island; National Park Service's
  North Manitou Island brochure

When a trail on the west side of North Manitou Island swung close to the Lake Michigan shoreline, the beach route was too inviting for a pair of backpackers to resist. They left the trail and took to the beach, hiking several miles along the sandy avenue until they reached the rugged, northwest corner of this fifteen thousand-acre island. Here they pitched their tent on a bluff, then climbed high onto a wind-blown sand dune where, miles from anybody, they watched the oranges, reds, pinks, and purples of a spectacular sunset melt into the Great Lake. It was almost 11 P.M. before the show was over.

North Manitou Island offers hikers the best wilderness experience in southern Michigan. The island is not only isolated from the mainland and undeveloped but is preserved by the National Park Service (NPS) as part of the Sleeping Bear Dunes National Lakeshore. Among the strict rules the NPS enforces is a ban on motors, off-road vehicles, mountain bikes, even wheeled carts used for portaging boats to Lake Manitou.

Although some visitors reach the island in private boats, the island offers no protected anchorage, and the vast majority of hikers arrive at this Lake Michigan wilderness through a ferry service out of Leland. The ferry runs only three times a week, forcing hikers to stay at least two nights, but any less time here would be a mistake.

North Manitou is seven-and-a-half-miles long, four-miles wide, and laced with more than twenty-two miles of designated trail, posted with directional and mileage signs. Even more unsigned trails exist, and all paths are either old roads or railroad grades. The trails wind through impressive stands of maple and beech, through clearings that used to be farm fields, past serene Lake Manitou, and over the open dunes at the southern end of the island. The highest point on North Manitou is 1,001 feet above sea level, a rather remote spot in the northwest corner that few hikers ever reach. Overall, the hiking is surprisingly level, and the trails are not difficult to follow. But the park service urges

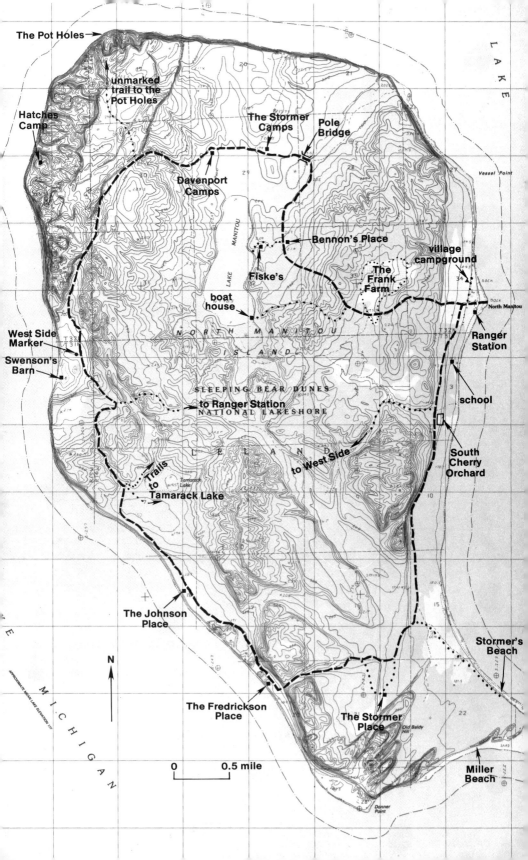

everybody visiting the island to pack along a compass, especially those who plan to hike cross-country or follow the unsigned paths.

Along with the dunes, great sunsets, and scenic places to pitch a tent, another intriguing aspect of North Manitou is the visible signs of its past. A trip around the island reveals abandoned buildings, old cemeteries, forgotten orchards, and other relics. The heyday of North Manitou was at the turn of the century when loggers arrived and cut much of the island's original stand of timber. Others followed to farm the area or plant apple and cherry orchards. The U.S. Lifesaving Service manned a station here, including a lighthouse on Dimmick's Point, to protect shipping through the wicked Manitou Passage.

By the 1920s, however, most of the island was under single ownership, and it was used primarily as a private hunting preserve until the park acquired control in 1984. To improve the hunting, seven whitetail deer—five bucks and two does—were released in 1927, and the small herd, without any natural predators, exploded to more than two thousand by the 1980s. Today, parts of North Manitou's forests, particularly in the rugged northwest corner, are almost devoid of an understory, giving them a park-like appearance. Controlling the herd is the main reason the state of Michigan conducts special deer hunts on North Manitou every year.

Other wildlife that might be seen include chipmunks and raccoons, both of which are encountered too frequently to be natural. Raccoons have become very troublesome to backpackers since they invade packs and food supplies. There are stories every summer of how they even unzipped tents to steal food bags and packs. For this reason, rangers urge visitors to hang food between two trees, five feet from the ground and five feet from the nearest branch, almost as if you were in bear country.

Keep in mind that fires are not allowed on the island outside of a community fire ring in the Village Campground. Bring a backpacker's stove or feast on cold meals. The only safe water supply is at the ranger station; all other water should be treated. You can camp anywhere on the island except within sight or sound of a building, a major trail, or another camper, within three hundred feet of an inland water source (lake or stream), or on the beach along Lake Michigan. Pack all trash out; if you bury it, the raccoons will dig it up. And don't bring your pet.

The ranger station is located in what is referred to as the "Village," a cluster of buildings on the east side of the island. There are no stores or accommodations here, but there is an eight-site campground and a dock. At one time the ferries from Leland landed here, but in recent years a sand bar developed in front of the dock, forcing them to make an on-beach landing at the southeast corner of the island. There is talk of extending the dock out beyond the sand bar, but since it would be a one million dollar project, it probably won't happen anytime soon. For that reason, this hike is described in a counterclockwise direction and as a three-day walk, beginning with the trek to the Village.

Access: Manitou Island Transit provides ferry transportation to both Manitou islands and departs from Leland, a small resort town on the west side of the Leelanau Peninsula, 24 miles north of Traverse City via MI 22 and MI 204. Tickets can be purchased at The Pot Hole gift shop, located in Leland's quaint Fishtown area, and ferries depart from the wharf right behind it. Either write to Manitou Island Transit, P.O. Box

591, Leland, MI 49654; or call the ferry at (616) 256-9061 or (616) 271-4217 to get exact sailing times and to make reservations. The boat runs from May through November but only maintains a scheduled service from June through August, when it departs at 9:30 A.M. on Sunday, Wednesday, and Friday. It reaches the island at about 11 A.M. and immediately turns around and heads back.

Until either the dock in front of the ranger station is extended or the sand bar miraculously disappears, the ferry to North Manitou makes a beach landing at the southeast corner of the island. Depending on wind and weather conditions, the boat lands either on the east side of Dimmick's Point at what is referred to as Stormer's Beach or on the west side at Miller's Beach. Rangers meet every boat and lead backpackers through a quick orientation, which includes filling out backcountry permits. Hikers leaving the island meet at Bourniques farm, where a ranger leads the departing group to the proper beach.

For more information on North Manitou, either stop at the Sleeping Bear Dunes National Lakeshore Visitor Center in Empire or call the park headquarters at (616) 326-5134.

Trail: Once on the island, you can hike the trails in any direction, and many backpackers make a beeline to the west side where some of the most scenic campsites in Michigan are found. But the entire loop is covered here and described in a counterclockwise direction. This direction is the easiest way to hike the route, and it puts you in the southwest corner of the island the night before the ferry departs. The next morning you are faced with only a two- or three-mile walk to catch the boat, which departs at about 11 A.M. This is one

ferry you don't want to miss. It can be a long three days if you do.

East Side

Distances from Bourniques:
To Village Campground: 4 miles
To Lake Manitou: 6.7 miles
To Pole Bridge: 7.2 miles

After landing, a ranger greets all backpackers, and, among other things, informs them that Dimmick's Point is closed to the public from May 1 to August 15 because of the endangered piper plover, who uses it as a nesting area. The lighthouse and lightkeeper's residence were located here, but the tower has long since fallen into the lake and little remains. Heading north from Stormer's Beach, you follow an old road that skirts the lake and, in .7 mile, comes to Bourniques Place, where there is a picturesque weathered farmhouse and barn in a clearing. Here is where departing visitors gather, and a sign announces which beach the boat will arrive at that day.

The trail remains in the clearing and soon passes an old cemetery, where two family graveyard fences can be seen along with several headstones that date back to as early as 1906. Two miles from Dimmick's Point, or 1.3 miles from Stormer's Beach where the ferry lands, you reach the first posted junction of the route. Here signs point to the ranger station, 3.3 miles to the north (right), and to the Fredrickson Place, a popular camping area, 2 miles to the west (left). Turn right for the ranger station.

You are now on the main trail, which at this point is a wide, unmistakeable path heading north through a beech-maple forest. It is surprisingly level, considering that you are skirting the base of a seventy- to two hundred-foot-high ridge. The trail does make a short climb, though, 1.3 miles from the trail junction. You finally break out of the forest after the climb to pass through the South Cherry Orchard, where a few of the old trees can still be seen. The next posted junction is around the bend. Heading west (left) is a signed trail that cuts across the center of the island to reach the clearing around the old Swenson's farm in 5 miles. To the north is the ranger station, reached in 1.3 miles. But you first pass through another orchard, where a sign indicates a spur to an old school. The ruins lie just a short walk off the main trail and amount to little more than a pile of lumber and a few bricks on a stone foundation. There is, however, a good view of Lake Michigan and plenty of space to make a camp. In fact, camping opportunities are plentiful on the northeast side of Manitou Island. They include setting up your tent near the Great Lake, staying at the Village Campground, following the trail just north of the Village to spend the night near Vessel Point, or camping near Lake Manitou.

In less than a mile farther north, you break out of the woods into the twenty-seven-acre clearing around the Village, much of it an old airstrip. Along the lakeshore is a row of white buildings, including the ranger station where, on the side of the old house, is a water faucet with the only safe drinking water on the island. Next door is the oldest building on the island, which once served the U.S. Lifesaving Service. Later, according to some folks, it was known as the "Loaf House," where island residents gathered in the evening to play cards and socialize. The beach along the Village, like along most of the island, is a beautiful stretch of sand decorated with small pebbles and bleached driftwood. Across the lake is the light blue water of the Manitou Passage and the mainland on the horizon. A map box can be found next to the National Park Service dock.

Leave the Village on a trail that heads west past the maintenance building and its trash containers, quickly to come to a posted four-way junction. To the north a short way is the Village Campground, where you'll find eight numbered sites and community fire rings. Another signed trail continues from the campground to the junction at Pole Bridge. To the south, the Fredrickson Place lies 8.5 miles away, while due west, though it's not posted, is the signed trail to Lake Manitou. The lake is a serene body of water and a nice alternative to setting up a tent in the campground. The trail makes a gentle climb across the old airstrip in the middle of the Village clearing and then returns to the woods. Within a mile from the dock, you break out into the old apple orchard of the Frank Farm. Just beyond it is an old sign that says simply "Lake." This is the side trail to a spot on Lake Manitou known as the Boat House. Though the structure is no longer there, the area is still a nice spot to camp.

In another mile from the junction to the Boat House, you arrive at the clearing known as Bennon's Place. Heading west (left) from here is another foot trail to the lakeshore. You can camp here at Bennon's, in a small clearing closer to the lake known as Fiskes, or anywhere that is three hundred feet from the water. Be wary of the raccoons, however, for they are more aggressive and plentiful along the lake than anywhere else on the island.

The trail from Fiskes ends at the water, but a rough trail skirts the lakeshore in both directions. To the south is an old boathouse and even a boat rotting away on the bank, indications that the fishing here is pretty good. Large schools of perch and panfish can be found in Lake Manitou, and largemouth bass as well. The most successful anglers are those who haul in a belly boat or an inflatable raft, or even those that wade to reach the deeper sections of the lake away from the shore. If those options are not open to you, hike along the lake and find a drop-off or weedline within casting distance.

Continuing along the main trail from Bennon's Place, you head north through two more clearings. In .8 mile, you reach the posted junction at the Pole Bridge, which really isn't a bridge at all but rather a culvert over a stream in a large swamp. Here another signed trail to the right leads back to the ranger station.

West Side

Distances from Pole Bridge:
To Swenson's: 4.5 miles
To Fredrickson Place: 8 miles
To Bourniques: 10 miles

Backpackers passing packs to shore

At the Pole Bridge, a sign points left to the west side, technically a marker in the middle of the Swenson's clearing, 3.5 miles away. The trail departs due west and begins as a level route. Within .6 mile it breaks out in the Stormer Camps. The grassy clearing features a handful of old cars and even a set of wagon wheels half hidden along its edge. The hike remains level for another .5 mile, when the trail reaches the Davenport Camps. From here you begin a steady ascent.

Just before a bluff closes in on each side of the trail, you pass an unsigned trail to the Pot Holes. The spur is hard to spot and easy to miss if you're not looking for it. It's a rugged mile to the depressions and involves a little bush-whacking at the end. If you make the attempt to reach them, have a compass in hand and veer left when you come to a junction. Eventually, you'll stumble over them. Whether they are worth the effort is debatable. Some say the Pot Holes are little more than "forested gullies."

The main trail begins to curve south as it passes through the most rugged section of North Manitou. The route is actually an old railroad grade, and it's easy to envision the tracks running through the hills to a logger's camp

somewhere. Here, more than anywhere on the island, deer have consumed almost every plant and sapling on the ground. It's eerie to be able to see so well in a forest with trees so old. This overbrowsing by the animals is of much concern to the National Park Service, since it does not allow new trees to replace the old ones that die.

Two miles from the Pole Bridge, the trail begins a rapid descent, which provides the rationale for walking this stretch from east to west. Within a mile you break out into a long, narrow clearing. On the other side of the clearing, you re-enter the woods briefly, then reach the northern edge of Swenson's clearing. This clearing is huge, more than .5-mile long, and a favored spot among backpackers to spend the night. Even from the trail you can see glimpses of Lake Michigan, but if you cut across to the beach, you'll be greeted with an excellent view of South Manitou Island and the perched dunes on its west side.

In the middle of the clearing is the "West Side" marker, while at the south end are the ruins of the Swenson's farm, including a very impressive barn. All around are wild strawberry plants and raspberry patches. Camping spots abound here, and a pleasant afternoon can be spent hiking the beach north to view the steep bluffs at this corner of the island and climbing the dunes that cut into them. Two miles to the north along the beach is Hatches Camp, a group of three buildings that are not marked and difficult to find. If you camp in Swenson's, it's 5 miles to Bourniques or about a 3-hour hike to reach the ferry the next morning.

The main trail cuts through the clearing, swings back into the woods before reaching the Swenson's barn, follows what is obviously the raised bed of the old railroad line, and within .5 mile reaches a posted junction. To the east is the signed trail that cuts across the middle of the island to reach the ranger station in 5.5 miles. The main trail heads west at first, then south, before coming to an unmarked junction with three more trails, 1.6 miles from Swenson's clearing. The first two veer off to the east and southeast towards Tamarack Lake; with a little searching for an old trail on the lake's north side, you can make a loop out of these trails. The main trail is easy to identify and heads due south. Within .5 mile, views of Lake Michigan open up between the trees.

You are actually on a bluff above the lake, and you remain on this bluff until you descend into the Johnson Place, reached 2.6 miles from the Swenson's clearing or 6.1 miles from the Pole Bridge. The trail departs from here and, at one point, passes some dunes pouring down between the trees, an indication that you are close to the lakeshore, but the trail then swings inland. It's 1.2 miles from the Johnson Place to the Fredrickson Place along the trail. Given a little adventurous spirit, you could just as easily follow the beach from one clearing to the next. In fact, there have been hikers who have walked the entire beach around the island and skipped the trails altogether, a 27-mile trek.

There are no buildings at Fredrickson Place, but there are some beautiful spots in which to pitch a tent. Here you can set up camp on a grassy bluff high above the lakeshore and have an incredible view of South Manitou Island and the mainland from your sleeping bag. A scenic walk, after dropping the pack, is to head south along the beach to Donner's Point, stopping along the way to climb Old Baldy, an open dune

Trail marker on North Manitou Island

that rises almost 140 feet above Lake Michigan.

The North Manitou Island loop is completed by a 2-mile hike on to Bourniques Place on the trail to Dimmick's Point. There is a short climb as you ascend into Cat Hole clearing, but soon the trail levels out. The rest of it remains a pleasant, wooded hike. Along the way, you pass two unmarked trails that form a loop to the south through the Stormer Place. Soon after the second trail enters the main trail, you reach the junction to Dimmick's Point, where you turn right to meet the ranger in charge of the day's departure at Bourniques Place.

South Manitou Island

Place: Sleeping Bear Dunes National Lakeshore
Total Distance: 9 miles
Hiking Time: 4 to 5 hours (two-day stay)
Rating: Challenging
Highpoints: Scenic vistas, beach hiking, shipwreck
Maps: USGS South Manitou Island

No other hike in southern Michigan matches this trek on South Manitou Island. Within a nine-mile loop, you pass a shipwreck, travel through a virgin stand of white cedar, trudge up sand dunes to spectacular views, rest on isolated beaches, and end it all by climbing up the tower of a historic lighthouse. What more could you possibly want in a hike? How about backpacking opportunities at some of the most scenic campsites in the state? An inland lake that never experiences much fishing pressure? Spectacular sunsets?

South Manitou Island is a day hiker's paradise much like its sister island, North Manitou, is a haven for backpackers. The 5,260-acre island is administered by the National Park Service as part of the Sleeping Bear Dunes National Lakeshore but is only about a third of the size of North Manitou. Located only seven miles off Sleeping Bear Point on the mainland, South Manitou is the southernmost island of a Lake Michigan archipelago that stretches all the way to the Straits of Mackinac. The island's west side features perched dunes that rise more than four hundred

feet above Lake Michigan. Florence Lake lies on the south side, old farms and other remains of the island's past are scattered throughout, and some of the most beautiful beaches in Michigan form the shoreline.

Like North Manitou, the vast majority of campers and hikers reach the island on a ferry that departs from Leland's Fishtown. It's a ninety-minute trip, and along the way you will view Sleeping Bear Dunes, North Manitou's scenic west shore, and North Manitou Shoal Light in the middle of the Manitou Passage. The trip is very scenic on a nice day and an excellent way to begin any island adventure.

Unlike North Manitou, you can only camp in three designated campgrounds: Weather Station, Bay, and Popple. But all three are extremely scenic, each overlooking Lake Michigan or lying a few steps away from its golden beaches. They provide fire rings, water pumps, and numbered sites. You hike to the campgrounds from the ferry dock. Weather Station is the closest at 1.1 miles, and Popple, the furthest is 3.5 miles away and, thus, is the least used.

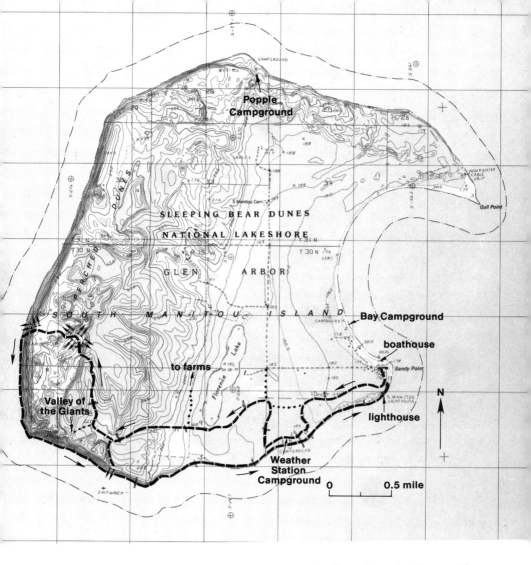

Although camping is restricted to the campgrounds, they are strategically located so that an excellent two- or three-day trek can be planned by walking the shoreline from Weather Station to Popple and eventually back to the ranger station and dock. The only potential problem with this twenty-mile hike would be the log jams between the steep shoreline bluffs and Lake Michigan.

Most visitors simply hike to the *Francisco Morazan,* the shipwrecked freighter along the south shore, then head back. They thus miss the most impressive area of the island — the perched dunes. The nine-mile hike described here extends beyond the shipwreck and crosses the dunes before returning to Lake Michigan. You return along the shoreline for an excellent beach hike and the best view of the grounded freighter.

Technically, this walk is a day hike. But note that the ferry arrives around 11:30 A.M. and leaves at 4 P.M. You thus have roughly four hours to walk nine miles. Those in good hiking shape will be able to complete the loop, but most people will find themselves standing on the shore, watching the boat head back toward Leland. The best way to undertake this route, then, is to camp at Weather Station. That afternoon you can hike the rest of the loop, timing your return along the shoreline so that you catch the sun setting over Lake Michigan.

Camping is free on the island, but you must pick up a backcountry permit at the ranger station after arriving there. The station and ferry dock are located at Sandy Point, along with the trailhead for all routes across the island. Also located here is a visitor's center with historical displays, a modern bathroom, picnic tables, and the historical South Manitou Island Lighthouse. There is no store on the island, so bring all your own supplies, food, and equipment.

Access: Manitou Island Transit provides passenger ferry transportation to South Manitou Island. The ferry departs from Leland, a small resort town on the west side of the Leelanau Peninsula 24 miles north of Traverse City via MI 22 and MI 204. Tickets can be purchased at The Pot Hole gift shop, located in Leland's quaint Fishtown area. The ferries depart from the wharf right behind the shop. Either write to Manitou Island Transit, P.O. Box 591, Leland, MI 49654 or call the ferry at (616) 256-9061 or (616) 271-4217 to get exact sailing times and to make reservations. The boat runs daily from June through August, and on Friday through Monday along with Wednesday in May, September, and October. It departs at 10 A.M. and reaches the island around 11:30 A.M., where it docks until its departure between 3:30 P.M. and 4 P.M.

There are approximately three miles of dirt road on South Manitou, and Manitou

Island Transit runs a motorized tour past sights such as the old school, the farms, and the cemetery of a farming community that once existed here. The company also offers a lift to hikers out to where the trail swings close to the road, which shaves off the first mile of the walk. Check with transit officials on the way over for details.

For more information on South Manitou before your trip, either stop at the Sleeping Bear Dunes National Lakeshore Visitor Center in Empire or call the park headquarters at (616) 326-5134.

Trail: After stepping off the ferry, you head up the dock to the boathouse that was built in 1901 as part of the U.S. Lifesaving Station established here. South Manitou was once a crucial place for Great Lakes shippers, who used Manitou Passage to shave off fifty to sixty miles of travel. The bay where you landed was the only deep water harbor from here to Chicago, and from 1860 to the early 1900s, so many ships sought its protection that it was often referred to as the "Forest of Masts."

The surf boat used to rescue sailors still sits inside the boathouse, but of more interest to many hikers is the three-dimensional map that shows the rugged contour of the island. Rangers conduct a brief orientation for both hikers and campers, hand out backcountry permits and maps, and send the newly arrived visitors on their way. Head towards the lighthouse, going past the visitor's center with the old farm equipment on display outside, and within 200 yards is the posted junction to Weather Station Campground.

The trail quickly leaves the open shoreline of the island and becomes a cool forest walk, passing an old cottage along the way. In less than a mile you come to a posted junction with a spur that heads south to the campground. It's still another .5 mile to the facility, which features more than thirty group and individual sites along with a water pump and vault toilets. Some of the sites are in a lightly shaded area where you can stand on the bluff and view Sleeping Bear Dunes across the passage or a beautiful bay and beach below you. These are spectacular campsites, some of the best in the state, and are always the first to be occupied.

From this group of campsites, a trail heads due north, past the hand pump for water, and ends at a posted junction with the main trail in .4 mile. Head west (left) and in a few steps you reach a second junction where a sign says that the perched dunes are still a 2.1-mile walk away. The main trail is actually an old road, so it's wide and level, making for pleasant hiking. In a mile from the campground, you skirt the south end of Florence Lake. The long, narrow, but scenic lake has an undeveloped shoreline, clear water, and a sandy bottom. Bass anglers, especially those who pack in a belly boat, will be attracted to the patches of pencil reeds and other aquatic plants just off the shore.

A posted trail heads north to the farms at the next junction, reached in .2 mile, while the main route west passes an open field, site of the first farm on the island. Both are testimonies to the rich farming history South Manitou enjoyed from the turn of the century until the late 1940s. The early settlers quickly discovered that the island was an excellent place to raise experimental seeds and crops, because the plants were isolated from alien pollens on the mainland. South Manitou farmers soon became known throughout the Midwest as producers of prize Russian rye and hybrid beans and peas. At the 1920 Chicago International Livestock Exposition, a crop of South Manitou Russian

Hiker viewing a ship-wrecked freighter

rye won top honors. By 1948, however, due to the dwindling shipping traffic, only two farms were still active.

In another .5 mile from the junction to the farms, you reach the spur to the shipwreck. The side trail is a short walk and ends at an overlook and interpretive display, with the boat visible out in Lake Michigan. Before you shoot a roll of film, keep in mind that the best views of the wreck are seen from the beach on the return portion of the trip. The next posted junction is only .3 mile further down the trail and is the spur to the Valley of the Giants. Bugs can be murderous here, but these trees should not be missed. The stand of virgin white cedar, estimated to be more than five hundred years old, is impressive, especially the North American champion white cedar that is only ninety feet but has a trunk that measures more than seventeen feet in circumference.

Just the fact that these trees are still standing is amazing. From 1840 to 1917, South Manitou was an important refueling stop for the woodburning steamships that sailed the Great Lakes. Almost all the island's original timber was cut for those boilers, except for this stand. Why the sailors passed over these cedars has been debated. Some believe they were too remote from the docks at Sand Point, while others say that the dune sand embedded in the bark discouraged loggers.

Campsite overlooking lake Michigan

After the spur to the cedars, the main trail narrows again in .2 mile, indicating that the majority of hikers have already turned back. In another quarter mile, you begin a steep climb up a soft, sandy path. You ascend almost 150 feet, then break out of the trees and into the perched dunes. It's an amazing scene. When you top off on a dune at 924 feet, you can view all of South Manitou as well as North Manitou to the north, the bluffs of Sleeping Bear Dune to the south, Pyramid Point and Leland to the east, and much of the mainland shoreline. A million dollar view that cost you only the price of a ferry ticket.

Most of the dunes are covered by grass, but here and there are the stark white trunks of the "Ghost" forests, stands of trees that were killed by the migrating sand. Continuing west towards Lake Michigan, you see one dune crowned by trees. Referred to by some as the "Island of Trees," this is South Manitou's highpoint at 1,014 feet. Even more impressive is the bowl of sand you climb through that ends at the edge of the steep bluff. More than three hundred feet almost straight down is the Lake Michigan shoreline. The bluff ranks right up there with those seen at Pyramid Point, Sleeping Bear Dune, or the Log Slide at Pictured Rocks in the Upper Peninsula. Many people feel like running and jumping down it while yelling "Look Ma! I can fly!" It's best not to, though. This high ridge was formed by a tilted layer of limestone that the glaciers buried under a blanket of glacial debris. Winds off Lake Michigan have built these rare perched dunes, and their existence is fragile. When descending to the beach, it is best to avoid running straight down, which promotes erosion, but rather to hike diagonally toward the water to avoid disturbing the sand as much as possible. At the bottom, you'll

discover one of the most remote beaches in Michigan, and if you're not in a hurry to catch the ferry, plan to spend a few hours here.

Skinny dipping, anyone?

By following the beach to the north, you will reach Popple Campground after a 6-mile hike. To the south (left) is the shipwreck and a quick return to Sand Point. Hike south along the beach, with that impressive bluff towering over you on one side and Lake Michigan lapping at your boots, or maybe by now your feet, on the other side. In .5 mile, the sandy beach becomes more rocky as you begin to hike around the southwest corner of the island, and eventually you clear the point to see the wreck.

It's another .5 mile to get directly across from the grounded ship, the middle third of which still stands above the water less than one hundred yards offshore. The *Francisco Morazan* departed Chicago on November 27, 1960, and was bound for Holland with 940 tons of cargo, a crew of thirteen, its captain, and his pregnant wife. The next day it ran into forty-mile-per-hour winds, snow, and fog that made a virtual whiteout. The captain thought he was rounding Beaver Island, more than one hundred miles away, when he ran aground. A Coast Guard cutter and helicopter rescued the fifteen persons, but the wreck was left behind to be forever battered by Lake Michigan. Now it's probably the most popular destination for hikers on the island.

The wreck moves out of view when you round the next point south, and then you come to the only log jam on this side of the island. Here a mass of cedars have tumbled down the bluff to block the beach. You must either get your feet wet by wading around them or climb the bluff. For me, getting my feet wet and stubbing a few toes on rocks beats climbing any day. In the middle of this bay is one of the many abandoned buildings still remaining on the island. Around the next point is Weather Station Campground, a 3-mile walk from where you descended from the dunes. Actually, the campground is up on the bluff, but you'll know the spot. There'll be more than one camper lying out on the beach.

You can either rejoin the trail or continue along the shore. The beach is actually the shorter route to Sand Point and maybe a more scenic one. For most of the way, you can see the top of the lighthouse sticking out above the trees. The original tower was built here in 1839 — the first light on Lake Michigan and one of the earliest ones on the Great Lakes. This one replaced it in 1871, and its one hundred-foot tower and Fresnel lens from Paris made it a superior structure. It could well withstand the violent winds of Lake Michigan. The walls of the tower are eighteen-feet thick at the base and taper to two feet, four inches at the top, and they are hollow inside, allowing them to sway in the wind. The spiral staircase inside is not attached to the walls, which allows it to move as well.

It's 125 steps to the top platform, but the view is worth every one of them. The lighthouse is usually locked, but several times a day rangers give a presentation about it that ends with a climb to the top. Check the bulletin board near the boathouse for the exact times each day.

Mud Lake Trail

Place: Leelanau State Park
Total Distance: 4 miles
Hiking Time: 2 to 3 hours
Rating: Moderate
Highpoints: Lake Michigan shoreline, scenic overlook
Maps: USGS Northport; Leelanau State Park map

Most people heading to Leelanau State Park drive to the northern tip of Michigan's "Little Finger" so that they can view the historic Grand Traverse Lighthouse, look for Petoskey stones along the pebbled beach, or pitch a tent in the rustic campground. Hikers, however, stop four miles short of Lighthouse Point and head west towards Cathead Bay. Surrounding the scenic bay is the bulk of the 1,253-acre park, including its six-mile network of trails.

Other than a parking lot, this non-motorized area is undeveloped, consisting of low dunes forested predominately in hardwoods of maple, beech, white ash, and paper birch. Towards the water, the forest gives way to open dunes covered only by patches of beachgrass, shrubs, and a few cottonwoods. Then, at the shoreline itself, you find a beautiful beach with fine sand and often a gentle surf. The other spectacular aspect of this area is the sunsets, where on a clear evening the fiery orb melts in Lake Michigan, silhouetting the nearby Fox Islands.

Although there are five named trails within the network, the system basically forms a four-mile loop using the Lake Michigan Trail and Mud Lake Trail, with three crossover spurs in the middle. Loops as short as 1.5 miles can thus be enjoyed, while the trek described here makes for a pleasant three-hour walk or even a full day outing if combined with an extended break on the beach.

Birders congregate here in the spring to walk out to an old observation dock on Mud Lake, which attracts a variety of waterfowl, while the hardwoods, whose colors generally peak in early October, make this trail an excellent choice in the fall. The most popular use of this undeveloped tract is for cross-country skiing in the winter; but come summer, it's hard to imagine a better destination for a hike than the somewhat isolated beaches of Cathead Bay.

Access: The park is located at the northern tip of the Leelanau Peninsula, a 30-mile drive from Traverse City along MI 22. In Northport, continue north along MI 201 and then County Road 629 for another 4 miles. A sign for the trailhead is posted on County Road 629, just past Woolsey Airport, and is reached by turning left on Densmore

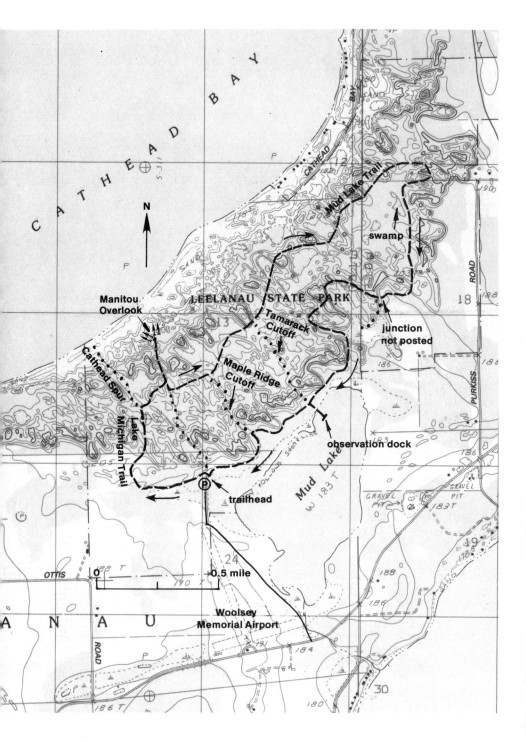

C A T H E A D   B A Y

N

Mud Lake Trail

swamp

Manitou
Overlook

LEELANAU STATE PARK

Tamarack
Cutoff

junction
not posted

Cathead Spur

Maple Ridge
Cutoff

Lake Michigan Trail

observation dock

Mud Lake

trailhead

GRAVEL
PIT

GRAVEL
PIT

OTTIS

0   0.5 mile

24

Woolsey
Memorial Airport

A N A U

ROAD

202 *Sleeping Bear Dunes*

Road and following it to a parking area at the end.

The rest of the park and the park office (616-386-5422) is another 4 miles north on County Road 629. A daily vehicle permit or annual state park pass are required to enter either section, and there is an additional fee for those who want to spend a night in the campground at Lighthouse Point. No camping is allowed in the Cathead Bay area.

Trail: In the parking area is a large display map of the trail system, and smaller but similar ones are placed at most of the junctions. The maps will indicate an approximation of where you are, but keep in mind that the network has been re-routed slightly since they were posted. Three trails depart from near the trailhead sign: Mud Lake Trail, a direct route to the Manitou Overlook, and Lake Michigan Trail (the recommended beginning for this hike). The latter is marked by a light blue bootprint and departs the area due west (left).

Lake Michigan Trail provides the shortest avenue to the beach and begins as a level walk through a pine/hardwood stand that keeps you well shaded from the sun. At .6 mile, you pass the first of several benches and hike through a series of forested dunes. The ridges actually rise above you on both sides of the trail, but the trek remains surprisingly level. Within a mile from the trailhead, you arrive at the junction with Cathead Spur, the beach access trail.

Regardless of what the park map says, it's close to .5 mile out to the bay, along a path that begins in the forest but suddenly breaks out of the trees into open dunes. If it's summer, you'll make the transition from cool forest to the brilliant sunlight and hot sand of the dunes in three steps or less. Yellow posts lead you across the low, rolling dunes to Cathead Bay, a spectacular spot to unroll a beach towel. Only a few cottages are visible to the east; to the west is Cathead Point, and out on the horizon of Lake Michigan lie the Fox Islands.

Backtrack on the spur trail and turn left to continue on Lake Michigan Trail. The trail climbs over a low dune and, in .25 mile, reaches the next junction, Manitou Overlook Spur. This side trail to the left is an uphill walk, including a long staircase at the end, to a wooden observation platform and bench from where you can view the edge of the forest, open dunes, and the shoreline. Although it's called Manitou Overlook, the most prominent landmark you see in Lake Michigan is the Fox Islands, and in the still of a quiet morning, they often appear to be floating on a layer of mist and fog.

Back on Lake Michigan Trail, the junction to Mud Lake Trail, marked by orange bootprints, is just beyond (south of) the spur to the overlook and heads northeast (left). Turn onto Mud Lake Trail and hike a level, .2 mile to Maple Ridge Cutoff. There, near the posted map, is a bench overlooking several impressive paper birch trees. The crossover trail leaving to the right heads .75 mile south to the parking area. To continue this hike, stay on Mud Lake Trail as it travels its level course to Tamarack Cutoff, reached in another .2 mile. Stay on Mud Lake Trail here as well.

Most of the trails are wide tracts to accommodate both hikers and skiers, but the northern half of Mud Lake suddenly changes to a true footpath as it winds among several forested dunes. No views of the water can be had from here, but the terrain is still interesting, and at one point, you seem to be in a natural amphitheater as the ridges tower above you on three sides. At 2.5 miles from the trailhead (not including spurs to

Cathead Bay

the beach or overlook), the trail swings south and begins the steepest climb of the day. You descend to a marsh, skirt it, and then follow a boardwalk to cut across the middle of it.

Across the swamp, you quickly come to the first junction not posted with a map. One trail extends along a level course straight ahead, and the other climbs the ridge. Despite what common sense tells you, start climbing. The trail was recently rebuilt, with the new stretch a scenic walk along the crest of a dune. Three times you cross boardwalks built to prevent excessive erosion to the deli-cate sides of the dune by hikers. You then descend to the marshy north end of Mud Lake.

The trail parallels the lake, and within .3 mile, you pass the southern end of Tamarack Cutoff. Nearby, but not marked, is a spur to the observation dock that extends out onto the water. The dock can sometimes be partially under the water, but it still provides the best view of this shallow lake. From here, it's less than .5 mile until Mud Lake Trail emerges into the open area around the parking lot.

Pere Marquette

41

Pine Valleys Pathway

Place: Pere Marquette State Forest
Total Distance: 4.1 miles
Hiking Time: 3 to 4 hours
Rating: Moderate
Highpoints: Inland lakes, backcountry campsites
Maps: USGS Stewart Lake; Pine Valleys Pathway map

Lake County's Lost Lake isn't really lost, just well hidden in Pere Marquette State Forest by a shoreline of high bluffs. Travelers zipping along nearby MI 37 may be oblivious to this small but scenic body of water; but for hikers who make an effort to locate the trailhead, the lake is easy to find and well worth the effort expended to reach it.

The water of Lost Lake is clear, and the shoreline is sprinkled with fallen trees and other structures, making this an attractive destination for any walk-in angler. All but one corner of the lake has a shoreline of steep bluffs, and on that corner the DNR's Forest Management Division has built a five-site backcountry campground where the door of every tent has a scenic view of the water.

Built in the mid-1970s, Pine Valleys Pathway is actually a network of three loops, with the northern and southern loops passing near or through numerous clear-cut areas. The most pleasant hike is the 4.1-mile middle loop, which travels the bluffs above Lost Lake before heading back.

Keep in mind that 7 Mile Road continues as a dirt road beyond the trailhead and runs near the trail at certain points. For this reason, no doubt, off-road-vehicle (ORV) destruction is very noticeable in places, particularly along the southern loop. The pathway also draws an occasional mountain biker or horseback rider from the camp on Stewart Lake. If you walk this trail in the middle of the summer, however, you'll probably have the path as well as the lakeside campground to yourself.

Access: The pathway is in the northern portion of Lake County, 13 miles north of Baldwin or a half-hour drive west of Cadillac. From MI 55, head south for 9 miles along MI 37, then turn east onto 7 Mile Road, which is posted for the park. The dirt road passes a few homes and then comes to a large, grassy parking area on its south (right) side. The trailhead is posted here by the locator map.

If coming from the south, keep in mind that the DNR Baldwin field office (616-745-4651) is located just north of town right along MI 37 and can provide maps and other information about the pathway.

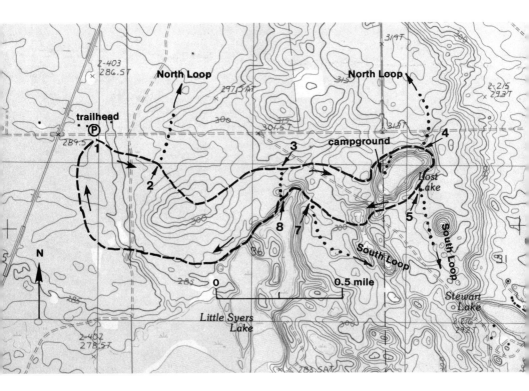

Trail: From the trailhead and post 1, you head east (left) and cross an ORV trail. In .2 mile, you'll come to post 2, where the northern loop splits off to the north (left). Continue straight. The forest walk becomes more hilly on the way to post 3, and you soon pass signs of logging activity, including old stumps and brush piles. But the area isn't a wholesale clearcut that some hikers consider an eyesore, rather it appears to be selective cutting that leaves the resemblance of a forest around the trail.

The pathway is marked in a mixture of fading blue blazes on trees, blue DNR pathway triangles, and blue bootprints. In .8 mile from the trailhead, you arrive at post 3. At this point, the forest is predominately oak and maple, and the trail will usually be covered with acorns and, thus, deer prints. The trail follows an old vehicle track at first, then veers to the

right when it crosses the dirt road to Stewart Lake where it is clearly posted on both sides.

On the east side of the road, the pathway swings to the southeast. Within .5 mile of post 3, it gently climbs a bluff for the first view of Lost Lake. You skirt the lake on the bluff to arrive shortly at a pair of vault toilets, indicating the campground. A path descends to the five lakeshore sites, passing a water pump along the way. Lost Lake is a clear body of water ringed in by shoreline bluffs, a beautiful spot to pitch a tent. Even better is the campground's walk-in status, the reason for its light use during the summer. It appears that not many anglers fish the lake, but the habitat looks promising and the lake probably holds populations of panfish if not a few bass.

From the campground, the trail con-

Marsh along the Pine Valleys Pathway

tinues to skirt Lost Lake from above, with many unofficial trails leading down to the water. The number of gnawed stumps indicate that the majority were probably made by hungry beavers rather than shore fishermen. You soon skirt 7 Mile Road, seen through the trees, and arrive at post 4, where the northern loop re-enters. The trail continues to traverse the lakeside bluffs, and .2 mile from post 4, arrives at the locator map at post 5.

The fork heading south (left) is the southern loop, which leads in .6 mile to Stewart Lake, a small body of water with cottages and a church camp on it. The southern loop then returns to the middle loop through some clearcut areas. Take the fork that heads west (right) from post 5. It continues to skirt the south shore of Lost Lake before crossing the road to Stewart Lake. From there, it remains a forested walk, reaching the locator map at post 7 .6 mile from post 5, where there is a skier's bench so high off the ground it's useless for most hikers.

The next post and locator map (post 8) is only a hill or two away. From there, the trail swings southwest to arrive shortly at what appears to be a flooded pond. Actually, it's an arm of Syers Lake that has been heavily dammed up by beavers. The trail skirts the water where a variety of wildlife, especially birds and waterfowl, is often spotted. You swing away on an old logging track, coming to the edge of a wildlife project. The grassy clearing, actually a planting of rye grass, was created by the DNR Wildlife Division for the benefit primarily of deer, which feed in such open areas. The trail never crosses the clearing, though undoubtedly a few hikers mistakenly have, but rather skirts the edge of it.

Keep an eye out for blue bootprints as the pathway crosses three logging roads and cuts through a second rye grass clearing during the next .5 mile. Eventually the trail swings near MI 37, where at times it's possible to hear the trucks rumble by, but quickly arrives at the trailhead.

Cadillac Heritage Nature Study Area

Place: Mitchell State Park
Total Distance: 3 miles
Hiking Time: 1 hour
Rating: Easy
Highpoints: Wetlands, birding
Maps: USGS Cadillac North and Cadillac South; Mitchell State
  Park map

Cadillac Heritage Nature Study Area offers you an opportunity to hike through an area most people want to avoid — a wetland. The idea of sloshing through a swamp or marsh is enough to make most hikers bronze and mount their boots. But in this 110-acre wetland on the edge of Cadillac, you can hike through the middle of it, look closely at the plant life that thrives there, study the birds and other wildlife that make their home in it, . . . and still keep your feet dry.

The nature preserve is part of Mitchell State Park but is a world away from the campground and day-use area most people think of as the park. The campground here is popular; one of the few state park facilities open year-round and filled most weekends from June through August. Situated between Lake Cadillac and Lake Mitchell and bordered on one side by a canal running between the two bodies of water, the campground is a scenic place to park the trailer, and there are even fast-food restaurants and convenience stores just down the road.

But the rows of recreational vehicles,

the water skiers on the lakes, and the crowds of sunbathers on the beach all disappear when you enter the nature study area. Occasionally you can hear the traffic nearby, especially on a Sunday afternoon when everybody is heading home and MI 115 resembles the Indianapolis 500. But considering how close this trail lies to the city, it's rather remarkable that you can still enjoy a quiet walk in a natural area like Cadillac Heritage.

There are two ways to reach the main trail loop. One begins near Lake Cadillac at Kenwood Heritage Park from an access road. The other begins near Lake Mitchell and is a scenic spur to the main trail. The 3-mile walk described here begins with that spur, which you then backtrack to your vehicle. Spring is an excellent time to be on the trail to enjoy the wildflowers; fall is when the greatest number of birds will be seen. On a still summer day, though, you'd better douse yourself with insect repellent. After all, dry footing or not, you're still hiking through a marsh.

Access: Mitchell State Park is 2.5

miles west of downtown Cadillac on MI 115. At the corner of MI 115 and North Boulevard, reached just north of the park campground, the trailhead is posted with a "Cadillac Heritage Nature Study Area" sign. You can park at the day-use area and enjoy a refreshing swim after the hike, but a daily vehicle permit or annual state park pass will be needed to enter.

Kenwood Heritage Park is reached by following North Boulevard around Lake Cadillac. Just after crossing Black River, you pass a dirt road posted with a "Nature Area" sign, which leads to the second trailhead into the area. For more information, stop at the Mitchell State Park headquarters or call (616) 775-7911.

Trail: The trail departs from the corner of MI 115 and North Boulevard as an old logging road, heading east for a short way before arriving at post 1 and a display map. At this point, the trail swings north, crosses two bridges through low-lying forests, and becomes a most pleasant wood chip path winding through a stand of pines and hardwoods. Within .7 mile, you cross another bridge, reach post 2, and head west (left) into a change of scenery.

On one side of you is the marsh, on the other, the Black River that flows around it. You are walking on an earth dike built by fishery biologists from the Department of Natural Resources (DNR) in 1973. Originally, the Black River was a shallow and winding waterway that meandered through the middle of the marsh from Lake Mitchell to Lake Cadillac. In the mid-1800s, loggers used it to move timber from one lake to the

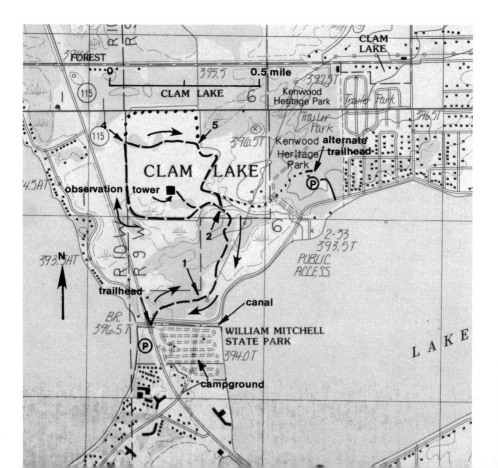

sawmills on the other. It was a slow and laborious task, not to mention the bugs they must have encountered, so in 1873, they built the present canal.

A century later, DNR biologists came along, diked the marsh, installed a water control structure, and began using the area as a northern pike spawning grounds. They would remove the two-inch fingerlings after several weeks and plant them in other lakes. Modern hatcheries, where higher production is achieved by raising the pike in concrete raceways, made this fish-rearing technique obsolete, and the area was closed in the late 1970s. The marsh was declared a nature study area in 1979, and six years later the DNR, with the help of the Michigan Conservation Foundation and many local groups, began to develop the area by marking trails, building bridges, and posting maps.

One feature they added is reached by taking a spur to the right that appears shortly after post 2. The path leads a quarter mile through a stand of maple, with a few impressive paper birch mixed in, and ends at a twelve-foot-high observation tower. From the platform on top, you can survey the entire marsh and observe that it is actually part of a larger wetland. The importance of this wetland, and wetlands in general, are often underestimated by the public. This one serves the surrounding urban area as a filter, for it captures runoff water and removes harmful phosphates, nitrates, and pesticides before they reach the two adjacent lakes. It also stores surplus water in time of floods while helping to replenish groundwater during a dry summer. To think that at one time no one gave a second thought to filling in wetlands and covering them with a shopping mall or parking lot!

The main trail continues to border the Black River as it heads west, and the observable wildlife can be plentiful at times. Along the way, a beaver dam can be viewed from a few feet away. Birds commonly seen include yellow finches, great blue herons, mallards, wood ducks, and a variety of other waterfowl. Eventually the dike and the trail swing north, and here you hear the traffic on MI 115 roaring by. Just up the trail, post 4 is reached 1.9 miles from the trailhead. At this junction, you can either keep heading north to skirt the marsh or cut across the middle of it by heading east.

The far more interesting route is through the middle of the marsh. You begin by hiking into a stand of impressive black spruce, so tall that the noise of speeding cars suddenly disappears. You emerge from the grove of pine at a long boardwalk, often bordered by a profusion of wild calla with its distinctive single-petaled white flower. You return to the dike and the Black River at post 5, turn right, and curve around the marsh before reaching the final post and map after .3 mile. Here and there on both sides of the trail will be pockets of open water, and in the fall, every one seems to have a duck or two resting in it.

At the final junction, you can either head north (left) to cross a bridge and end up at Kenwood Heritage Park in .5 mile or head south to cross a bridge and return along the first leg you hiked.

North Country Trail—Manistee Segment

Place: Manistee National Forest
Total Distance: 20.2 miles
Hiking Time: 2-3 days
Rating: Moderate
Highpoints: Scenic vistas, backcountry camping
Maps: USGS Yuma, Marilla, and Brethren

Possibly one of the least hiked trails in this book is the Manistee Segment of the North Country Trail. Surprisingly, it's also one of the most scenic walking routes in lower Michigan. Few trails match the natural beauty, the number of scenic vistas passed, or the rugged terrain that this section of the national trail has. The problem with the Manistee Segment is the remoteness of the trailheads and the fact that it's a point-to-point path. Unless you arrive with two cars, getting back to your vehicle is a hassle. It's also a twenty-mile route that only hikers in great shape or marathon runners can complete in one day. Everybody else needs to spend a night or two in the backcountry to make it from Hodenpyle Dam Pond to High Bridge over the Manistee River.

The problem of returning to your vehicle will be partially solved when the U.S. Forest Service completes another trail on the east side of the Manistee River. That one will extend from Hodenpyle Dam to Red Bridge near the halfway point of the Manistee Segment. Called the Manistee River Trail, when combined with a portion of this hike it will form a twenty- to twenty-five-mile loop and pass one of the two waterfalls in the Lower Peninsula. The new trail is presently being built and is expected to be ready for hikers in 1992 or 1993.

But why wait for the new trail? The Manistee Segment is worth the trouble of driving two cars and hauling a backpack around for a couple of days. Most of the trail follows a ridge of hills that parallels the Manistee River. Throughout the hike you climb to one high point after another, coming to breaks in the trees and panoramas of this rugged corner of Michigan. When you're not gazing at the river valley or more hills on the horizon, you're plunging deep into the forest or skirting the high banks of the Manistee River.

The entire trail is worth hiking, but if twenty miles is a bit much, the route can be broken up into three smaller segments. The northern trailhead at Beers Road to Coates Highway equals 9.1 miles; Coates Highway to Drilling Road is 5.3 miles; and Drilling Road to the southern trailhead at High Bridge, 5.8 miles. The most impressive vistas, including the Red Hill outlook, are seen along the first portion to Coates Highway.

You can camp anywhere as long as you pitch the tent two hundred feet off the trail. There are good camping spots all along. There are no hand pumps or any other sources of safe water, but a number of streams are passed along the way as well as the Manistee River. Be sure to treat the water before drinking it.

Access: The entire route lies in Manistee County. The southern trailhead at High Bridge, where you will leave one car if you follow this description, is 30 miles west of Cadillac. Head west from

Fiddleheads

Cadillac on MI 55 through the town of Wellston, then turn north (right) in 2 miles at High Bridge Road (also labeled County Road 669). Within 2.5 miles you reach a National Forest boat launch on the north side of the bridge with parking and vault toilets, while directly across the road is one end of the trail.

To reach the northern trailhead, head northwest from Cadillac on MI 115, reaching Mesick in 18 miles. Continue another 2 miles beyond the town and turn south (left) on Hodenpyle Dam Pond Road (also known as County Road 598). Follow it for 5.5 miles to the posted trailhead on the south (left) side of the road. If traveling east from Marilla, County Road 598 is labeled Beers Road.

To reach the halfway point, continue north on High Bridge Road. In the hamlet of Brethren, turn east (right) on Coates Highway for 7 miles. The trail crosses the paved road here and is marked best on the north side.

There are no fees to camp, hike, or park near the trailheads. For more information call the U.S. Forest Service offices in Manistee at (616) 732-2211 or in Cadillac at (616) 775-8539. Write to North Country Trail, P.O. Box 311, White Cloud, MI 49349.

Trail: The trail can be hiked in any direction but is described here from north to south, beginning near Hodenpyle Dam. This direction puts you in sync with the mileage posts that are remarkably accurate. The trail is also marked by blue painted blazes and grayish diamonds posted on the trees.

Northern Trailhead to Coates Highway

The trailhead off Beers Road (or Hodenpyle Dam Pond Road) offers parking for

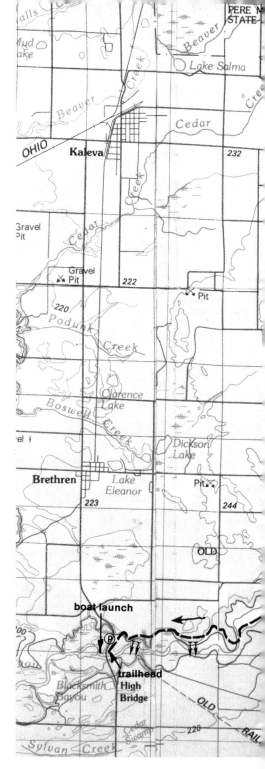

a dozen cars and has a picnic table and display sign. From here, the trail wanders into a pine plantation. It soon enters a stand of oak, maple, and other hardwoods as it skirts the ridge along the river valley. It doesn't take long to reach the first scenic vista. In only .5 mile, you find yourself on the edge of the steep ridge gazing down at the Manistee River, with the dam pond off in the distance.

At this point, you actually begin paralleling a two-track road but are unaware of it until the trail crosses it at 1.1 miles. By now, the off-road-vehicle barriers are painfully evident, and the damage these motorized mosquitoes causes is a little shocking. To keep the vehicles off the soft, sandy ridges, logs six inches in diameter have been pounded into the ground, making some areas look like a war zone—which it probably is in some respects. At 1.4 miles, the trail descends to cross Eddington Creek where it runs down a beautiful wooded ravine on its way to the Manistee River. You head upstream in this hollow, cross a footbridge, then climb out the other side to resume skirting the ridge.

The trail descends a second time at 2.7 miles to cross a junction of three dirt roads. Somewhere around here is a creek, but it's hard to spot at times. You reclimb the ridge and follow its edge for the next mile, getting views through the trees of the valley below. Eventually you swing inland and, after passing the post for mile 4, begin the long descent into Sweets Ravine. It's a good .5 mile down into the steep-sided ravine, and the trail bottoms out at the next mileage post.

Then it's a real climb back out, although this is an intriguing part of the trail. You cross a dirt track and begin an almost mile-long ascent, where several times you climb into a ravine before crossing over to the next slope. It's im-

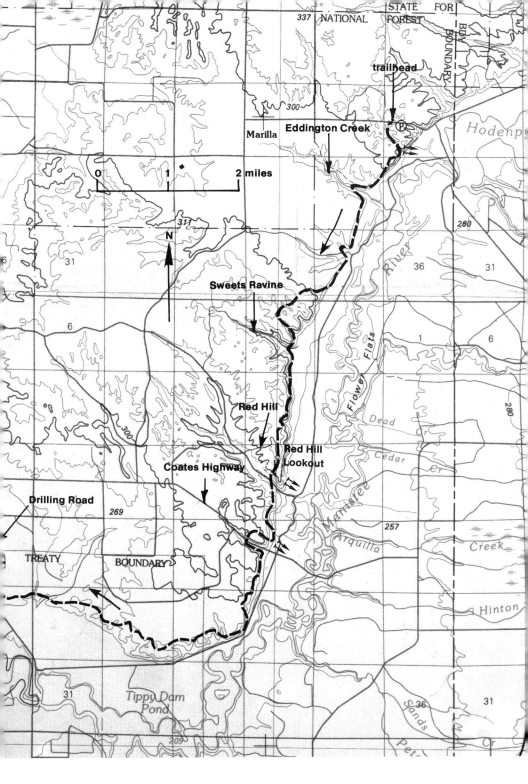

pressive country, and it makes you feel like you're a million miles from anywhere. Eventually you swing inland, then return to the edge of the ridge before arriving at the mile 7 post, where the trail parallels a dirt road for a short spell. In 7.3 miles from the trailhead, you reach the junction posted "Red Hill Overlook." It's a climb of about two hundred yards to the 1,105-foot highpoint, where you can see for miles to the southeast. It's hard to spot the Manistee River, but looming in front of you are several steep ridges indicating what lies ahead.

Back at the junction are some spots to pitch a tent, but if you can resist stopping for the day, a better area is a mile down the trail. From the spur, the main trail swings almost 180 degrees around Red Hill, then descends to an old and very overgrown forest road where the trail passes the mile 8 post on the other side. You resume climbing and within .5 mile pass a wooded ravine with some excellent spots to pitch a tent. Just up the trail is another scenic vista, the third one of the day, and I suspect more than one party of backpackers have enjoyed their morning coffee here while watching the sun rise over the ridges to the east. The trail departs the clearing, skirts the ridge for a short spell, then descends to mile 9 reached right before you cross Coates Highway, the first paved road the trail crosses.

Coates Highway to Drilling Road

The trail on the south side of Coates Highway can be hard to spot; it's directly across from where the trail emerges on the north side. This portion of the hike begins with a steep climb, the path paralleling the road for a short spell before swinging away with the ridge. Within a mile you pass the next

mileage post and are greeted with a view of a wide body of water—the east end of Tippy Dam Pond. The dam itself is actually another seven miles downstream and is well known around the state by steelheaders. The spawning trout are stopped by the dam, and in March and April, anglers line the banks shoulder-to-shoulder to entice the fish with salmon eggs or spinners.

From the viewpoint, you swing inland and cut through a small clearing where some logging has taken place. There are stumps and brush piles everywhere. It's the first clearcut of the trip, though, and considering that you have walked

Bridge over a creek

more than 10 miles, it's rather amazing there have not been more. The trail swings out to the edge of the ridge again for another and better view of Tippy Dam Pond, then begins a descent, passing the post for mile 11 and bottoming out near a powerline right-of-way.

The trail winds through the trees along this man-made intrusion, but in .5 mile merges with an old two-track road and swings away from the electric towers. You begin a gentle climb, continuing on the old road until you reach a well-marked junction. Here the two-track heads south, and the trail goes west as it skirts the base of a low ridge forested predominately in maple. This level stretch continues for almost a mile as a nice forest walk. Right before reaching the post for mile 14, the trail resumes climbing and skirts the edge of the ridge before descending to a forest road. Continuing west, you hike over several small hills and then break out at Drilling Road, the second paved road of the journey.

Drilling Road to High Bridge

The trail resumes directly across the road and begins as a level path. It passes the post for mile 15 and then comes to the edge of a bluff for a good view of the Manistee River and its floodplains. The trail descends to the grassy clearing, marked by scattered shade trees. For almost the next mile, the trail stays close to the river while skirting Leitch Bayou, a marshy area. It's a scenic mile. In the summer, it might be buggy at times, but the opportunity to pitch a tent on the edge of the steep riverbank with shade trees overhead and the Manistee flowing below are almost unlimited. Here the river is a good fifty- to seventy-yards wide and clear enough

to see logs and deadheads on its sandy bottom. This is steelhead country, and in spring and fall anglers in waders can be seen stalking the holes or running a driftboat through this stretch in an effort to land rainbow trout which often exceed ten pounds.

Eventually the trail crosses the clearing and re-enters the woods where it makes a steep climb up a ridge. You pass the post for mile 17 along the way, then top off where you can view the river and the area you just hiked between the trees. The trail follows the edge of this ridge, which protrudes to the south, swings north along its other side, then skirts a narrow crest where there is a steep drop on both sides of you.

To the south are wetlands and sapling forests that border the river. You merge into an old two-track, but the trail quickly climbs away and comes to another vista. You are less than eight hundred-feet high here, but the view is one of the best of the trip and includes the Manistee winding through miles of National Forest. In October, this is a picture postcard painted in autumn colors.

You pass the post for mile 18 and resume skirting the ridge. At one point, the path swings near a snowmobile trail, marked in orange diamonds. You might have a tendency to follow that route, but the North Country Trail never crosses it. Instead, it descends away from it, staying close to the river. You stay so close to the river, in fact, that with a mile to go, you find yourself directly above the water, treading a steep bluff. By now you can hear the traffic on High Bridge Road and even catch a glimpse of the bridge. The last leg of this incredible hike is a descent to the edge of a wetland that the trail skirts before climbing to High Bridge Road, right across from the entrance to the public boat launch.

Marl Lake Trail

Place: South Higgins Lake State Park
Total Distance: 5.5 miles
Hiking Time: 2 to 3 hours
Rating: Easy
Highpoints: Inland lake
Maps: USGS Lyon Manor; South Higgins Lake State Park
  map

South Higgins Lake State Park is an amazing park. A slice of it lies north of County Road 100, and within those three hundred acres you find the park's campground, beach, boat launch, picnic area, and the vast majority of the 450,000 annual visitors who come here. On the south side of the road is Marl Lake and the park's other half. The shallow lake here is in the middle of a seven hundred-acre forest, and wrapped around most of its shoreline is a 5.5-mile trail of three loops that makes an easy and level day hike.

Talk about apples and oranges. In midsummer when the campground is filled and Higgins Lake is buzzing with motor boats and jet skis, when there's a line of cars waiting to get into the beach area, you can cross the road and enjoy a quiet, wooded path and encounter only a handful of other people. In the winter, the loops are groomed once a week for skiers, and in October the hardwoods mixed in with white and red pine provide brilliant fall colors.

Not only does Marl Lake lie totally in the park, freeing its shoreline from cot-

tages and resorts, but its deepest section is only three feet, limiting anglers to canoes or small motorboats. The lake does hold populations of perch, bass, and northern pike and has an unimproved boat launch, but angling activity is light and shore fishing is usually unproductive due to the shallow depth.

All this works to the advantage of the hiker who is looking for a quiet retreat. The trail is divided by two crosscuts, with the shortest route marked in green dots. That route is only a 2-mile walk, making it ideal for children as young as three- or four-years old. The red loop is 3.5 miles and reaches a bench on the lakeshore, a scenic spot for lunch. The entire trail, which is described here, is a 5.5-mile round trip out to the Cut River. Sections near the lake can be muddy in spring or after a recent rainstorm, but otherwise the blue loop is a pleasant walk and a great escape from the campers, crowds, and congestion north of the road.

Access: To reach the trail from I-75, exit at Roscommon (exit 239). Head south, away from the town, and immediately turn west (right) onto County Road 103, where there is a state park sign. Follow County Road 103 for 3 miles, then turn south (left) onto County Road 100 for 3 more miles. The Marl Lake parking lot is located right before the main entrance to the state park on the east (left) side of County Road 100. You need a vehicle permit to enter the park, which can be purchased at the main entrance contact station or from the park headquarters (517-821-6374), across from the boat launch parking area.

Trail: From the parking area is a view of the lake, picnic tables, and a large trail sign next to a footbridge that marks the beginning of the trail. From here, the trail heads south. The first .75 mile of the walk is delightful as you hug the lake for a good view of the water through the fringe of pine trees. Right before the first cutoff, you cross two long bridges that provide dry access between the lake to the east and an interesting swamp to the west. The cutoff is posted with green dots that swing south (right) to reach the return trail; the red and blue dots continue along the lakeshore.

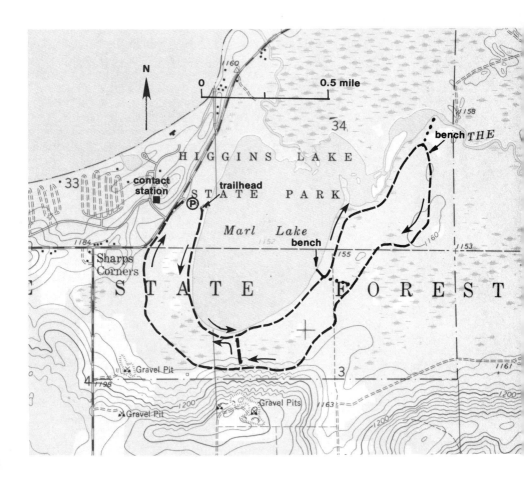

The red and blue loop stays close to the lake for a short way, then swings away from it slightly. You can still catch slivers of blue between the green pines and the white trunks of the paper birch trees, as well as any wind off the lake. The next cutoff is reached in .6 mile, or 1.4 miles from the trailhead, where a short path leads left down to the shoreline. At the bench here, you can sit and look across the weedy lake to watch others just starting out at the parking area.

At this point, the vast majority of hikers begin their return, which is too bad. The longer blue loop takes you past the oldest and most impressive trees of the forest, and it is from this section of the trail that hikers have their best chance of sighting whitetail deer, especially in the early morning or at dusk. Even if you don't see the animals themselves, their tracks often cover the path.

The blue loop immediately moves out of view of the water into a mixed forest of pine, maple, oak, and beech. It can get wet and muddy in places, but it's not too bad as long as you're not worried about the color of your hiking boots. The blue diamonds embedded in the trees are mostly six to seven feet off the ground. In the winter, skiers might have trouble following the route after a fresh snowfall, but hikers encounter few problems.

In 2.5 miles from the trailhead, you arrive at a spot where the trail merges into an old two-track road and begins its return journey. But to the north (left) is a short trail that leads down to the Cut, the channel that flows between Higgins Lake and Houghton Lake, passing through the north end of Marl Lake along the way. The waterway is a popular canoe route, and you might hear or see a few rental canoes banging their way down the channel. The river also holds populations of bass and pike, and from the few Twister Tails that can be seen on the riverbank, it's evident that an occasional angler stops here to fish.

The return trip on the loop follows an old vehicle track and is considerably wider, and drier, than the first half. It winds through mostly hardwoods, but in .6 mile passes through a stand of pine with one particularly impressive white pine towering right above the trail. In another .3 mile, you come to the junction with the second cutover spur (you can actually see the bench on the lake). The main trail continues southwest along the old two-track road. A post with blue and red dots clearly marks the trail where another old road merges with it, and in 1.6 miles from the Cut, you arrive at the first cutover spur.

At this point, you are a mile from the parking lot, whether you follow the return loop or backtrack along the shoreline portion. The return loop swings near a gravel pit, winds through some clearings, and ends up paralleling County Road 100, where on a summer weekend the traffic roars by. The alternative is to follow the cutover spur to the right past an interesting marsh and then to rehike the most scenic stretch of the trail. For most hikers, that's no choice at all.

Lake Ann Pathway

Place: Pere Marquette State Forest
Total Distance: 3.4 miles
Hiking Time: 2 hours
Rating: Moderate
Highpoints: Views of lakes and Platte River
Maps: USGS Lake Ann and Platte River; Lake Ann Pathway
*   map from the DNR's Forest Management Division*

Lake Ann Pathway lies in the Pere Marquette State Forest and is known primarily as an excellent Nordic ski trail, featuring many loops and some challenging hills. When it was first built in the late 1970s, however, it was called Chain 'O Lakes Pathway, was part of the Betsie River State Forest, and was designed as an interpretive trail, not a ski run.

Much has changed over the years. The old interpretive posts are nowhere to be found. Trail users now include mountain bikers, and the path has even been widened and re-routed in places to make the hills more manageable for novice skiers. What hasn't changed, and what is most important to hikers, are the scenic overlooks from the trail and the quiet nature of the area. In less than four miles, you view four lakes, skirt three bogs, and follow a stretch of the Platte River. From swamps and lakes to a trout stream, few trails in southern Michigan display so much water in such a short distance.

The hiking season runs from early May to late November, but keep in mind that the low-lying swamps and bogs found here are bug factories during the summer, especially from mid-June through July, and that a potent insect repellent is a requirement then. Fall colors are excellent, and the bogs are a profusion of wildflowers in the spring. Anglers will find the fishing difficult in the Platte, but Shavanaugh and especially the deeper Mary's Lake can be productive at times for panfish and perch.

The network is actually four loops, but the one located in the campground on the east side of Reynolds Road is of little interest to hikers during the summer. To the west, the first loop is a trek of 1.2 miles from the posted trailhead; the second is a 1.8-mile walk. The entire circuit on the west side of the road is a 3.4-mile hike and, without a doubt, makes for the most interesting afternoon in the woods.

Access: The trailhead is located in a Lake Ann State Forest campground, a rustic facility of thirty sites many of which are on a high, wooded bluff overlooking the water. The campground has

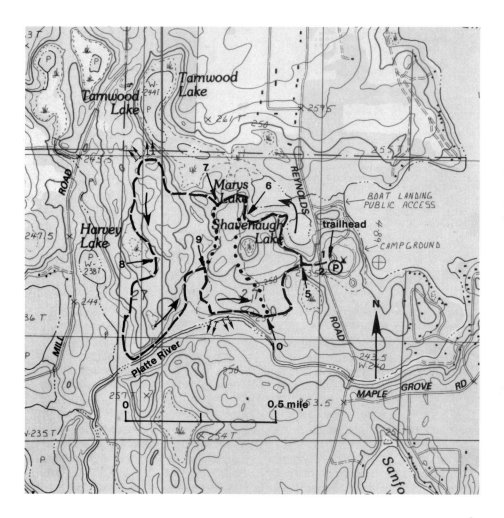

a boat launch but no developed swimming area, and there is a per night fee for campers.

From US 31, 18 miles southwest of Traverse City, turn north onto Lake Ann Road (County Road 665). This road ends in the small town of Lake Ann, where you turn west (left) onto Almira Road for 1.5 miles to skirt the north end of Lake Ann. Then turn south (right) onto Reynolds Road and travel .5 mile to the campground. The campground is posted from both Almira and Reynolds roads, and the trailhead is in a small parking area with a large display board and a registration box. Another 4 miles west along US 31 is the Platte River Fish Hatchery and DNR field office (616-325-4611), where you can obtain a rough map to the trail system and learn more about Michigan's coho salmon.

Trail: From the parking area and display board, blue pathway triangles mark the trail, which immediately crosses Reynolds Road and comes to a numbered post and map. By heading north (right) at post 5, you'll skirt a bluff forested in maples and oak, spot Shavanaugh Lake, and then drop down to the water .4 mile from the trailhead. From one lake, it's only a few steps to the next, as the trail immediately skirts the southern shore of Mary's Lake. The latter is actually the next body of water in the chain, connected to Lake Ann by a stream, whereas Shavanaugh is isolated. Mary's is a beautiful and completely undeveloped lake with crystal clear water that is framed by paper birches leaning over the shoreline.

From Mary's Lake, the trail climbs through an older stand of paper birch already being replaced by saplings of maple and beech. There's a skier's bench at post 6 and an opportunity to head back to the trailhead and shorten the hike by way of a cutoff spur. If you do head back, note the small bog the spur passes from above. A pond many years ago, this and other bogs in the area have no outlets. Marsh grass gradually filled in the open water and, in turn, is being replaced by shrubs and trees such as red osier dogwood, black spruce, tamarack, cedar, and aspen.

If continuing on the longer loop, turn right at post 6. The trail travels along a bluff above Mary's Lake, but the water is only visible in early spring or in November when the heavy foliage isn't obscuring the view. Along the way, the trail passes by a few remnants of the white pine that once covered most of northern Michigan. These pines are thought to be more than a century old and possess the size and straightness that made the species so desirable to loggers in the late 1800s. Soon the trail breaks out to views of the low-lying wetlands that stand between Mary's and Tarnwood

lakes, then descends to the swamps to reach post 7.

This area is a good spot to look for deer tracks or even the animals themselves, for they are frequently seen moving between the swamps and small lakes to the uplands to feed on acorns. The second cutoff spur departs here for post 9, which lies .2 mile to the south. The longer loop to the west (right) resumes climbing, and you cross a couple of hills before reaching the high point of 860 feet. There it's possible to see both bodies of water that make up Tarnwood Lake and the swamp that lies between them. In spring or after a heavy downpour, the swamp will be flooded and Tarnwood will look like one lake. The fine view on the edge of a forested ridge is spoiled only by a fence and the "No Trespassing" sign in front of you.

At this point, the trail swings 180 degrees to the south and follows the crest of a ridge, with steep slopes on each side of it. Within another .3 mile, you approach another swamp, thick with marsh grass and standing dead trees, and arrive at an unmarked junction. The trail to the west (right) is a recently built loop to assist novice skiers down the ridge. The trail to the south (straight ahead) is a rapid descent to the bog below. Here is another great spot to search for wildlife (if the bugs allow you to), especially for deer.

The trail skirts the wetlands, quickly arrives at post 8, then heads due south. You continue through the hilly terrain before descending to the Platte River for the first time. The headwaters for this trout stream lie only 1.5 miles to the east where Lake Ann and several smaller streams feed it. Because this stretch is so close to the lake, the stream tends to be too warm to support many trout. Downstream, closer to the

Foot trail

hatchery, springs and feeder creeks have lowered the temperature of the river enough to support a good fishery of brown trout. But the Platte is best known around the state as the first Michigan river to receive a planting of coho salmon in 1966, which marked a new era in Great Lakes fishery.

The trail swings east here and follows the river for the next .3 mile in a interesting stretch. On one side of you is a steep hillside covered with beech and maple, on the other, is the flat bank of the Platte forested in cedar and tamarack. Eventually the trail swings away from the clear, gently flowing river and ascends the ridge it has been skirting to arrive at post 9. Turn south (right), and the trail drops into the river valley again. Along the way, observant hikers might spot a large stump or two. These are the remains of the white pines that were logged in the late 1800s and pulled out by horses to the north across frozen Tarnwood Lake. Within .2 mile of post 9, you climb to a bench along the trail overlooking the river valley. It's a scenic spot even though trees prevent a clear view of the river itself. But if it's a windless day, you can hear the Platte flowing through the valley below.

The trail follows the ridge above the river and shortly arrives at post 10, located in a natural forest opening. If it's August, look around this spot for blackberry bushes! The last leg back to post 5 (straight ahead) re-enters the woods and passes a second bog, though this one is hard to identify due to the bigger shrubs and trees that have already taken hold. The trail skirts the bog from above and then ascends to the junction, where you head east (right) to return to the parking lot or your campsite.

Muncie Lakes Pathway

Place: Pere Marquette State Forest
Total Distance: 8 miles
Hiking Time: 5 to 6 hours
Rating: Moderate
Highpoints: Inland lakes, trout stream, backcountry camping
Maps: USGS Jack's Landing; Muncie Lakes Pathway map
 from the DNR Forest Division Management

Muncie Lakes Pathway was built in 1971 as the first segment of the State Forest Pathway System, a trail network designed to meet the growing demands of cross-country skiers as much as to provide hikers with additional routes in the summer. The ten miles of trail wind through an area loaded with natural scenery, heading past the undeveloped Muncie Lakes and along a stretch of the Boardman River, one of Michigan's blue-ribbon trout streams.

But like many state forest areas, this tract of the Pere Marquette State Forest is heavily used by a variety of users and groups. Along with hikers and skiers, equestrians pass through on the Shore-to-Shore Trail during the summer, and snowmobilers use the trail in the winter. Rough dirt roads and gas line access routes criss-cross the area, along with electric powerlines, due to the area's close proximity to Traverse City. Throw in an occasional clearcut and it becomes obvious why the Pathway is a less than a pristine area for foot travel. In fact, the Pathway is a far better network for skiers, when a blanket of snow

hides the traces of other user groups.

Foreknowledge of these intrusions of civilization, however, will reduce the disappointment of seeing them and allow you to enjoy the highpoints of this trail. And the best part of this trek, without a doubt, is a night spent camping near Muncie Lakes. Backcountry camping is allowed anywhere in this area, but the lakes make a scenic retreat for a quiet evening of fishing or simply of watching the wildlife pass through. Though a rough woods road reaches the main lake, few people find their way back here to disturb the tranquility of those who walked in.

The network is basically an 8.6-mile loop from Ranch Rudolf Road, with three cutoff spurs and the Shore-to-Shore Trail merging with it from the south and departing at its north end. I use the Shore-to-Shore Trail from Supply Road to access the Pathway here, for the most scenic section by far is the top half of the loop. Also, many of the clearcuts in the south can be avoided by entering the network from this trailhead and returning by way of the spur from post 11 to post 4. The main trailhead for the Pathway is located off Ranch Rudolf Road. From post 1 to post 4 is a hike of 1.6 miles, and the return from post 11 to 12, 12 to 2, and 2 to 1 is also a walk of 1.6 miles.

If you plan to spend a night along the trail, either carry in water or be prepared to treat what you take from the inland lakes or Boardman River.

Access: The trail is located in the Pere Marquette State Forest, 16 miles southeast of Traverse City in Grand Traverse County. From MI 72, turn south on County Road 605 (Williamsburg Road), 5 miles east of the junction with US 31 or 12 miles west of Kalkaska. Within 6 miles, the road merges with Supply Road. Just beyond that point, look for a post on the east (left) side of the road with a boot and horseshoe symbol. Here is where the Shore-to-Shore Trail crosses Supply Road. By following this path to the west (right), you

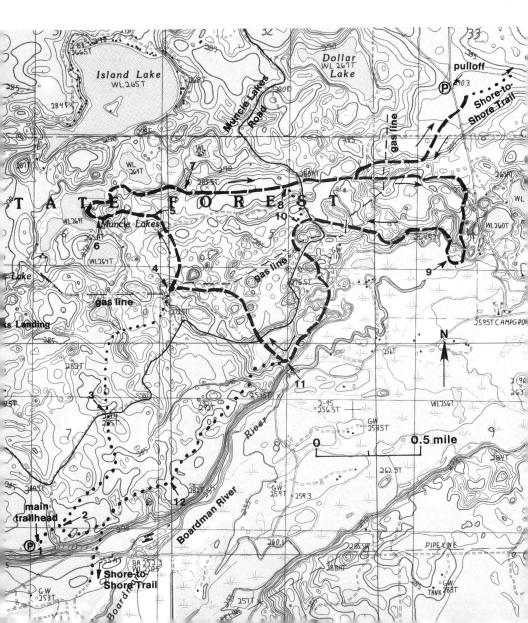

will meet Muncie Lakes Pathway. Cars can be left at a pulloff just north of where the trail crosses Supply Road.

To reach the main trailhead, continue south on Supply Road until just after it crosses the Boardman River. Then turn west (right) on Brown Bridge Road. Within 2 miles, the road crosses the Boardman again and comes to a V-junction. Head right on Ranch Rudolf Road and climb steeply up a bluff. At the top is a posted parking area with vault toilets and a map box.

Just west of Kalkaska on MI 72 is a Department of Natural Resources field office (616-258-2711). The office is open Monday through Friday from 8 A.M. to 5 P.M., and additional information about the trail can be obtained there.

Trail: From the Shore-to-Shore Trail at Supply Road, head west (right) to reach the junction with Muncie Lakes Pathway in 1.1 miles. The trail is marked by blue boot/horseshoe symbols and winds its way over the hilly terrain. Along the way, you cross four dirt roads, a gas line right-of-way marked by yellow posts, and then one more dirt track before arriving at the footpath junction. There is a Shore-to-Shore post here, while the Pathway is marked by faded blue blazes in the trees. Head east (left) and within almost 100 yards you'll spot the first blue DNR pathway triangle.

Heading east towards post 9 on the Boardman River, the trail crosses a snowmobile trail twice, marked by orange triangles, and then recrosses the gas line—a right-of-way that has been cleared of all vegetation and abused by off-road vehicles in recent years. Between snowmobile routes, gas lines, horse trails, and a few paths made by hunters in the fall, this stretch can get confusing at times. But the Pathway always heads east here and is marked by blue triangles. Eventually the trail follows

an old two-track road and climbs to a highpoint, where you are greeted with a view of the Boardman River Valley to the southeast.

You follow the crest of a ridge for a short way, then break out at a knob with the best views found anywhere on the Pathway. The Boardman River winds along directly below, while to the southeast, miles of Michigan stretch to the horizon. A post directs you off the ridge for a rapid descent to the river, where you bottom out at post 9, reached 2 miles from Supply Road. This scenic spot on the banks of the Boardman is equipped with a picnic table and bench nearby. Here is the only place where the Pathway reaches the banks of the Boardman, a blue-ribbon trout stream known for its excellent fishery of brown trout.

The trail resumes by heading west away from the river and passing through a low-lying wet area, which might be muddy in the spring and early summer. This marshy stretch is short, however, and the handful of paper birch here is an impressive stand of trees. From here, the trail begins a long climb out of the river valley, crosses the gas line within .7 mile from the river, and then continues climbing. Just on the other side of Muncie Lakes Road is post 10. The spur trail to the right (north) quickly reaches post 8, where a right turn leads back to the trailhead in 1.5 miles.

For a longer hike, turn left (south). The trail crosses a clearcut and in .3 mile arrives at the gas line for the fourth time. Believe it or not, you'll cross it two more times before the hike is over. The trail climbs away from the right-of-way, crosses Muncie Lakes Road again, and ascends a ridge covered predominately with pine. Within .7 mile of post 10, you cross the electric line. There is also a road here, but the trail is well posted.

The latter skirts a wet area, then makes a long march to the next junction. The climb to post 11 ends at the edge of a ridge, where you cross an old two-track road for a view of the Boardman River Valley. The view in the distance is nice, but the river is almost completely hidden by trees.

Post 11 is a three-way junction. To circle back by way of Muncie Lakes, head west (right) toward post 4. The trail gently descends off the ridge through the forest and breaks out at Muncie Lakes Road. On the other side of the road is a clearcut, and this spot can be confusing because of the logging roads that pass through it. The trail departs the clearcut to the northwest and quickly skirts a small lake from above before arriving at post 4, reached .7 mile from the last junction.

The gas line crosses the trail at this junction, and you head north of it (to the right) where the Pathway is well marked and appears as a footpath into the woods. It climbs through an impressive stand of birch, levels out, and in .3 mile crosses the powerline right-of-way. On the other side of the powerline, you descend to the rough dirt road leading to the lakes and arrive at post 5, less than .5 mile from the last locator map.

Swing due west here as the trail skirts a grassy meadow and crosses another

Backcountry campsite

powerline. The trail climbs a hill through a hardwood forest to descend on the other side, providing a glimpse of the largest Muncie Lake before bottoming out at its east end. Many choose to camp near this lake (the reason for the vault toilet here). A skier's bench along the shore provides a nice view of this crystal clear lake, totally ringed by trees. Anglers work the lake for largemouth bass and panfish and are most success-ful if they have some way to reach the lake's deep areas near the middle.

The Pathway resumes near the toilet, where it is marked by a blue DNR trian-gle. It begins by climbing a ridge for a good view of the lake and its many arms and inlets. The trail descends to one of these arms, often a separate lake during a dry summer, and follows its shore to a powerline at its east end. You cross the right-of-way and emerge at a large marshy area with pockets of open water, the remaining Muncie Lakes. In the fall, the grass and cattails make golden waves surrounding the dark

brown muskrat lodges, while ducks can often be spotted resting in the openings.

The trail climbs the side of the ridge south of the marsh for an overview of the wetlands, then swings away and ar-rives at post 7. You have just finished the most scenic stretch of the pathway, and, although the leg from the largest Muncie Lake to post 7 was less than .7 mile, to many it is worth crossing all the clearcuts and gas lines to reach it. The trail continues east to post 8 by leveling out through a forest predominately of oak. The many acorns on the ground at-tract deer in September. You might also see a few illegal deer stands in the trees, maintained by bowhunters who return for the October archery season.

Post 8 is reached .5 mile from the last junction, and from there the trail quickly descends to Muncie Lakes Road. On the other side of the road, continue east until you return to the junction with the Shore-to-Shore Trail, which is back-tracked to reach the vehicle pulloff on Supply Road.

Sand Lakes Quiet Area

Place: Pere Marquette State Forest
Total Distance: 8 miles
Hiking Time: 3 to 5 hours or two days
Rating: Moderate
Highpoints: Lakes, backcountry camping
Maps: USGS South Boardman; DNR Forest Management
  Division "Sand Lakes Quiet Area" map

Sand Lakes is not dramatic; it doesn't have the stunning scenery of a Sleeping Bear Dunes, nor is it the pristine wilderness that draws people to Isle Royale National Park. It's just a quiet group of small lakes scattered in a forest where motors aren't allowed and development has been postponed indefinitely. It's a place that was heavily logged at one time, abandoned, and now used to escape a man-made world that too often resembles a cheeseburger served in a styrofoam box.

The only man-made facilities in Sand Lakes Quiet Area are the logging roads, which are slowly turning into foot trails, a dozen or so posted maps, and a vault toilet. Otherwise, what you'll find there are stands of towering red pine, deer tracks crossing the path, possibly a bass at the end of your line, and hopefully a little quiet. It's this soul-soothing solitude, not the stunning scenery, that makes a hike or a night at Sand Lakes worthwhile.

Classified as a quiet area in 1973 by the Department of Natural Resources, Sand Lakes is a 2,500-acre preserve of low, forested hills, interspersed with twelve lakes and ponds that are connected to one another by a twelve-mile network of trails and old fire lanes. For the most part, the trails form a 6.2-mile loop, with eight trailheads providing access from four different roads.

The trails are wide, well marked with locator maps, and generally easy to follow. The posts are numbered in a clockwise direction, with post 1 located at a parking area on the corner of Sand Lake and Broomhead roads. But by beginning at Guernsey Lakes State Forest Campground, you can turn this walk into a two-day trek and spend the night at a backcountry campground located on the west shore of Sand Lake No. 1. By following the posts in sequence, you complete a 4.4-mile walk the first day and a 2.6-mile hike the second to return to your vehicle.

A wide range of wildlife inhabits the forest environment, including large numbers of whitetail deer, while the lakes offer hike-in fishing opportunities. Most anglers are seen on the western Guernsey Lake due to a boat launch facility in

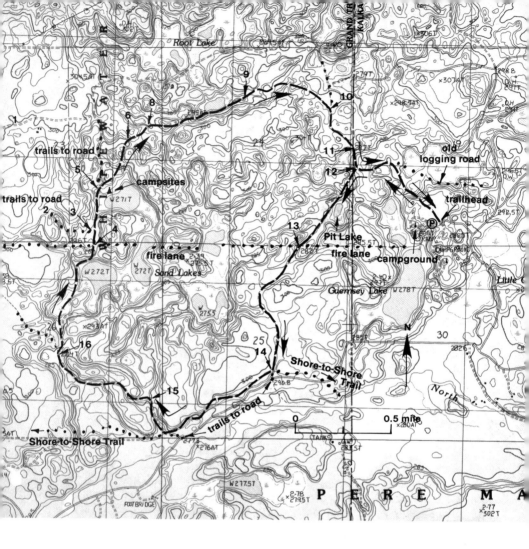

the state forest campground. The rest of the lakes can only be reached on foot. Occasionally, anglers are seen fishing Sand Lake No. 3 for bass or panfish, while Sand Lake No. 2 is a designated trout lake. Most intriguing, perhaps, is Sand Lake No. 5, which isn't connected to the network of trails and fire lanes. This body of water can only be reached by bushwhacking a short way through the woods or finding (and trusting) someone else's unmarked and unmapped trail. But who knows what

lunkers lie beneath the surface of Sand Lake No. 5?

Access: Guernsey Lakes can be reached from Kalkaska by heading west from MI 72 on Island Lake Road for 8 miles, then turning south on Guernsey Lake Road to the posted state forest campground. On the entrance drive to the campground, you will pass a parking area with a trailhead and a map box across from it. This trail is the forested spur to post 12 on the main loop and is where this trail description starts. The rustic campground further down Guernsey Lake Road has twenty-six sites, including many that overlook the lake from a high bank, and a boat launch.

To reach the trailhead from Traverse City, take MI 72 23 miles east to Cook Road. Turn south (right) here, swinging east and then south again and ending up on Broomhead Road. After 4 miles, turn left on Island Lake Road, then right on Guernsey Lake Road to the trailhead parking area.

Post 1 of the trail is accessed through a parking area at the corner of Broomhead and Sand Lakes roads. Other trailheads located off Island Lake Road, River Road, and Broomhead Road are marked by locked gates and provide different starting points onto the loop, including quick access to the lakes. The shortest trek to the lakes begins at post 17 located just off Broomhead Road, .6-mile south of Sand Lakes Road. From there it is under a mile to either Sand Lake No. 3 or No. 1. The wide trails are also ideal for cross-country skiing. Most skiers begin from the parking lot at post 1 at the corner of Sand Lakes Road and Broomhead Road. For more information on the area, call the state's Department of Natural Resources office in Kalkaska at (616) 258-2711.

Trail: The spur to post 12 begins as a level path through a beautiful stand of red pine before descending to an old logging road. To the east are several small ponds, one visible from the junction. To the west (left), the wide path skirts the northern inlet (or separate pond during a dry summer) of Guernsey Lake.

The trail swings away from the water and in less than a mile gently descends to post 12. Like most of the network, the loop appears as an old dirt road through a forest of pines, oaks, and maples. Heading south (left), you quickly

come to a fire lane that veers off to the left. You then pass Pit Lake, a small, round body of water marked with a sign but not labeled on USGS quads or maps published by the state's Forest Management Division.

From the lake, the trail heads straight through a growth of pine for post 13, reached 1.2 miles from the start. It then continues south to post 14. Along the way, you pass unmarked trails that head west (right), presumably made by anglers seeking out Sand Lake No. 5. This spot might be a little confusing, but the main loop is marked with blue blazes on the trees, even though at times they are hard to spot. Eventually the trail straightens out, and you can see the yellow trailhead gate off River Road.

Just before the gate is post 14, where the loop swings west (right) and merges into a segment of Michigan's Shore-to-Shore Trail. One of the first statewide trails to be built in Michigan, the Shore-to-Shore Trail stretches 203 miles from Empire on Lake Michigan to Tawas City on Lake Huron, allowing hikers and horseback riders to cross the width of the state. The route passes ten state or national campgrounds, and much of it parallels two of the state's most famous trout streams, the AuSable and the Boardman.

While on the Shore-to-Shore, the loop trail appears to be more of a trail rather than an old road. The narrow path winds over gently rolling terrain, but watch your step during the summer! You are sharing this route with horses. The forest changes here to a stand that dominated by oaks, maples, and other hardwoods, and soon the trail begins to follow the edge of a low ridge. You skirt River Road from above, though you rarely see the dirt road, then descend to it at a well-posted junction. Head north (right) to reach post 15, .75 mile from

the last junction marker or 2.7 miles from the state forest campground.

The trail returns to an old logging road and eventually descends to an opening of tall shrubs and saplings, a good area to look for deer, especially near dusk. If you don't see the animals themselves, you're sure to spot their tracks in the sandy path criss-crossing in every direction. At post 16, the main loop swings to the north (right) and continues to follow the logging road for .2 mile. At one point, the old road ascends a ridge forested on top, and the loop, poorly marked here, veers off to the left.

You skirt a bog area, re-enter the woods, and emerge at Sand Lake No. 3, a clear body of water that can be fished for bass and panfish. The trail skirts the lake for a good view of it, then arrives at post 4. The first day's hike is almost over; the campground is a short walk beyond post 5. The facility is on the edge of Sand Lake No. 1 and has a pair of vault toilets, a table, and a water pump near the lake. It's a shady and very quiet area (what you would expect), with enough space for a half-dozen tents. The lake is oblong shaped,

shallow in most places, and surprisingly green at times.

The trail to post 6 is a .5-mile walk. You ascend quickly to post 8 and then swing east towards post 9. It is only a .5-mile walk between posts 8 and 9 but a scenic stretch. Along the way, the trail skirts another small, unnamed lake where on a still evening you can watch the panfish rise and snatch bugs off the surface. Mushrooms in an assortment of colors grow in profusion in early summer where the trail skirts the west end of the lake before ascending to the next junction.

The trail to post 10 returns to footpath status and is another enjoyable segment of the loop. It weaves its way through the gently rolling terrain, forested in hardwoods and pines. At one point, you follow the crest of a low ridge before emerging at a fire lane where post 11 is located, 1.9 miles from the backcountry campground. You are now less than a mile from your vehicle at the state forest campground via post 12 and the spur that made up the first leg of your journey.

Wakeley Lake (Orange Trail)

Place: Wakeley Lake Foot Travel Area
Total Distance: 3.5 miles
Hiking Time: 2 hours
Rating: Easy
Highpoints: Inland lake, backcountry camping
Maps: USGS Wakeley Lake; Wakeley Lake Opportunity Area
  map from the U.S. Forest Service

Most of the people who know and visit Wakeley Lake are anglers looking for a quality fishing experience. Because of special regulations such as walk-in access, the lake has developed a loyal following of fishermen who stalk its waters for trophy bluegill, bass, and northern pike.

The same regulations that allow the lake to produce twelve-inch bluegill also make the area surrounding it a hiker's delight. Walk-in access means that there are no motorhomes or off-road vehicles in this two thousand-acre tract of the Huron National Forest. A ban on outboard motors means that the mornings are quiet and the water is still, even when there is a handful of anglers working the shoreline. And the fact that you can't use live bait and have to carry your boat in keeps even most fishermen out of the area.

For hikers, Wakeley Lake makes for a quiet walk around a scenic body of water, with a good chance of encountering a variety of wildlife. I once watched three whitetail deer bound through the woods from the trail here while listening to a loon's eerie laugh across the water. Birding is so good within the preserve that the Michigan Audubon Society maintains a daily field checklist at the trailhead. One hundred fifteen different species have been spotted in the area, including blue herons, bald eagles, or loons that nest on the lake.

There are no cottages or other development along the shore line, for the entire lake was owned by a single family until the U.S. Forest Service purchased the tract in 1986. The area is laced with old logging roads and two-track forest roads, but a nine-mile network of trails has been marked into three loops. All three loops follow the same two-track road for the first 1.3 miles before splitting off into a yellow trail, roughly six miles in length, a five-mile-long blue trail, and the 3.5-mile orange loop described here.

The latter is by far the most scenic walk. It begins and ends at the trailhead off MI 72 and follows almost the entire shoreline of the lake. On this walk, you can enjoy good views of the water as well as measure anglers' successes.

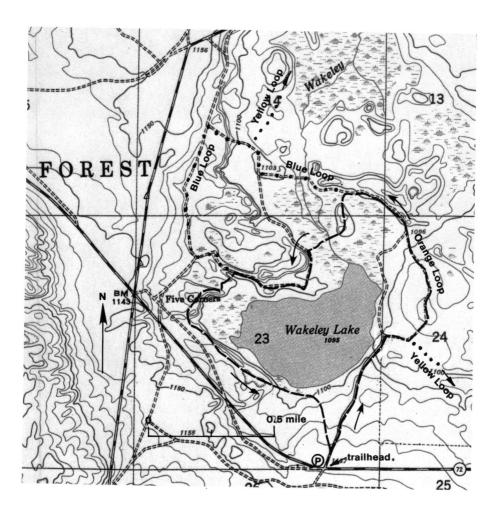

One count indicated that bluegills up to twelve inches were being landed, the northern pike being caught were up to twenty-eight inches, and more than half of the largemouth bass were twelve inches or larger.

The fishing season on Wakeley is from June 15 to August 31. The fishery is good not only because of the walk-in access, but also because of other strict regulations. Only artificial lures can be used, and there is a no-kill, catch-and-release regulation for all fish caught in the lake regardless of species or size.

Camping is allowed anywhere in the tract as along as you're at least two hundred feet from the shore. Some anglers make camp on a high grassy bluff on the lake's east side, but overall you see few campers along the trail. Part of the orange trail crosses a loon nesting area and is closed to the public from March 1 to July 31. The area is well posted, and, if you are walking the trail at that time, simply stay on the blue loop, which swings around the area before re-

Geese with Wakely Lake in background

turning to the orange route (the detour adds 1.5 miles to the hike).

Access: The trailhead is posted on the north side of MI 72, 10 miles east of Grayling, 22 miles west of Mio, or about a three-and-a-half-hour drive from Detroit. There is a map box at the display board in the parking area, but it's not always filled. If you're passing through Mio, you might want to stop at the U.S. Forest Service office (517-826-3252) on MI 72 to pick up a map or additional information.

Trail: A road, with a locked gate across it, leads straight to the lake. You reach the water in only .3 mile, and it's amazing that this short distance is enough to keep the fishing pressure light. You reach the lake at a grassy area, where USGS quads still show a number of buildings belonging to a private camp that has long since been removed. What you'll find now is a picnic table and fire ring in the shade of a few pine trees and, further up the grassy hill, a few more red pines that make a great spot to pitch a tent. If you plan to spend a night, pack in drinking water, for there is no hand pump here or elsewhere in the tract.

From this shore, you can view the entire lake. Chances are there will be a canoe or a belly boat or two on the banks. The best way to fish Wakeley is from a boat, for it's only twelve-feet deep at the deepest spots and much of it is choked with lily pads and aquatic weeds. The trail, marked on trees by three bands of yellow, blue, and orange, leaves the clearing as an overgrown two-track. You quickly pass the first junction, where the yellow trail veers off to the right, then wind through a predominately pine forest until the trail skirts a swamp within the first mile.

Old logging roads come and go, but the main trail is well marked. At 1.2 miles, you climb a low rise for a view of the lake from its north end. The junction where the orange loop swings south is just up the trail. It's posted "Wildlife Habitat Area" and managed for the protection of the loons and eagles that nest in the area every year. If the orange trail is closed, continue on the blue loop, which skirts the large swamp to the west and then winds through the woods to add 1.5 miles to the walk before re-joining the shoreline trail.

If the orange trail is open, it makes an interesting walk here. You cross a dike, really a sandy bridge between two swamps, then climb a low, forested ridge that provides good views of the lake to the east and the huge cattail marsh to the west. The trail drops down to the lake's northwest corner, where on a still morning you can see mist rising off the surface of the water while a motionless canoe and angler sit in the middle of it. This ridge is actually a forested island in the middle of a swamp, and from here you cross two more dikes and then skirt the shoreline for another .7 mile. The trail stays just inside the trees, and there are glimpses of the water and an access trail for shoreline anglers. Eventually, the path swings away from the lake and arrives at where the blue trail returns, 2.4 miles from the trailhead.

For the first time, the trail actually looks like a trail as it swings around the western corner of the lake. Keep an eye out for the trail's color bands, for the tendency here is to head south on an old two-track until you are paralleling MI 72, completely out-of-sight of the water. The trail stays near the shore and, on the south side of the lake, climbs a bluff that puts you above the water. It's a nice view and not a bad stretch in which to set up camp either. The trail remains on the shoreline bluff for almost .5 mile, until you descend to the water and follow a narrow path with the lake on one side and a lily-covered pond on the other. From here, you swing into the woods and arrive at the parking area in .2 mile.

Mason Tract Pathway

Place: AuSable River State Forest
Total Distance: 9.5 miles one-way
Hiking Time: 4 to 6 hours one-way
Rating: Moderate
Highpoints: Blue-ribbon trout stream
Maps: USGS Roscommon North and Eldorado; Mason Tract
Pathway map by DNR Forest Management Division

The most famous trout waters in Michigan are the Holy Waters, a stretch of the AuSable River east of Grayling that is revered by fly fishermen throughout the Midwest. But auto magnate George Mason loved the river's South Branch.

Mason made his fortune in the automobile industry and, in the 1930s, purchased a large tract of land that borders the South Branch from another auto magnate, Clifford Durant of the Durant Motor Car Company. It became his personal wilderness, an area of undeveloped woods and clear water where he would go with a flyrod in hand to escape the daily routine of Detroit. Mason loved to fish his river. The grayling were no longer there, having been obliterated by the loggers in the mid-1800s, but the stream had been stocked with brook and brown trout, which thrived in the cold, clear water of the South Branch.

Mason loved his river so much that upon his death in 1954 he bequeathed it to the state of Michigan on three conditions. The land had to be a permanent game reserve, never to be sold; camping was to be banned for twenty-five years; and the state had to accept the gift within two years of Mason's death. The conservationist's plan was to preserve his wooded retreat by opening it up to everyone who loved the Northwoods, and Michigan accepted the responsibility to maintain it that way.

The original gift of 1,500 acres has since been enlarged to 2,860 acres, and officially it's called the South Branch AuSable River Area. Fly fishermen and canoeists, however, know it simply as the Mason Tract, a beautiful spot in northern Michigan that is undeveloped, forested in pines and hardwoods, and split in the middle by eleven miles of some of the finest trout waters in the state. These qualities and the conditions Mason put in his will almost half a century ago have also made the area a good destination for hikers.

Paralleling the west bank of the river is the Mason Tract Pathway, an 11.5-mile network of trails, most of which is a 9.5-mile, one-way hike from MI 72 to Chase Bridge on Chase Bridge Road (also known as County Road 519). The river moves in and out of view along

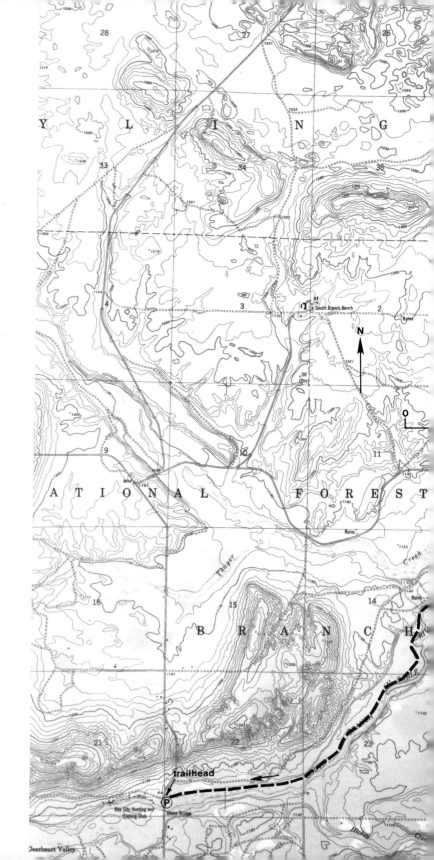

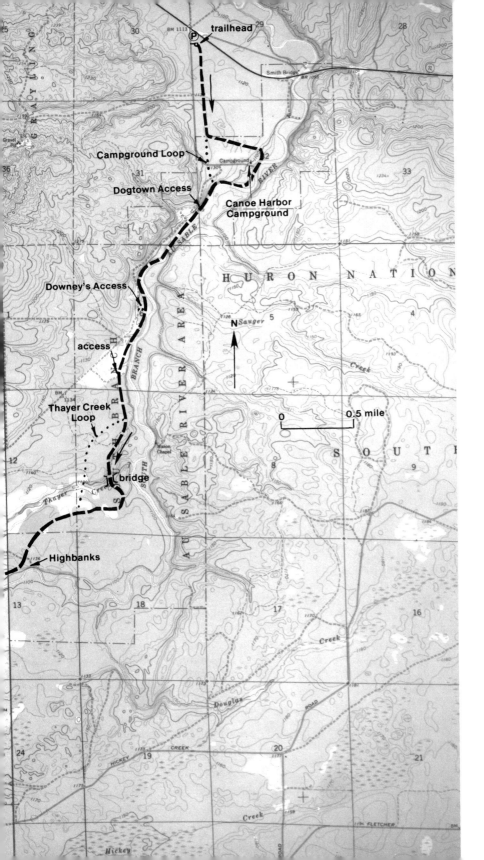

this trek, as the trail works its way across the bluffs the South Branch flows between. For many, beginning at one road and ending at the other presents a transportation problem. Beyond backtracking the entire way or using two vehicles, the only other solution is to walk only a portion of the pathway. The best section of trail for this choice is the northern half, where two small loops have been set up. This stretch is also the most scenic. A hike from the MI 72 trailhead, around the small loop around Canoe Harbor, and back is 2.8 miles. Adding the next loop, around Thayer Creek, would make an 8.7-mile day from MI 72.

Few hikers attempt this trail carrying waders, a flyrod, and a fishing vest. But even if you don't know a dry fly from a housefly, the trout and fly fishing that goes on here adds an intriguing aspect to this walk. Tackle the trail in the morning or early evening after canoers have departed for the day, and you can sit quietly on the banks and watch trout rise to feed on insects. Or spend some time studying a fly fisherman work a floating line and delicate fly with such precision that he or she is able to drop it in the smallest pockets of water between deadheads and sweepers.

Watch that angler hook and land a trout, and you'll be stopping at the first sport shop on the way home.

Access: The pathway is within a half-hour drive of Grayling and Roscommon and is under a three-hour journey from such major metro areas as Detroit, Flint, Lansing, and Grand Rapids (undoubtedly the reason for its heavy use by canoers during the summer). From I-75, depart at Roscommon (exit 239) and head east on MI 18 through town. To leave a car at the southern trailhead, turn north (left) on Chase Bridge Road (County Road 519) 2.5 miles out of

Roscommon. The South Branch is 2 miles up the road, and the posted trailhead is on the north side of the river. On the south side of the bridge is a canoe landing, vault toilet, and a well.

To reach the northern trailhead (where this description starts), continue on MI 18, and the road will swing north and reach MI 72. Head 2 miles west (left) on MI 72 to reach the posted entrance to the Mason Tract. Turn south (left) on the dirt road into the area, and you will soon pass a parking lot and large trail sign to the east (left). If you continue on the dirt road past the trailhead, within .5 mile, you will pass the posted entrance to Canoe Harbor Campground, the only place where camping is allowed in the river retreat. Canoe Harbor was exempt from Mason's camping ban because the area was federally owned at the time and not part of the original gift. The state forest campground has forty-five sites, well water, vault toilets, and a canoe landing on the river. There is a fee to camp.

Trail: Next to the large trail sign is a metal cylinder for leaving trail maintenance donations. Please give. If hikers and skiers don't contribute to the maintenance of the state's trails, we really can't expect anybody else to either. The trail is well marked with blue dots and triangle pathway markers, and along the way there are eleven "You Are Here" maps, though some might be missing.

The trail begins by winding through a sparse stand of pine. It crosses a two-track, dirt road in .5 mile and enters a thicker forest on the far side. In another .2 mile, you reach the junction with the loop around Canoe Harbor Campground. Heading east (left), you begin by following a two-track road, then veering off it where a pathway map has been posted. The trail is now skirting the campground and soon dips down to

Fly fisherman along Mason Tract Pathway

provide the first sight of South Branch.

Here is a classic Michigan trout stream. The river is twenty to thirty yards wide, less than four feet deep in most places, bordered along the banks by sweepers and deadheads, and is crystal clear. The trail follows the river briefly, then at 1.2 miles from the beginning, comes to the campground's canoe landing, picnic area, and vault toilets. The trail heads southwest, skirts a high bank forested in red pine and hardwoods, and arrives at the junction with the return loop to the campground at 1.7 miles. Located here there is a posted map and a bench, where on a quiet morning you can sit and listen to the river below.

Continuing south (left), the pathway winds over several small hills and swings away from the river to within sight of the dirt access road. It then descends back into view of the South Branch and arrives at a parking area at 2.1 miles, from which several trails lead to the water's edge. This is the Dogtown access point and marks the spot where market hunters in the nineteenth century used to gather. Dogtown picked up its name from all the dogs the commercial hunters used to kill grouse, pheasant, and other wildlife for sale to restaurants in the cities.

For the next .5 mile, the trail stays within sight of the river as it passes through a pine/beech forest with a thick understory of ferns. It arrives at another parking area for anglers at 2.7 miles, the Downey's Access Site. A display sign informs anglers that the water is a

"Quality Fishing Area," and by law they must use artificial flies. Charles Downey was one of the first sportsmen to own the tract after buying the land from an exclusive fishing club of which he was a member. For a while, this section was known as Downey's Club, but after his death in 1921, his widow sold the tract to her nephew, Clifford Durant. A spur leads from the parking area down the high bank to the South Branch.

The trail stays close to the road for a spell, then swings away and continues to hug the river as you pass through two grassy openings. Eventually you arrive at a grassy bluff with a stone staircase leading down to the water and a beautiful view of the South Branch. The trail is marked along the grassy bluff with six-foot posts. In another .2 mile, you arrive at another parking area and "Quality Fishing Area" sign that marks an access site for anglers. The cedar stairway that leads down to the river was built by a Trout Unlimited Club in 1976.

The junction to the Thayer Creek loop is reached at 3.6 miles from the MI 72 trailhead and is marked by a map and a bench. Stay left here, and the pathway re-enters a forest of primarily paper birch, beech, and assorted pine. Most of the time, you are close to the river, but you can't see it until the trail swings past the riverbank at 4 miles and you get a splendid view upstream. On the other side of the South Branch (nearly impossible to see), is the Mason Chapel, built in 1960 with funds from the Mason trust as a place of reverence for anglers. Ironically, the beautiful structure has since become a stop for canoers, who have most fly fishermen cursing under their breaths.

The trail swings away from the South Branch, enters a low-lying wet area, and at 4.1 miles crosses a bridge over Thayer Creek. After ascending from the creek slightly, the trail merges into an old logging road where there is a posted map and continues to cut through the forest, well away from the river. At 4.7 miles, you arrive at the junction with the return spur of the Thayer Creek loop, where there is a map and a bench.

The main trail swings to the southwest (left) from the junction as it follows a logging road briefly, then veers to the left at a well-marked spot. You climb into a small, grassy clearing, re-enter the woods, and eventually emerge at a parking area and access. On the other side of the lot, the trail re-enters the forest and quickly begins skirting the bluffs known to fly fishermen as the High Banks—for good reason. The South Branch is far below you, seen every now and then between the towering pines.

At 5.5 miles, the pathway arrives at a prominent hill overlooking the river where there is a map, long stairway to the water, and a bench. The South Branch forms a sharp bend here, and the view from the bench is of flowing water and towering red pines that shade the bluffs. This is the High Banks access site, and from here the trail gradually descends until it cuts across a low-lying wet area and comes to the banks of the South Branch.

The river is briefly followed until the trail arrives at the remains of Durant's Castle at 6 miles. Only parts of a stone foundation and a fireplace are left, but in 1931 this site held a $500,000 home built by the automaker. The forty-two-room castle was a retreat for Durant, and included a drawing room, music room, library, barber shop, gymnasium, and seven fireplaces. What amused locals the most, though, was a ticker tape that kept the millionaire in contact with the New York stock market even in this getaway in the woods. The house only lasted a year, for it was destroyed by fire in February 1932.

From the ruins, you ascend to a parking area with vault toilets and a covered sign. A well-built trail leads down to a wooden landing deck on the river for canoeists. The trail resumes in the woods directly across from the covered display sign and resembles a two-track road here. You follow the track through the forest and, at 6.4 miles, come to a map and bench at the edge of a steep bluff. Just beyond, the trail veers off the logging road and ascends into an old clearcut that takes .5 mile to cross.

There are no trail markers in the clearing, but on the other side a blue map box appears.

You re-enter the woods, pass an access to the South Branch, and follow the rolling terrain to a map and bench at 8 miles. Here a spur leads down to the river. The trail levels out in the final mile, staying in the woods and not allowing many views of the South Branch. You do pass two more road access points before you enter the final .5 mile of the trail, the traffic on Chase Bridge Road becoming louder with every step. At mid-day in the summer, there's bound to be considerable activity around the road bridge, with canoe liveries dropping off boats and paddlers.

AuSable River Foot Trail

Place: Hartwick Pines State Park
Total Distance: 3 miles
Hiking Time: 1 to 2 hours
Rating: Easy
Highpoints: Trout stream, virgin pines
Maps: USGS Big Bradford Lake; AuSable River Foot Trail
 map

At 9,762 acres, Hartwick Pines is the largest state park in the Lower Peninsula, but its best known trail, Pines Loop, is its shortest. Only a mile long, the path winds through the park's interpretive area, which includes virgin white pines, a reconstructed logger's camp and a museum dedicated to Michigan's lumbering era. The trail allows a fascinating look at lumberjacks, but for a quieter, less crowded, and true escape into the woods, many hikers choose the AuSable River Foot Trail on the west side of MI 93.

This three-mile trail crosses the East Branch of the AuSable River twice, passes through its own stands of virgin timber, and sports thirteen interpretive posts with an accompanying brochure available at the park headquarters or contact station. A bit of climbing is involved, and a few wet spots must be crossed; but overall the trail is not difficult and can be easily hiked in tennis shoes. It also serves as an access for anglers, who enjoy the challenges of fishing small trout streams.

A daily vehicle permit or an annual state park pass is required to enter the park, and there is an additional fee to stay overnight in the campground. Presently the campground is located near the trailhead for the AuSable River Trail, but future plans call for moving it to the east side of MI 93. Hartwicks is a popular stop for travelers, and campsite reservations are strongly recommended for most weekends from late June through late August.

Access: Hartwick Pines is 9 miles north of Grayling and is reached from I-75 by departing at exit 259. Head north on MI 93 for 3 miles, and at the park entrance, turn east (right) towards the headquarters. The trailhead is posted along Scenic Trail, just past the entrance to the DNR office (616-238-9392).

Trail: The trail is marked in deer track symbols. It begins by passing through a stand of pines to the junction with the return loop, where you continue straight. You cross an old vehicle track .4 mile from the trailhead and, in another .25 mile, reach the East Branch of the AuSable River. Interpretive posts 2, 3, and

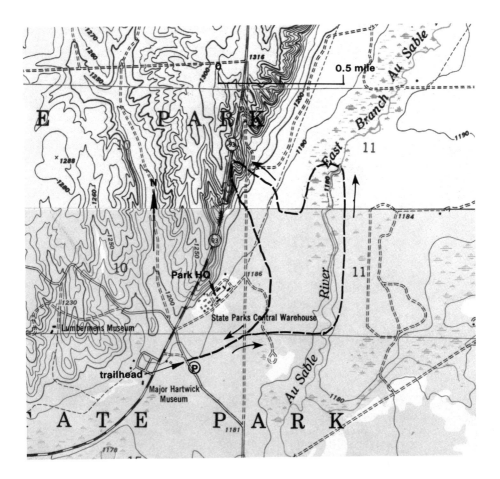

4 are clustered here. There is also a bench, and if you sit quietly for long enough, you might see the rings of rising trout dissipate down the stream. Post 4 marks an old "C.C.C. swimming pool," and trout fingerlings can often be seen darting around in its still water.

The East Branch flows sixteen miles from its source to the southwest and into the main stream of the AuSable River, the most famous trout stream east of the Mississippi. In Hartwick Pines, the East Branch is especially scenic, a crystal clear stream that gurgles between gravel banks and through cedar swamps and undercuts the banks

around deadheads. Too narrow to be a good canoeing waterway, the stream ranges between fifteen- and twenty-feet wide in most places and holds a good brook trout fishery that is overlooked by many anglers. Fly fishermen turn to short rods and roll casts exclusively, but still much of their time is spent picking flies out of overhanging branches. Most anglers are spin or bait fishermen using worms or small spinners to entice the brookies, and, sometimes, brown trout.

From the bridge, the trail swings away from the stream and into a mixed forest of white, red and jack pine along with maple, balsam, fir, and paper birch. You

Looking up into a stand of virgin Hemlock trees

pass several benches, including a pair at the second bridge over the East Branch reached 1.3 miles from the trailhead. The trail might get a little wet on the other side of the river, and post 7 explains the reason; you're in a white cedar swamp where the groundcover is a soft cushion of sphagnum moss. The best stand of trees, however, is reached 1.7 miles from the trailhead when you pass through an area of virgin hemlock. This stand of huge eastern hemlocks towers above the trail, enjoyed today only because in the nineteenth century the market price of tan bark fell before they did. The low return on hemlock bark, which was used for tanning leather, no longer paid the loggers even to cut them.

The relatively level walk crosses the dirt track reached earlier, then turns into a true climb when you begin ascending a glacial moraine, which tops off at post 11 at 1,240 feet. The scenic overlook described in the brochure has been significantly reduced by a growth of saplings, but some glimpses are still possible of the ridgeline four miles away. After a descent from the ridge, the final leg of the trail is a level walk past a railroad grade of the Lewiston Railroad and a rectangular-shaped mound that many believe was a former barn in the area.

At this point, the trail continues south to re-cross the dirt track for the fourth time and return to the only junction on the route, where you turn right to reach the trailhead.

Appendix

Helpful Resources

The Michigan Department of Natural Resources (DNR)
Information Services Center
P.O. Box 30038
Lansing, MI 48909
Tel. (517) 373-1220

The DNR, through both its Parks Division and Forest Division, manages all of Michigan's state parks, recreation areas, and forests, including the miles of trails that traverse them. The Information Services Center can provide a variety of materials, including trail maps, state park brochures, and listings of state forest campgrounds. The office also sells the USGS topographical quads that cover Michigan.

Huron-Manistee National Forest
421 South Mitchell
Cadillac, MI 49601
Tel. (616) 775-2421

This U.S. Forest Service center has information and handouts on trails, campgrounds, canoe routes, and fishing opportunities for the two national forests in the Lower Peninsula. There are also many regional offices scattered around the state that are an excellent resource for material and trail maps. Check the "Access" section of each hike for the closest one, but three of the principal ones are:

Manistee National Forest
Manistee Ranger District
1658 Manistee Highway
Manistee, MI 49660
Tel. (616) 723-2211

Manistee National Forest
Baldwin Ranger District
P.O. Drawer D
Baldwin, MI 49304
Tel. (616) 745-4631

Huron National Forest
Harrisville Ranger District
P.O. Box 289
Harrisville, MI 48740
Tel. (517) 724-5431

Sleeping Bear Dunes National Lakeshore
P.O. Box 277
Empire, MI 49630
Tel. (616) 326-5134

The National Park Service headquarters can provide information and maps for any of the hikes within the national lakeshore as well as a list of campgrounds.

North Country Trail Association
P.O. Box 311
White Cloud, MI 49349
No Phone

More of this national trail lies in Michigan than in any other state, and this citizen's group was set up to assist in its development. Write to the association for a brochure on what has been completed or to find out about the volunteer work parties that are building the trail.

Manitou Island Transit
P.O. Box 591
Leland, MI 49654
Tel. (616) 256-9061 or (616) 271-4217

This is the ferry company that provides transport to both North and South Manitou islands from Leland. Call for the current rates and departure times.

Michigan United Conservation Clubs (MUCC)
P.O. Box 30235
Lansing, MI 48909
Tel. 1-800-777-6720

The MUCC, the largest conservation organization in the state, sells a variety of reference material, including the USGS quads that cover Michigan.

Michigan Travel Bureau
P.O. Box 30226
Lansing, MI 48909
Tel. 1-800-543-2937

Contact the travel bureau for a state highway map or information on lodging and other attractions in the area. You can also contact a regional travel association:

West Michigan Tourist Association
136 Fulton Street, East
Grand Rapids, MI 49503
Tel. (616) 456-8557

Books and Guides

Daniel, Glenda, and Jerry Sullivan. *The North Woods: A Sierra Club Naturalist's Guide.* Sierra Club Books, 1981.

DuFresne, Jim. *Michigan State Parks.* Mountaineer-Books, 1989.

DuFresne, Jim. *Michigan's Best Outdoor Adventures with Children.* Mountaineer-Books, 1990.

DuFresne, Jim. *Michigan: Off the Beaten Path.* Globe Pequot Press, 1990.

Favored Outings of the Huron Valley Sierra. Sarah Jennings Press, 1986.

Hart, John. *Walking Softly In The Wilderness.* Sierra Club Books, 1984.

Korn, Claire V. *Michigan State Parks: Yesterday through Tomorrow.* Michigan State University Press, 1989.

Michigan Trail Atlas & Gazetteer. DeLorme Mapping Company, 1987.

Also from The Countryman Press and Backcountry Publications

The Countryman Press and Backcountry Publications, long known for fine books on travel and outdoor recreation, offer a range of practical and readable manuals.

Hiking Series:

50 Hikes in the Adirondacks, $11.95
50 Hikes in Central New York, $11.95
50 Hikes in Central Pennsylvania, $10.95
50 Hikes in Connecticut, $11.95
50 Hikes in Eastern Pennsylvania, $10.95
50 Hikes in the Hudson Valley, $10.95
50 Hikes in Massachusetts, $11.95
50 More Hikes in New Hampshire, $12.95
50 Hikes in New Jersey, $11.95
50 Hikes in Northern Maine, $10.95
50 Hikes in Ohio, $12.95
50 Hikes in Southern Maine, $10.95
50 Hikes in Vermont, $11.95
50 Hikes in West Virginia, $9.95
50 Hikes in Western New York, $12.95
50 Hikes in Western Pennsylvania, $11.95
50 Hikes in the White Mountains, $12.95

Other books of interest:

25 Bicycle Tours in Ohio's Western Reserve, $11.95
Pennsylvania Trout Streams and Their Hatches, $14.95
Vermont: An Explorer's Guide, $16.95
New Hampshire: An Explorer's Guide, $14.95
Maine: An Explorer's Guide, $16.95
New England's Special Places, $12.95
Family Resorts of the Northeast, $12.95

We offer many more books on hiking, walking, fishing and canoeing in the Midwest, New England, New York State, and the Mid-Atlantic states— plus books on travel, nature, and many other subjects.

Our titles are available in bookshops and in many sporting goods stores, or they may be ordered directly from the publisher. When ordering by mail, please add $2.50 per order for shipping and handling. To order or obtain a complete catalog, please write The Countryman Press, Inc., P.O. Box 175, Woodstock, Vermont 05091.